Marcia Nelson

Taste of Home's
BREAD
RECIPES

A bread box full of the country's family favorites...including yeast breads, quick breads, muffins, rolls, biscuits, scones, doughnuts and breadsticks ...selected from thousands of recipes shared by subscribers to *Taste of Home, Quick Cooking* and *Country Woman* magazines.

And the winner is... "Golden Sesame Braid"
from Barbara Sunberg of Camden, Ohio.
(See details on page 6 and the recipe on page 37.)

Let the Baking Begin...

Here's a picture preview of this book's contents and some of the winning recipes in each category—family favorites to suit every taste and time schedule.

We dug into our files...page 6
The story behind the book

Muffin Mania...page 12
A medley of morsels

Quick Breads...page 24
Loaves with little work

Editor: Julie Schnittka
Food Editor: Janaan Cunningham
Associate Food Editors: Coleen Martin,
Diane Werner
Senior Recipe Editor: Sue A. Jurack
Recipe Editor: Janet Briggs
Associate Editors: Kristine Krueger, Jean Steiner
Art Director: Bonnie Ziolecki
Test Kitchen Assistant: Suzanne Hampton
Photography: Rob Hagen, Dan Roberts, Jim Wieland
Food Photography Artist: Stephanie Marchese
Graphic Art Associate: Ellen Lloyd
Publisher: Roy Reiman

© 2005 Reiman Media Group, Inc.
5400 S. 60th St., Greendale WI 53129
International Standard Book Number: 0-89821-471-8
Library of Congress Control Number: 2005935273
All rights reserved. Printed in China.

Pictured on Back Cover. Top to bottom: Cheese-Filled Ginger Bread (p. 25), Little Texas Corn Bread (p. 26) and Cranberry Streusel Loaf (p. 25).

Classic Yeast Breads…page 36
Tried-and-true favorites

Biscuits and Beyond…page 94
Small in size, big on flavor

Savory Yeast Breads…page 56
Specially seasoned breads

Breads in Brief…page 106
"Homemade" breads in a hurry

Sweet Yeast Breads…page 74
Treats for your sweet tooth

Looking for a certain bread? The index begins on page 112.

Visitors Got Their Two Scents Worth

Most "judges" took a second breath when they walked in the door and helped us with our search for "The Best Bread in the Country".

COME ON IN! That's our company Visitor Center (top photo) in downtown Greendale, Wis. In the foreground are some of the 37,000 flowers planted annually along the village's main street. Above, food staffers at work in the Center's test kitchen. Note the large overhead mirror that provides visitors a clear view.

ONE of the best things about working on this *Taste of Home's Bread Recipes* cookbook was the aroma.

The bulk of the testing was done in the modern test kitchen at our company Visitor Center in downtown Greendale, Wisconsin. And when the scent of freshly baked bread drifted out the front door, it drew people in like popcorn at the movies.

"*Mmm!*" we'd hear them say as they stepped inside, then stopped in their tracks and lifted their head for a second breath of it. That kind of regular reaction led one of our food staffers to say, "If we could package this aroma, we could sell a lot of that, too!"

Visitors to the Center—we're glad to say an average of over 250 per day come to see us—enjoyed more than the aroma. They enjoyed tasting and helping us "judge" the fresh-out-of-the-oven entries we tested for this bread contest each day.

Likewise, our home economists appreciated the hands-on input of these friendly visitors. This helped our staff select the recipes for this book with the confidence that these were the breads a good cross section of our readers would like most.

Choosing the best for this book was no easy task, considering that we had *several thousand* recipes to choose from, each of which was a family favorite contributed by subscribers to *Taste of Home*, *Quick Cooking* and *Country Woman* magazines.

In fact, the selection was so huge, our food staff took more than 6 months to screen, file, test, taste and retest these bread recipes! Then, at our Visitor Center, they got "What do you think?" opinions from eager tasters who tested at least one of these breads every day.

Each taster was asked to fill out a small "Judge's Rat-

SOME OF OUR "JUDGES". Subscribers who tour our Visitor Center (average of over 250 a day) help select recipes for our magazines and our books (including this one). They taste, then fill out a "Judge's Rating Sheet" to indicate which they like best.

ing Sheet" (as the lady is doing in the photo above) to tell which bread she or he liked best. This daily reaction was then tallied by the test kitchen staff to gradually determine the finalists.

Queen for a Day

We announced early on that the winner would be given a free trip for two to Greendale to tour our company headquarters, meet our editors and home economists, see how we go through the recipe testing process and be given real "celebrity" treatment during the entire visit.

Our winner (shown at right) is Barbara Sunberg of Camden, Ohio. Her delicious "Golden Sesame Braid" (featured on page 37) is sure to be a winner at your house, too.

THE WINNER! From several thousand recipes, Barbara Sunberg's was selected the best bread of them all!

So...to give you an idea of the kind of tour Barbara is going to experience, we'll now give you a *photo-tour* of our home offices...our test kitchens and photo department...the flower-laden grounds around our headquarters...and our new Visitor Center. This way, "by proxy", *you* can take pretty much the same tour Barbara will be taking in person.

The pictures here and on the following pages provide photo evidence that we take great pride in our company grounds. Flowers abound!

The suntanned members of our landscaping crew plants more than *37,000* new annuals in our flower beds each year. That's in addition to the multiple flower baskets hanging throughout the property, along with hundreds of perennials that come up to greet us each spring. Our front entrance is lined with hundreds of tulips and daffodils in late April. And when those fade, geraniums, marigolds, salvia and petunias take over. It's not uncommon for our receptionist to see people stopping halfway up the walk, to not only take a closer look, but to take a deep breath as well.

There's a fairly large pond on our property with a gazebo on a small "island" near the edge. Our more than 400 staff members find it a great place to relax during the noon hour on a summer day.

There's also a blacktop walking trail that meanders around the perimeter of our grounds, through all the trees and the flower beds. The path is measured, so our employees know exactly what distance they've covered when they complete the route.

It's the belief of our company's management that if you provide employees with modern conveniences and beautiful surroundings, they'll look forward to coming to work and they'll be more productive once they get there.

We're proud to say that our company grounds "set a pleasant mood", and to an extent reflect the kind of pretty places and pretty pictures that are featured in our magazines throughout the year.

Inside this headquarters facility we have more

COMPANY ENTRANCE. The colorful walkway below greets our employees each morning, and this is where Barbara will enter our offices while enjoying her free trip to Greendale.

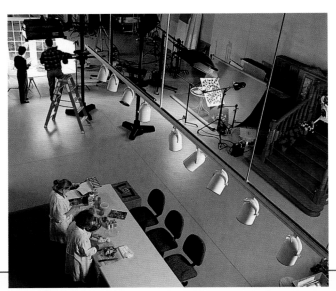

THIS IS OUR HEADQUARTERS. Above you see a side view of our front entrance and part of the colorful grounds of Reiman Publications. At left, part of our editorial staff selects photos for the next issue of one of our magazines. Our large photo department at lower left is where all of our food photos (including those for this bread book) are taken. Food "stylists" in foreground ready items to be photographed.

than 400 busy people who seem to love what they do. Barbara will likely be most interested in our test kitchens, our art directors' facilities and our photography department. We've included photos of those areas for you as well.

While we'll be glad to give Barbara a personal tour of our offices, this is a special opportunity for her that, unfortunately, we can no longer offer the hundreds of subscribers who write to ask whether they can do the same.

We learned that tours are simply too difficult to handle in our small offices and compact hallways. What's more, our kind of creative work requires a quiet environment. And, since any enjoyable tour includes laughter and loud voices, such tours are too disruptive and interfere with deadlines.

More Flowers Downtown

That's the main reason we constructed our company Visitor Center in downtown Greendale, which is within walking distance of our offices (many of our staffers stroll down there during the noon hour). The Center duplicates the main elements of our headquarters and was built to facilitate tours. There, we *wel-*

come laughter—it's a sign our visitors are enjoying themselves. In fact, there's a large lounge (shown at right) that encourages visitors to sit down, have a cup of coffee and get acquainted.

The Center has a large film room, which shows a video of our company's roots and history…there are many fascinating wall displays…the *Country's Reminisce Hitch* wagon (which was horse-drawn 10 miles a day from Maine to California and was ridden for short distances by over 50,000 of our subscribers) is on exhibit.

There's much more—a display of a variety of creative items sent in by our subscribers, including nearly a hundred handcrafted birdhouses entered in our national birdhouse contest...a colorful display by our art directors, portraying the contents of each of our magazines…and other fascinating exhibits.

And, on the lower level there's a Bargain Center, where you can get slightly damaged books and other closeout items, some at *less than 1/8* of their original prices.

Visitors Love the Test Kitchen

But the "star" of the Visitor Center is its large, modern test kitchen, where visitors can watch our home economists busily preparing and testing food through the windows and in the large mirror over the center island.

And these cooks aren't just there for "show", they're there for "dough", especially testing recipes for this cookbook and our various publications. In other words, this is a *working* test kitchen, where the recipes being screened and selected will show up later in our magazines and cookbooks.

So, that's the kind of tour our winner, Barbara Sunberg, will get of both our headquarters and our Visitor Center. You're welcome at the latter whenever you can fit it into your schedule. The Center is open 9 a.m. to 5 p.m. Monday through Saturday. Greendale is located on the south edge of Milwaukee just off the I-894 bypass. Exit at 60th Street and head south about a mile to Grange Avenue.

Then continue south as 60th becomes Northway and curves right into the village, where the Center is located at the corner of Northway and Broad Street.

We'd love to have you come for a "taste" of Greendale …in more ways than one. But for now, you have a *lot* of tasting to do right in your own home…of the recipes for more than 200 *best breads in the country*!

LOTS TO SEE. The above scenes offer a photo-tour of the Reiman Publications Visitor Center. At top is the lounge where subscribers from across the country get acquainted. Next, a couple looks over one of the wall displays. Third is the wagon that crossed America. Just above, a shopper in our Bargain Center on the lower level. At left, guests check out our test kitchen.

THESE GREAT BREADS NEARLY WON IT ALL!

Here are half a dozen fabulous finalists that were just one step away from being the overall winner. These recipes— along with the "Golden Sesame Braids" grand-prize winner—are marked in the book with a stalk of wheat.

Lemon Raspberry Jumbo Muffins (page 13)
shared by Carol Thoreson, Rockford, Illinois

These are my favorite muffins because they can be made with blueberries instead of raspberries with the same delicious results. Friends often request the recipe.

Pumpkin Cranberry Nut Bread (page 31)
shared by Darlene Conger, Greenville, Texas

This bread has a terrific combination of flavors that's perfect for the holidays. I like to make and freeze loaves to share with friends and neighbors.

eddar Batter Bread *(page 57)*
red by Debbie Keslar, Seward, Nebraska

ve batter breads because I can offer my family
cious homemade bread without the hassle of
ading and shaping the dough. This is terrific
h chili.

Danish Kringle *(page 75)*
shared by Lorna Jacobsen, Arrowwood, Alberta

This traditional yeast bread wonderfully reflects my
Scandinavian heritage. Flaky layers of tender dough are
flavored with almond paste. The unique sugar cookie
crumb coating adds the perfect amount of sweetness.

shed Potato Doughnuts *(page 95)*
red by Tammy Evans, Nepean, Ontario

a special treat in winter, my parents would make a
ble batch of these doughnuts to welcome us six
s home from school. This recipe from my great-
t has been handed down through the generations.

Speedy Cinnamon Rolls *(page 107)*
shared by Nicole Weir, Hager City, Wisconsin

On special occasions when we were growing up, my
mother would make as many as four batches of these
delicious cinnamon rolls to satisfy the appetites of her
eight ravenous children. Today this recipe is still a hit.

Muffin Mania

The combination of flavors in muffins is unbeatable and nearly unlimited. So make your day with these melt-in-your-mouth morsels.

LEMON RASPBERRY JUMBO MUFFINS

Carol Thoreson, Rockford, Illinois

(Pictured at left)

These are my favorite muffins because they can be made with blueberries instead of raspberries with the same delicious results. Friends often request the recipe.

> 2 cups all-purpose flour
> 1 cup sugar
> 3 teaspoons baking powder
> 1/2 teaspoon salt
> 2 eggs
> 1 cup half-and-half cream
> 1/2 cup vegetable oil
> 1 teaspoon lemon extract
> 1 cup fresh *or* frozen unsweetened raspberries*

In a large bowl, combine the flour, sugar, baking powder and salt. In another bowl, combine the eggs, cream, oil and extract. Stir into dry ingredients just until moistened. Fold in raspberries. Fill greased jumbo muffin cups two-thirds full. Bake at 400° for 22-25 minutes or until a toothpick comes out clean. Cool for 5 minutes before removing from pan to a wire rack. Serve warm. **Yield:** 8 jumbo muffins. *****Editor's Note:** If using frozen raspberries, do not thaw before adding to the batter. Sixteen regular-size muffin cups may be used; bake for 18-20 minutes.

APPLE STREUSEL MUFFINS

Michele Olsen, Wessington Springs, South Dakota

(Pictured at left)

Pieces of tender apples appear in every bite of these pretty muffins. The streusel topping is nicely seasoned with cinnamon and sugar.

> 2 cups all-purpose flour
> 1 cup sugar
> 3 teaspoons baking powder

FRUIT-FILLED TREATS. Pictured at left, top to bottom: Apple Streusel Muffins (recipe on this page), Aunt Betty's Blueberry Muffins (recipe on page 14) and Lemon Raspberry Jumbo Muffins (recipe on this page).

> 1-1/4 teaspoons ground cinnamon
> 1/2 teaspoon baking soda
> 1/2 teaspoon salt
> 2 eggs
> 1 cup (8 ounces) sour cream
> 1/4 cup butter *or* margarine, melted
> 1-1/2 cups chopped peeled tart apples
> **TOPPING:**
> 1/4 cup sugar
> 3 tablespoons all-purpose flour
> 1/4 teaspoon ground cinnamon
> 2 tablespoons cold butter *or* margarine

In a large bowl, combine dry ingredients. In another bowl, beat the eggs, sour cream and butter. Stir into dry ingredients just until moistened. Fold in apples. Fill greased or paper-lined muffin cups two-thirds full. For topping, combine sugar, flour and cinnamon. Cut in butter until mixture resembles coarse crumbs. Sprinkle a rounded teaspoonful over each muffin. Bake at 400° for 18-20 minutes or until a toothpick comes out clean. Cool for 5 minutes before removing from pans to wire racks. Serve warm. **Yield:** 16 muffins.

LIME MUFFINS

Robin Christmas, Charlotte, North Carolina

I bake muffins every Sunday morning, so I'm always trying different ingredients to make them interesting. These citrus muffins are my husband's favorite.

> 2 cups all-purpose flour
> 1 cup sugar
> 2 teaspoons baking powder
> 1/2 teaspoon salt
> 1 egg
> 1/4 cup milk
> 1/4 cup vegetable oil
> 3 tablespoons lime juice
> 1-1/2 teaspoons grated lime peel

In a bowl, combine the first four ingredients. In another bowl, beat the egg, milk, oil, lime juice and peel. Stir into dry ingredients just until moistened. Fill paper-lined muffin cups two-thirds full. Bake at 400° for 18-20 minutes or until a toothpick comes out clean. Cool for 5 minutes before removing from pan to a wire rack. **Yield:** 1 dozen.

AUNT BETTY'S BLUEBERRY MUFFINS

Sheila Raleigh, Kechi, Kansas

(Pictured above and on page 12)

My Aunt Betty bakes many items each Christmas, but I look forward to these mouth-watering muffins the most. She gives me enough so that I can freeze and enjoy them for weeks.

      1/2 cup old-fashioned oats
      1/2 cup orange juice
      1 egg
      1/2 cup vegetable oil
      1/2 cup sugar
      1-1/2 cups all-purpose flour
      1-1/4 teaspoons baking powder
      1/2 teaspoon salt
      1/4 teaspoon baking soda
      1 cup fresh *or* frozen blueberries*
TOPPING:
      2 tablespoons sugar
      1/2 teaspoon ground cinnamon

In a large bowl, combine oats and orange juice; let stand for 5 minutes. Beat in the egg, oil and sugar until blended. Combine the flour, baking powder, salt and baking soda; stir into oat mixture just until moistened. Fold in blueberries. Fill greased or paper-lined muffin cups two-thirds full. Combine topping ingredients; sprinkle over batter. Bake at 400° for 20-25 minutes or until a toothpick comes out clean. Cool for 5 minutes before removing from pan to a wire rack. **Yield:** about 1 dozen. *****Editor's Note:** If using frozen blueberries, do not thaw before adding to the batter.

VIDALIA MUFFINS

Kelly Hom, Brighton, Michigan

These slightly sweet onion muffins are a snap to make and are great when served with homemade stew or soup. I hope this recipe becomes a favorite with your family as much as it has with mine.

      1 cup self-rising flour*
      1 cup quick-cooking oats
      1/4 cup sugar

      1 egg
      3/4 cup milk
      1/3 cup vegetable oil
      3/4 cup shredded cheddar cheese
      1/2 cup chopped Vidalia *or* sweet onion

In a large bowl, combine the flour, oats and sugar. In another bowl, beat the egg, milk and oil. Stir into dry ingredients just until moistened. Fold in cheese and onion. Fill greased muffin cups three-fourths full. Bake at 400° for 15-20 minutes or until a toothpick comes out clean. Cool for 5 minutes before removing from pan to a wire rack. Serve warm. Refrigerate leftovers. **Yield:** 1 dozen. *****Editor's Note:** As a substitute for 1 cup self-rising flour, place 1-1/2 teaspoons baking powder and 1/2 teaspoon salt in a measuring cup. Add all-purpose flour to measure 1 cup.

RHUBARB MUFFINS

Alma Hansen, New Denmark, New Brunswick

A cousin in Maine gave me this recipe. I take these slightly tart treats to meetings where lunch is being served and always come home with an empty plate. It's a good way to use up plentiful rhubarb.

2-1/2 cups all-purpose flour
      1 cup packed brown sugar
      1 teaspoon baking powder
      1 teaspoon baking soda
      1/2 teaspoon salt
      1/4 teaspoon ground nutmeg
      1 egg
      1 cup buttermilk
      1/2 cup vegetable oil
      2 teaspoons vanilla extract
      2 cups diced fresh *or* frozen rhubarb

In a large bowl, combine the dry ingredients. In another bowl, beat the egg, buttermilk, oil and vanilla. Stir into dry ingredients just until moistened. Fold in rhubarb. Fill paper-lined muffin cups two-thirds full. Bake at 350° for 22-25 minutes or until a toothpick comes out clean. Cool for 5 minutes before removing from pans to wire racks. Serve warm. **Yield:** 16 muffins

CONFETTI MUFFINS

Nancy Piram, St. Cloud, Minnesota

These savory herb and vegetable muffins are a nice break from the usual sweet muffins. Serve them with soups, barbecued entrees or main-dish salads for a meal your family will love.

1-1/2 cups all-purpose flour
  2 tablespoons sugar
  2 teaspoons baking powder
1/2 teaspoon baking soda
1/2 teaspoon salt
1/2 teaspoon dried basil
1/4 teaspoon dried tarragon
1/3 cup chopped green onions
1/3 cup minced sweet red pepper
1/4 cup minced green pepper
1/2 cup butter *or* margarine
1/4 cup minced fresh parsley *or* 4 teaspoons dried
    parsley flakes
  2 eggs
2/3 cup sour cream
  1 tablespoon Dijon mustard

In a large bowl, combine the first seven ingredients. In a skillet, saute onions and peppers in butter until tender. Stir in parsley; cool for 10 minutes. In a bowl, beat eggs, sour cream and mustard. Add onion mixture. Stir into dry ingredients just until moistened. Fill greased or paper-lined muffin cups two-thirds full. Bake at 400° for 15-20 minutes or until a toothpick comes out clean. Cool for 5 minutes before removing from pan to a wire rack. Serve warm or at room temperature. **Yield:** 1 dozen.

ROASTED RED PEPPER MUFFINS

Fancheon Resler, Bluffton, Indiana

In 1998, I was the chairman of the 4-H committee designated to assemble a cookbook. This recipe was submitted by an 11-year-old boy, who used it for one of his baking projects.

  1 teaspoon cornmeal
1-3/4 cups all-purpose flour
  3 tablespoons sugar
  2 teaspoons baking powder
1/2 teaspoon coarsely ground pepper, *divided*
1/4 teaspoon salt
  1 egg
3/4 cup buttermilk
1/4 cup vegetable oil
2/3 cup chopped roasted sweet red pepper
1/2 cup shredded mozzarella cheese

Grease muffin cups and sprinkle with the cornmeal; set aside. In a large bowl, combine flour, sugar, baking powder, 1/4 teaspoon pepper and salt. In another bowl, beat the egg, buttermilk and oil. Stir into dry ingredients just until moistened. Fold in red pepper and cheese. Fill prepared muffin cups two-thirds full. Sprinkle with remaining pepper. Bake at 400° for 20-25 minutes or until a toothpick comes out clean. Cool

for 5 minutes before removing from pan to a wire rack. Serve warm. Refrigerate leftovers. **Yield:** 1 dozen.

POPPY SEED POUND CAKE MUFFINS

Glenda York, Wichita, Kansas

Muffins are one of my favorite foods, and these are so good! I enjoy making several varieties of muffins at one time to have on hand for breakfast or lunch.

1-1/2 cups butter *or* margarine, softened
  1 cup sugar
  2 eggs
  1 cup (8 ounces) plain yogurt
  1 teaspoon vanilla extract
  2 cups all-purpose flour
  1 tablespoon poppy seeds
1/2 teaspoon salt
1/4 teaspoon baking soda

In a mixing bowl, cream butter and sugar. Beat in eggs, yogurt and vanilla. Combine the flour, poppy seeds, salt and baking soda. Stir into creamed mixture just until moistened. Fill paper-lined muffin cups two-thirds full. Bake at 400° for 20-25 minutes or until a toothpick comes out clean. Cool for 5 minutes before removing from pans to wire racks. **Yield:** 14 muffins.

MAPLE BACON MUFFINS

Louise Biela, Hamburg, New York

These hearty muffins combine the fabulous flavors of pancakes and bacon. They're great for breakfast on the run.

  1 cup quick-cooking oats
3/4 cup all-purpose flour
3/4 cup whole wheat flour
1/2 cup packed dark brown sugar
  2 teaspoons baking powder
  1 teaspoon baking soda
1/2 teaspoon salt
  2 eggs
  1 cup buttermilk
  1 cup maple syrup
 10 bacon strips, cooked and crumbled

In a large bowl, combine the oats, flours, brown sugar, baking powder, baking soda and salt. In another bowl, beat the eggs, buttermilk and syrup. Stir into dry ingredients just until moistened. Fold in bacon. Fill greased or paper-lined muffin cups two-thirds full. Bake at 350° for 20-25 minutes or until a toothpick comes out clean. Cool for 5 minutes before removing from pans to wire racks. Serve warm. Refrigerate leftovers. **Yield:** 21 muffins.

PINEAPPLE SUNSHINE MUFFINS

Ann Bivins, Monticello, New York

Even though my children are grown, they still look for these muffins on Sunday mornings. I put the leftovers, if any, in my husband's lunch for a surprise treat.

> 2 cups all-purpose flour
> 1 cup sugar
> 2 teaspoons baking powder
> 1/2 teaspoon ground cinnamon
> 1/2 teaspoon ground ginger
> 2 eggs
> 1/2 cup butter *or* margarine
> 1 teaspoon vanilla extract
> 1 can (8 ounces) crushed pineapple, undrained
> 1/2 cup shredded carrot
> 1/2 cup sunflower kernels

In a large bowl, combine the flour, sugar, baking powder, cinnamon and ginger. In another bowl, beat the eggs, butter and vanilla; stir in pineapple. Stir into dry ingredients just until moistened. Fold in carrot and sunflower kernels. Fill greased or paper-lined muffin cups three-fourths full. Bake at 375° for 15-20 minutes or until a toothpick comes out clean. Cool for 5 minutes before removing from pan to a wire rack. Serve warm. **Yield:** 1 dozen.

SPICY SAUSAGE MUFFINS

Shirley Glaab, Hattiesburg, Mississippi

Ready for a change of pace? This muffin has a terrific spicy flavor with a good blend of herbs, sausage and cheese. It's very different from other savory muffins.

> 1/2 pound bulk hot pork sausage
> 1/4 cup chopped green onions
> 1/4 cup chopped sweet red pepper
> 3/4 cup all-purpose flour
> 1/2 cup cornmeal
> 1 tablespoon minced fresh cilantro *or* parsley
> 1 teaspoon baking soda
> 1/2 teaspoon salt
> 3/4 teaspoon minced fresh thyme *or* 1/4 teaspoon dried thyme
> 1 egg, beaten
> 1 cup buttermilk
> 3/4 cup shredded sharp cheddar cheese

In a skillet, cook sausage, onions and red pepper over medium heat until meat is no longer pink; drain and set aside. In a large bowl, combine the flour, cornmeal, cilantro, baking soda, salt and thyme. In another bowl, combine egg and buttermilk. Stir into dry ingredients just until moistened. Fold in cheese and sausage mixture. Fill greased muffin cups two-thirds

full. Bake at 375° for 25-30 minutes or until a toothpick comes out clean. Cool for 5 minutes before removing from pan to a wire rack. Serve warm. Refrigerate leftovers. **Yield:** 1 dozen.

POPPY SEED ORANGE MUFFINS

Cindy Kroon, Hartford, South Dakota

When our whole family has the day off together, we like to start our day with muffins for breakfast. This recipe made me a runner-up winner in the baked goods division at our county fair.

> 2/3 cup butter *or* margarine, softened
> 1 cup sugar
> 2 eggs
> 1 cup (8 ounces) plain yogurt
> 1/4 cup orange juice concentrate
> 1/4 cup grated orange peel
> 1 teaspoon orange extract
> 2-2/3 cups all-purpose flour
> 2 tablespoons poppy seeds
> 1 teaspoon baking soda
> 1 teaspoon salt

In a mixing bowl, cream butter and sugar. Add eggs, one at a time, beating well after each addition. Stir in the yogurt, orange juice concentrate, orange peel and extract. Combine the dry ingredients; add to creamed mixture just until moistened. Fill paper-lined muffin cups two-thirds full. Bake at 400° for 15-18 minutes or until a toothpick comes out clean. Cool for 5 minutes before removing from pans to wire racks. **Yield:** 16 muffins.

SPINACH CHEESE MUFFINS

Nancy Zimmerman
Cape May Court House, New Jersey

Muffins are my most favorite thing to bake because they're so fast and versatile. This version makes a great substitute for typical dinner bread and adds a little color to your table.

> 2 cups all-purpose flour
> 1/4 cup grated Parmesan cheese
> 2 tablespoons chopped green onions
> 1 tablespoon baking powder
> 1/4 teaspoon salt
> 1 egg
> 1-1/4 cups milk
> 1/3 cup butter *or* margarine, melted
> 1/2 cup chopped fresh spinach *or* 1/4 cup frozen chopped spinach, thawed and well drained

1/2 cup shredded Swiss cheese
Additional Parmesan cheese

In a large bowl, combine the flour, Parmesan cheese, onions, baking powder and salt. In another bowl, beat the egg, milk and butter. Stir into dry ingredients just until moistened. Fold in spinach and Swiss cheese. Fill greased muffin cups three-fourths full. Sprinkle with additional Parmesan cheese. Bake at 400° for 18-20 minutes or until a toothpick comes out clean. Cool for 5 minutes before removing from pan to a wire rack. Serve warm. Refrigerate leftovers. **Yield:** 1 dozen.

GREEN ONION MUFFINS

Janet Everson, Lake Mills, Wisconsin

I don't spend as much time in the kitchen as I did when our children were still at home. When I feel like baking these days, I share the goodies with neighbors.

1-3/4 cups all-purpose flour
1 cup crushed Rice Chex cereal
4 teaspoons baking powder
1 tablespoon sugar
1 teaspoon salt
2 eggs
1-1/4 cups milk
1/3 cup vegetable oil
1 package (3 ounces) cream cheese, cut into 1/4-inch cubes
1/2 cup chopped green onions

In a large bowl, combine the flour, cereal, baking powder, sugar and salt. In another bowl, beat the eggs, milk and oil. Stir into dry ingredients just until moistened. Fold in cream cheese and onions. Fill greased muffin cups two-thirds full. Bake at 400° for 15-20 minutes or until a toothpick comes out clean. Cool for 5 minutes before removing from pans to wire racks. Serve warm. Refrigerate leftovers. **Yield:** 1-1/2 dozen.

ALMOND PEAR MUFFINS

Frances Finegan, Gaithersburg, Maryland

I always bake muffins on the weekends and freeze them for breakfasts or snacks during the week. I take a few out in the morning, and they thaw by the time I get to work.

1 cup all-purpose flour
1 cup whole wheat flour
1/2 cup sugar
1 teaspoon baking powder
1 teaspoon baking soda
1 teaspoon ground cinnamon
1/4 teaspoon salt
1/4 teaspoon ground nutmeg
1/4 teaspoon ground cloves
2 eggs
1/2 cup plain yogurt
1/2 cup milk
1/2 cup vegetable oil
1 teaspoon almond extract
1 cup chopped peeled pear (about 1 medium)
1/2 cup chopped almonds

In a large bowl, combine the first nine ingredients. In another bowl, beat the eggs, yogurt, milk, oil and extract. Stir into dry ingredients just until moistened. Fold in pear and almonds. Fill greased or paper-lined muffin cups two-thirds full. Bake at 400° for 12-15 minutes or until a toothpick comes out clean. Cool for 5 minutes before removing from pans to wire racks. **Yield:** 15 muffins.

CITRUS DATE MUFFINS

Mary Ann Kerst, Wray, Colorado

These cake-like muffins have a nice balance of chewy dates and crunchy pecans. A sweet orange glaze is the perfect complement to the mild-flavored muffin.

1/2 cup chopped dates
1/2 cup chopped pecans
2 tablespoons plus 2 cups all-purpose flour, *divided*
1 cup shortening
1 cup sugar
2 eggs
1 teaspoon baking soda
1/4 teaspoon salt
2/3 cup buttermilk
GLAZE:
1/2 cup sugar
1/4 to 1/3 cup orange juice
2 teaspoons grated orange peel

In a bowl, combine dates and pecans; add 2 tablespoons flour. Toss to coat; set aside. In a mixing bowl, cream shortening and sugar. Add eggs, one at a time, beating well after each addition. Combine the baking soda, salt and remaining flour; add to creamed mixture alternately with buttermilk. Fold in the date mixture (batter will be stiff). Fill greased muffin cups two-thirds full. Bake at 375° for 18-20 minutes or until a toothpick comes out clean. Cool for 5 minutes before removing from pans to wire racks. Meanwhile, in a saucepan, combine glaze ingredients. Cook and stir over low heat until sugar is dissolved. Spoon over warm muffins. **Yield:** 16 muffins.

OLIVE PEPPERONI SNACK MUFFINS

Dorothy Swanson, St. Louis, Missouri

(Pictured at left)

Savory Italian-flavored treats will delight the sports fans in your family while they watch their favorite game. Try them as a perfect partner to a hot bowl of soup.

    3 cups all-purpose flour
    2 tablespoons sugar
1-1/2 teaspoons baking powder
1-1/2 teaspoons salt
    1/2 teaspoon dried oregano
    1/4 teaspoon baking soda
    1 package (8 ounces) cream cheese, softened
    2 eggs
    1 cup plus 2 tablespoons milk
    1/4 cup vegetable oil
    1 package (3-1/2 ounces) pepperoni, diced
    1/4 cup chopped stuffed olives

In a large bowl, combine the flour, sugar, baking powder, salt, oregano and baking soda. In a mixing bowl, beat the cream cheese, eggs, milk and oil until smooth. Stir into dry ingredients just until moistened. Fold in the pepperoni and olives. Fill greased or paper-lined muffin cups three-fourths full. Bake at 375° for 20-25 minutes or until a toothpick comes out clean. Cool for 5 minutes before removing from pans to wire racks. Serve warm. Refrigerate leftovers. **Yield:** 22 muffins.

BARBECUED CORN MUFFINS

Shawn Roland, Madison, Mississippi

(Pictured at left)

Being raised on a farm in Mississippi, I was encouraged to cook at an early age by my grandmother and mother. I rarely depend on written recipes, but this is a classic.

1/2 pound ground beef
1/4 cup packed brown sugar
1/4 cup ketchup
    1 tablespoon Worcestershire sauce
    1 teaspoon prepared mustard
1/2 teaspoon salt
1/4 teaspoon pepper
1/4 teaspoon garlic powder
    1 package (8-1/2 ounces) corn bread/muffin mix
2/3 cup shredded cheddar cheese

LIP-SMACKING SNACKS. Pictured at left, top to bottom: Olive Pepperoni Snack Muffins and Barbecued Corn Muffins (recipes on this page).

In a skillet, cook beef over medium heat until no longer pink; drain and place in a bowl. Add brown sugar, ketchup, Worcestershire sauce, mustard, salt, pepper and garlic powder. Prepare corn bread mix according to package directions. Fill greased muffin cups with a scant 2 tablespoons of batter. Top each with 2 tablespoons beef mixture; sprinkle with cheese. Top with remaining corn bread mix. Bake at 400° for 12-15 minutes or until a toothpick comes out clean. Cool for 5 minutes before removing from pan to a wire rack. Serve warm. Refrigerate leftovers. **Yield:** 1 dozen.

BANANA BRAN MUFFINS

Shelley Mitchell, Baldur, Manitoba

Our four daughters love these spiced moist muffins. With a little help from myself or my mom, the girls are all learning to be great cooks.

1-1/2 cups all-purpose flour
    1 cup oat bran
    1/2 cup whole wheat flour
    1 tablespoon ground cinnamon
    2 teaspoons baking powder
    2 teaspoons baking soda
    1/2 teaspoon ground nutmeg
    1/4 teaspoon ground allspice
    2 eggs
    1 cup orange juice
    1/2 cup sugar
    1/2 cup packed brown sugar
    1/2 cup vegetable oil
    1 cup mashed ripe bananas (2 to 3 medium)
    1/2 cup chopped walnuts

In a large bowl, combine the first eight ingredients. In another bowl, beat the eggs, juice, sugars and oil. Stir into dry ingredients just until moistened. Fold in bananas and nuts. Fill greased or paper-lined muffin cups two-thirds full. Bake at 400° for 15-18 minutes or until a toothpick comes out clean. Cool for 5 minutes before removing from pans to wire racks. Serve warm. **Yield:** 2 dozen. **Editor's Note:** Four dozen miniature muffin cups may be used; bake for 10-12 minutes.

MAKING MUFFINS

- *Mix the dry ingredients and liquids just until dry ingredients are moistened. A lumpy batter will yield tender muffins.*
- *If you don't have enough batter to fill all muffin cups, put some water in the empty cups so the muffins bake evenly.*
- *Muffins are done when a toothpick inserted near the center comes out clean.*

BREAKFAST IN A BISCUIT

Janeil Rasmussen, Pocatello, Idaho

This recipe brings back memories of my youth. My mother used to make these muffins as a special breakfast treat. My husband and I also have them for dinner.

> 2 cups all-purpose flour
> 1 tablespoon baking powder
> 1 teaspoon salt
> 1/4 cup shortening
> 3/4 cup milk
> 3/4 pound bulk pork sausage, cooked and drained
> 1/2 cup shredded Co-Jack cheese
> 2 tablespoons sliced green onion
> 2 eggs, beaten
> Melted butter *or* margarine

In a large bowl, combine flour, baking powder and salt. Cut in shortening until mixture resembles coarse crumbs. Stir in milk to form a soft dough. Divide into 12 portions. Roll each into a 6-in. circle; press each into a greased muffin cup. Fill each with 2 tablespoons sausage and about 1 teaspoon cheese. Sprinkle with onion. Spoon about 2 teaspoons beaten egg over each. Pinch crust together over filling to seal; brush with butter. Bake at 400° for 18-22 minutes or until golden brown. Cool for 5 minutes before removing from pan to a wire rack. Serve warm. Refrigerate leftovers. **Yield:** 1 dozen.

PUMPKIN STREUSEL MUFFINS

Barbara Nowakowski, North Tonawanda, New York

Their cream cheese filling and sweet crunchy topping make these moist muffins one of my most requested recipes. They smell so good while baking on a cold, snowy day.

> 1-3/4 cups all-purpose flour
> 1/2 cup sugar
> 3 teaspoons baking powder
> 1 teaspoon ground cinnamon
> 1/2 teaspoon salt
> 1/2 teaspoon ground nutmeg
> 1 egg
> 1/2 cup milk
> 1/2 cup cooked *or* canned pumpkin
> 1/3 cup vegetable oil
> 1 package (3 ounces) cream cheese, cut into 12 cubes
> **STREUSEL:**
> 1/4 cup packed brown sugar
> 1/2 teaspoon ground cinnamon
> 1 tablespoon cold butter *or* margarine
> 1/4 cup finely chopped nuts

In a large bowl, combine the flour, sugar, baking powder, cinnamon, salt and nutmeg. In another bowl, beat the egg, milk, pumpkin and oil. Stir into dry ingredients just until moistened. Fill greased or paper-lined muffin cups one-fourth full. Place one cream cheese cube in the center of each muffin cup; top with remaining batter. In a bowl, combine brown sugar and cinnamon; cut in butter until mixture resembles coarse crumbs. Add nuts. Sprinkle over batter. Bake at 400° for 18-22 minutes or until a toothpick comes out clean. Cool for 5 minutes before removing from pan to a wire rack. **Yield:** 1 dozen.

CHOCOLATE CHIP BANANA MUFFINS

Lois Gordon, Langley, British Columbia

These banana muffins are my kids' favorite. I adapt it for adults by adding chopped nuts or dried apricots.

> 1-3/4 cups all-purpose flour
> 3/4 cup sugar
> 1 teaspoon baking powder
> 1 teaspoon baking soda
> 1/2 teaspoon salt
> 1 egg
> 1/2 cup vegetable oil
> 1/2 cup plain yogurt
> 1 teaspoon vanilla extract
> 1 cup mashed ripe bananas (2 to 3 medium)
> 3/4 cup semisweet chocolate chips

In a large bowl, combine the flour, sugar, baking powder, baking soda and salt. In another bowl, combine the egg, oil, yogurt and vanilla. Stir into dry ingredients just until moistened. Fold in bananas and chocolate chips. Fill greased or paper-lined muffin cups two-thirds full. Bake at 350° for 22-25 minutes or until a toothpick comes out clean. Cool for 5 minutes before removing from pans to wire racks. **Yield:** 16 muffins.

NORTHWOODS MUFFINS

Kay Englund, Ham Lake, Minnesota

Even family and friends who aren't fond of wild rice rave about these golden muffins flecked with colorful blueberries and cranberries. They're a terrific take-along treat.

> 2 cups all-purpose flour
> 1/2 cup sugar
> 3 teaspoons baking powder
> 1/2 teaspoon salt
> 2 eggs
> 3/4 cup buttermilk
> 1/4 cup butter *or* margarine, melted
> 1 cup cooked wild rice
> 1/2 cup fresh *or* frozen blueberries*
> 1/2 cup fresh *or* frozen cranberries

In a large bowl, combine the flour, sugar, baking powder and salt. In another bowl, beat the eggs, buttermilk and butter. Stir into dry ingredients just until moistened. Fold in rice, blueberries and cranberries. Fill greased or paper-lined muffin cups two-thirds full. Bake at 375° for 20-25 minutes or until a toothpick comes out clean. Cool for 5 minutes before removing from pans to wire racks. **Yield:** 16 muffins. *Editor's Note:* If using frozen blueberries, do not thaw before adding to the batter.

CRANBERRY PECAN MUFFINS

Marilyn Gorham, Mora, Minnesota

I often serve these colorful muffins when my United Methodist circle meets at my home. They are always a hit.

    1/2 cup butter *or* margarine, softened
      1 cup sugar
      2 eggs
      1 teaspoon vanilla extract
      1 cup (8 ounces) sour cream
      2 cups all-purpose flour
      1 teaspoon baking powder
    1/2 teaspoon baking soda
    1/2 teaspoon ground nutmeg
    1/4 teaspoon salt
    3/4 cup coarsely chopped fresh *or* frozen
        cranberries
    1/2 cup chopped pecans
TOPPING:
      2 tablespoons sugar
    1/8 teaspoon ground nutmeg

In a mixing bowl, cream butter and sugar. Add eggs, one at a time, beating well after each addition. Add vanilla. Fold in sour cream. Combine the flour, baking powder, baking soda, nutmeg and salt; stir into creamed mixture just until moistened. Fold in cranberries and pecans. Fill greased or paper-lined muffin cups two-thirds full. Combine topping ingredients; sprinkle over batter. Bake at 400° for 20-25 minutes or until a toothpick comes out clean. Cool for 5 minutes before removing from pans to wire racks. **Yield:** 16 muffins.

PEANUT BUTTER MINI MUFFINS

Connie Barz, San Antonio, Texas

These bite-size muffins are perfect to send in our kids' lunches for snacktime. I make regular-size muffins for church functions and watch them disappear.

  1-3/4 cups all-purpose flour
    2/3 cup packed brown sugar
  2-1/2 teaspoons baking powder

    1/4 teaspoon salt
      1 egg
    3/4 cup milk
    2/3 cup chunky peanut butter
    1/4 cup vegetable oil
  1-1/2 teaspoons vanilla extract
    2/3 cup miniature semisweet chocolate chips

In a large bowl, combine the first four ingredients. In another bowl, combine the egg, milk, peanut butter, oil and vanilla. Stir into dry ingredients just until moistened. Fold in chocolate chips. Fill greased or paper-lined miniature muffin cups two-thirds full. Bake at 350° for 15-17 minutes or until a toothpick comes out clean. Cool for 5 minutes before removing from pans to wire racks. **Yield:** 4 dozen. **Editor's Note:** Twelve regular-size muffin cups may be used; bake for 22-25 minutes.

CARROT CHEESECAKE MUFFINS

Joyce Brash, New Richmond, Quebec

With a rich cream cheese filling and flecks of carrots, raisins and nuts, these moist muffins will certainly bring compliments to the cook.

      4 ounces cream cheese, softened
      2 tablespoons sugar
  1-1/2 teaspoons grated orange peel
BATTER:
    1/3 cup butter *or* margarine, softened
    1/2 cup packed brown sugar
      2 eggs
    1/2 cup evaporated milk
      2 tablespoons orange juice
  1-1/4 cups finely grated carrots
        (about 3 medium)
    1/2 cup raisins
    1/2 cup chopped walnuts
  1-1/2 cups all-purpose
        flour
      1 teaspoon
        baking powder
    1/2 teaspoon baking soda
    1/2 teaspoon ground cinnamon

In a mixing bowl, beat cream cheese, sugar and orange peel until smooth; set aside. In another mixing bowl, cream butter and brown sugar. Add eggs, milk and orange juice. Fold in the carrots, raisins and walnuts. Combine the flour, baking powder, baking soda and cinnamon; stir into creamed mixture just until moistened. Fill greased muffin cups with 2 tablespoons batter. Top each with 2 teaspoons filling; top with remaining batter. Bake at 350° for 23-25 minutes or until a toothpick comes out clean. Cool for 5 minutes before removing from pan to a wire rack. Store in the refrigerator. **Yield:** 1 dozen.

HAM 'N' CHEESE MUFFINS

Kati DeLaurier, Pine Mountain Club, California

While living in Oregon, I frequented a local restaurant that served these muffins. They wouldn't share the recipe, so I came up with my own creation.

1-3/4 cups all-purpose flour
2-1/2 teaspoons baking powder
  1 teaspoon ground mustard
  1/2 teaspoon ground cumin
    2 eggs
    1 cup buttermilk
    2 cups diced fully cooked ham
    2 cups (8 ounces) shredded cheddar cheese,
      divided

In a large bowl, combine the flour, baking powder, mustard and cumin. In another bowl, beat eggs and buttermilk. Stir into dry ingredients just until moistened. Fold in ham and 1-1/4 cups cheese. Fill greased muffin cups two-thirds full. Sprinkle with remaining cheese. Bake at 375° for 20-25 minutes or until a toothpick comes out clean. Cool for 5 minutes before removing from pans to wire racks. Serve warm. Refrigerate leftovers. **Yield:** 1-1/2 dozen.

LEMON YOGURT MUFFINS

Nicole Horne, Macon, Georgia

I only had this recipe a short time before it became a personal favorite. Folks like the light and tender texture of these muffins. I'm grateful to my mother, who taught me the goodness of baking from scratch.

1-3/4 cups all-purpose flour
  3/4 cup sugar
    1 tablespoon grated lemon peel
    1 teaspoon baking powder
  3/4 teaspoon baking soda
  1/4 teaspoon salt
    1 egg
    1 cup (8 ounces) lemon *or* plain yogurt
    6 tablespoons butter *or* margarine, melted
    1 tablespoon lemon juice
TOPPING:
  1/3 cup lemon juice
  1/4 cup sugar
    1 teaspoon grated lemon peel

In a large bowl, combine the first six ingredients. In another bowl, beat the egg, yogurt, butter and lemon juice. Stir into dry ingredients just until moistened. Fill greased muffin cups two-thirds full. Bake at 400° for 20-24 minutes or until a toothpick comes out clean. Cool for 5 minutes; leave muffins in pan. Using a toothpick, poke 6-8 holes in each muffin. In a saucepan, combine the topping ingredients. Cook

and stir over low heat until sugar is dissolved. Spoon over warm muffins. **Yield:** 1 dozen.

POPPY SEED MUFFINS

Susan Riediger, Oswego, Illinois

Spending time in the kitchen is one of the best ways I know how to relax. Since a crafting friend shared the recipe, I've made these traditional muffins with a spectacular glaze more times than I can count.

    3 cups all-purpose flour
2-1/2 cups sugar
4-1/2 teaspoons poppy seeds
1-1/2 teaspoons baking powder
1-1/2 teaspoons salt
    3 eggs
1-1/2 cups milk
    1 cup vegetable oil
1-1/2 teaspoons vanilla extract
1-1/2 teaspoons almond extract
GLAZE:
  3/4 cup sugar
  1/4 cup orange juice
    2 teaspoons butter *or* margarine, melted
  1/2 teaspoon vanilla extract
  1/2 teaspoon almond extract

In a large bowl, combine the flour, sugar, poppy seeds, baking powder and salt. In another bowl, beat the eggs, milk, oil and extracts. Stir into dry ingredients just until moistened. Fill greased muffin cups two-thirds full. Bake at 350° for 22-25 minutes or until a toothpick comes out clean. Cool for 5 minutes before removing from pans to wire racks. Combine glaze ingredients; spoon over warm muffins. Serve immediately. **Yield:** 2 dozen.

CHOCOLATE MUFFINS

Nellie Million Wimmer, Portage, Michigan

This recipe originally called for applesauce, but one time in a pinch, I substituted sour cream...it worked! Chocolate lovers can't resist these rich cake-like muffins.

2-2/3 cups all-purpose flour
1-1/2 cups sugar
  1/2 cup baking cocoa
1-1/2 teaspoons baking soda
  1/2 teaspoon salt
    3 eggs
    1 cup (8 ounces) sour cream
  1/2 cup water

1/2 cup milk
1/2 cup vegetable oil
 1 teaspoon vanilla extract
1/2 cup semisweet chocolate chips

In a large bowl, combine the flour, sugar, cocoa, baking soda and salt. In another bowl, beat the eggs, sour cream, water, milk, oil and vanilla. Stir into dry ingredients just until moistened. Fold in chocolate chips. Fill greased or paper-lined muffin cups two-thirds full. Bake at 325° for 20-25 minutes or until a toothpick comes out clean. Cool for 5 minutes before removing from pans to wire racks. **Yield:** 2 dozen.

BEST BRAN MUFFINS

Karen Hill, Willamina, Oregon

When my twin sister and I were in high school, these muffins were a staple in our home. I've made a few adjustments to the recipe, but it remains a winner.

1-1/2 cups old-fashioned oats
 1 cup All-Bran
 1 cup boiling water
1/2 cup sugar
1/2 cup packed brown sugar
1/2 cup butter *or* margarine, melted
 2 eggs, beaten
1/4 cup toasted wheat germ
2-1/2 cups all-purpose flour
2-1/2 teaspoons baking soda
1/2 teaspoon salt
 2 cups buttermilk

Place oats and cereal in a bowl; cover with boiling water. Let stand for 5 minutes. Stir in sugars, butter, eggs and wheat germ; mix well. Combine the flour, baking soda and salt; stir into oat mixture alternately with buttermilk just until moistened. Fill greased muffin cups two-thirds full. Bake at 375° for 18-20 minutes or until a toothpick comes out clean. Cool for 5 minutes before removing from pans to wire racks. **Yield:** 2 dozen.

BACON CHEESE MUFFINS

Deb Bowyer, Fort St. John, British Columbia

The first time I made these muffins, my husband thought he'd gone to heaven! I found the recipe in an old cookbook and added more spices for a little extra zip.

 2 cups all-purpose flour
 1 cup (4 ounces) shredded cheddar cheese
 8 bacon strips, cooked and crumbled

 2 tablespoons sugar
 3 teaspoons baking powder
1/4 teaspoon salt
1/8 teaspoon garlic powder
1/8 teaspoon lemon-pepper seasoning
 1 egg
 1 cup milk
1/4 cup vegetable oil

In a large bowl, combine the first eight ingredients. In another bowl, beat the egg, milk and oil. Stir into dry ingredients just until moistened. Fill greased muffin cups two-thirds full. Bake at 400° for 15-20 minutes or until a toothpick comes out clean. Cool for 5 minutes before removing from pan to a wire rack. Serve warm. Refrigerate leftovers. **Yield:** 1 dozen.

APPLE CRUNCH MUFFINS

Brenda Betz, Oakland, Maryland

These apple-filled muffins taste like little coffee cakes. I sometimes drizzle hot caramel over the muffins and serve them as dessert.

1-1/2 cups all-purpose flour
3/4 cup sugar
 2 teaspoons baking powder
 1 teaspoon ground cinnamon
1/4 teaspoon baking soda
1/4 teaspoon salt
1/4 teaspoon ground allspice
1/8 teaspoon ground nutmeg
 2 eggs
1-1/4 cups sour cream
1/2 cup butter *or* margarine, melted
 1 cup diced unpeeled tart apple
TOPPING:
1/2 cup chopped walnuts
1/4 cup all-purpose flour
 3 tablespoons sugar
1/4 teaspoon ground cinnamon
1/8 teaspoon ground nutmeg
 2 tablespoons cold butter *or* margarine

In a large bowl, combine the first eight ingredients. In another bowl, beat the eggs, sour cream and butter. Stir into dry ingredients just until moistened. Fold in apple. Fill greased or paper-lined muffin cups one-third full. For topping, combine the walnuts, flour, sugar, cinnamon and nutmeg. Cut in butter until mixture resembles coarse crumbs. Sprinkle about two-thirds of the topping over batter. Top with remaining batter; sprinkle with remaining topping. Bake at 375° for 20-25 minutes or until a toothpick comes out clean. Cool for 5 minutes before removing from pans to wire racks. **Yield:** 16 muffins.

Quick Breads

Whether they feature sweet fruits and chocolate or savory herbs and cheese, fast-to-fix quick breads round out meals from morning 'til night.

CHEESE-FILLED GINGER BREAD

Michelle Smith, Running Springs, California

(Pictured at left)

I very rarely make special trips to the store for one or two forgotten groceries. I prefer to "wing it" in the kitchen. It was during one of those cooking experiments that I created this variation of honey nut bread.

   1 package (8 ounces) cream cheese, softened
   1 cup sugar
   1/3 cup all-purpose flour
   1 egg
BATTER:
   3 cups all-purpose flour
   1/2 cup sugar
1-1/2 teaspoons baking soda
1-1/2 teaspoons salt
   1 teaspoon ground ginger
   2 eggs
   3/4 cup milk
   3/4 cup vegetable oil
   1/2 cup molasses
1-1/2 cups chopped walnuts
GLAZE:
   1 cup confectioners' sugar
   1 to 2 tablespoons milk

In a mixing bowl, beat the first four ingredients until smooth; set aside. In a large bowl, combine the flour, sugar, baking soda, salt and ginger. In another bowl, beat the eggs, milk, oil and molasses until smooth. Stir into dry ingredients just until moistened. Fold in walnuts. Spoon a third of the batter into a greased and floured 10-in. fluted tube pan. Top with the reserved cream cheese mixture. Carefully spoon remaining batter over filling. Bake at 350° for 40-50 minutes or until a toothpick comes out clean. Cool for 10 minutes before removing from pan to a wire rack. For glaze, combine confectioners' sugar and enough milk to achieve desired consistency. Drizzle over bread. Store in the refrigerator. **Yield:** 16-20 servings.

BREADS IN A JIFFY. Pictured at left, top to bottom: Cheese-Filled Ginger Bread (recipe on this page), Little Texas Corn Bread (recipe on page 26) and Cranberry Streusel Loaf (recipe on this page).

CRANBERRY STREUSEL LOAF

Lois McAtee, Oceanside, California

(Pictured at left)

I relied on this foolproof recipe when teaching our children to cook. Each slice is dotted with plump cranberries and flecks of orange peel.

   1/3 cup packed brown sugar
   3 tablespoons all-purpose flour
   2 tablespoons cold butter *or* margarine
   3/4 cup finely chopped pecans
BREAD:
   2 cups all-purpose flour
   3/4 cup sugar
1-1/2 teaspoons baking powder
   1/2 teaspoon ground nutmeg
   1/2 teaspoon ground allspice
   1/4 teaspoon salt
   1 egg
   3/4 cup orange juice
   3 tablespoons butter *or* margarine, melted
   2 tablespoons grated orange peel
   1 cup fresh *or* frozen cranberries
   1/2 cup golden raisins

In a bowl, combine brown sugar and flour. Cut in butter until crumbly. Stir in pecans; set aside. In a large bowl, combine the flour, sugar, baking powder, nutmeg, allspice and salt. In another bowl, beat the egg, orange juice, butter and orange peel. Stir into dry ingredients just until moistened. Fold in cranberries and raisins. Transfer half of the batter to a greased 9-in. x 5-in. x 3-in. loaf pan. Sprinkle with half of the streusel; repeat layers. Bake at 350° for 65-70 minutes or until a toothpick comes out clean. Cool for 10 minutes before removing from pan to a wire rack. **Yield:** 1 loaf.

QUICK BREAD BASICS

- *When making quick breads, be sure to only blend the liquid and dry ingredients just until moistened. Overmixing can create a coarse, tough texture.*
- *Test loaves for doneness 10 to 15 minutes before the end of baking time. The bread is done if a toothpick comes out clean. Most recipes instruct you to let the bread cool in the pan for a few minutes before removing to a wire rack.*

LITTLE TEXAS CORN BREAD

Mildred Sherrer
Bay City, Texas

(Pictured at left and on page 24)

Cheddar cheese, cream-style corn and green chilies dress up ordinary corn bread. Generous slices taste great with a bowl of chili. A friend gave me this recipe.

> 1 cup cornmeal
> 1 cup (4 ounces) shredded cheddar cheese
> 1 tablespoon baking powder
> 2 eggs
> 1 can (8-1/2 ounces) cream-style corn
> 1 cup (8 ounces) sour cream
> 1/2 cup vegetable oil
> 1 can (4 ounces) chopped green chilies, drained

In a large bowl, combine the cornmeal, cheese and baking powder. In another bowl, combine the eggs, corn, sour cream, oil and chilies. Stir into dry ingredients just until moistened. Pour into a greased 8-in. square baking pan. Bake at 400° for 30-35 minutes or until a toothpick comes out clean. Serve warm. Refrigerate leftovers. **Yield:** 8 servings. **Editor's Note:** This recipe does not contain flour.

SOUR CREAM COFFEE CAKE

Doris Rice, Storm Lake, Iowa

This coffee cake is a favorite for breakfast or brunch. I've also taken it to potlucks and served it as dessert. Tender slices feature an appealing crunchy filling.

> 1 cup butter *or* margarine, softened
> 1-1/2 cups sugar
> 3 eggs
> 1 teaspoon *each* almond, lemon and vanilla extract
> 2-1/2 cups all-purpose flour
> 2 teaspoons baking powder
> 1 teaspoon baking soda
> 1 cup (8 ounces) sour cream
> FILLING:
> 1/3 cup chopped pecans
> 3 tablespoons sugar
> 1 tablespoon ground cinnamon
> GLAZE:
> 1 cup confectioners' sugar
> 2 tablespoons milk

In a mixing bowl, cream butter and sugar. Add eggs, one at a time, beating well after each addition. Beat in extracts. Combine the flour, baking powder and baking soda; add to creamed mixture alternately with sour cream. Spread half of the batter in a greased and floured 10-in. fluted tube pan. Make a well in the center of the batter. Combine filling ingredients; sprinkle into well. Carefully cover with remaining batter. Bake at 350° for 45-50 minutes or until a toothpick comes out clean. Cool for 10 minutes before removing from pan to a wire rack. Combine glaze ingredients; drizzle over warm cake. **Yield:** 16-20 servings.

BOSTON BROWN BREAD

Shellie Robb, Cleveland, Ohio

Baking this bread in coffee cans lends to its interesting shape. At Christmas, I often make gift boxes for friends and family featuring this bread and various spreads.

> 2 eggs
> 2 cups packed brown sugar
> 1 cup molasses
> 1 quart buttermilk
> 4 cups whole wheat flour
> 2 cups all-purpose flour
> 2 teaspoons salt
> 2 teaspoons baking soda
> 1 cup raisins
> 1 cup chopped walnuts
> Butter *or* cream cheese, optional

In a mixing bowl, beat eggs and brown sugar. Add molasses and buttermilk; mix well. Combine the flours, salt and baking soda; stir into egg mixture just until moistened. Fold in raisins and walnuts. Transfer to five greased 13-oz. coffee cans. Bake at 325° for 75-80 minutes or until a toothpick comes out clean. Cool for 10 minutes before removing from cans to wire racks. Serve with butter or cream cheese if desired. **Yield:** 5 loaves. **Editor's Note:** Two 9-in. x 5-in. x 3-in. loaf pans may be used instead of the coffee cans; bake for 80-85 minutes.

COCONUT BREAD

Janis Hoople, Stanton, Michigan

Sprinkling sugar on top of this bread before baking gives it a delectable crunch. The flavor from almond extract pairs nicely with the coconut.

> 1/4 cup butter *or* margarine, softened
> 1 cup sugar
> 1 egg
> 1/2 teaspoon vanilla extract
> 1/2 teaspoon almond extract
> 2 cups all-purpose flour

3 teaspoons baking powder
1/4 teaspoon salt
1 cup milk
3/4 cup flaked coconut
Additional sugar

In a mixing bowl, cream butter and sugar. Beat in the egg and extracts. Combine the flour, baking powder and salt; add to creamed mixture alternately with milk. Fold in coconut. Pour into a greased 9-in. x 5-in. x 3-in. loaf pan. Sprinkle with sugar. Bake at 350° for 50-55 minutes or until a toothpick comes out clean. Cool for 10 minutes before removing from pan to a wire rack. **Yield:** 1 loaf.

BEST CHEESE BREAD

Joanie Elbourn, Gardner, Massachusetts

My husband and I often make a meal of bread and salad. We enjoy the garlic, dill and cheddar flavors in this savory bread. We think it's best served fresh from the oven.

3-3/4 cups all-purpose flour
2-1/2 cups (10 ounces) shredded cheddar cheese
5 teaspoons baking powder
1/2 teaspoon dill weed
1/2 teaspoon garlic powder
2 eggs
1-1/2 cups milk
1/3 cup vegetable oil
3 tablespoons honey

In a large bowl, combine the flour, cheese, baking powder, dill and garlic powder. In another bowl, beat the eggs, milk, oil and honey. Stir into dry ingredients just until moistened. Pour into a greased 9-in. x 5-in. x 3-in. loaf pan. Bake at 350° for 55-65 minutes or until a toothpick comes out clean (top will have an uneven appearance). Cool for 10 minutes before removing from pan to a wire rack. Serve warm. Refrigerate leftovers. **Yield:** 1 loaf.

BANANA SPLIT BREAD

Janice Allnatt, Rochester, New York

I developed this recipe in an effort to add pizzazz to my plain banana bread. I was pleased with the results, and so were my family and friends.

2/3 cup shortening
1-1/4 cups sugar
4 eggs
3-1/2 cups all-purpose flour
2-1/2 teaspoons baking powder

1 teaspoon baking soda
1/2 teaspoon salt
1-1/2 cups mashed ripe bananas (about 4 medium)
2 cans (8 ounces *each*) crushed pineapple, drained
2 cups (12 ounces) semisweet chocolate chips
1 jar (10 ounces) red maraschino cherries, well drained and chopped
1 cup chopped walnuts

In a mixing bowl, cream shortening and sugar. Add eggs, one at a time, beating well after each addition. Combine the flour, baking powder, baking soda and salt; add to creamed mixture alternately with banana and pineapple. Fold in the chocolate chips, cherries and walnuts. Pour into two greased 9-in. x 5-in. x 3-in. loaf pans. Bake at 350° for 60-65 minutes or until a toothpick comes out clean. Cool for 10 minutes before removing from pans to wire racks. **Yield:** 2 loaves. **Editor's Note:** Four 5-3/4-in. x 3-in. x 2-in. loaf pans may be used; bake for 50-55 minutes.

SWEET 'N' SAVORY DATE LOAVES

Diane Card, Hilliard, Ohio

My family and I were thrilled when this won "best of show" for quick breads at the state fair a few years ago. I sometimes substitute peach nectar for the apricot nectar with terrific results.

1-1/2 cups apricot nectar
1-1/2 cups chopped dates
1/2 cup chopped dried apricots
1 tablespoon grated orange peel
1-1/4 teaspoons dried rosemary, crushed
1/2 cup butter *or* margarine, softened
1 cup sugar
1 egg
1/3 cup evaporated milk
2-1/4 cups all-purpose flour
1-1/2 teaspoons baking soda

In a saucepan, bring the apricot nectar, dates and apricots to a boil. Reduce heat; cover and simmer for 5 minutes. Remove from the heat; add orange peel and rosemary. Cool for 10 minutes. In a mixing bowl, cream butter and sugar. Beat in egg and milk. Combine flour and baking soda; add to creamed mixture alternately with date mixture. Pour into three greased 5-3/4-in. x 3-in. x 2-in. loaf pans. Bake at 375° for 30-35 minutes or until a toothpick comes out clean. Cool for 10 minutes before removing from pans to wire racks. **Yield:** 3 mini loaves.

ORANGE CHOCOLATE CHIP BREAD

Luene Byers, Salt Lake City, Utah

The classic combination of flavors in this recipe reminds me of the orange and chocolate candy my grandmother made for the holidays. We like to snack on this bread throughout the day.

- 1 medium navel orange
- 2 cups all-purpose flour
- 1 cup sugar
- 1 teaspoon baking powder
- 1/2 teaspoon salt
- 1/2 teaspoon baking soda
- 1 egg
- 2 tablespoons butter *or* margarine, melted
- 1 teaspoon vanilla extract
- 1 cup (6 ounces) semisweet chocolate chips

Wash and grate orange. Place orange peel in a small bowl. Juice orange. Add enough boiling water to the juice to measure 1 cup. Pour over orange peel; let stand for 10 minutes. Meanwhile, in a large bowl, combine the flour, sugar, baking powder, salt and baking soda. In another bowl, beat egg, butter, vanilla and reserved orange mixture; mix well. Stir into dry ingredients just until moistened. Fold in chocolate chips. Pour into a greased 8-in. x 4-in. x 2-in. loaf pan. Bake at 350° for 55-65 minutes or until a toothpick comes out clean. Cool for 10 minutes before removing from pan to a wire rack. **Yield:** 1 loaf.

BLUEBERRY STREUSEL COFFEE CAKE

Eunice Sawatzky, Lowe Farm, Manitoba

My sister-in-law made this coffee cake with the fresh blueberries we picked while our families were vacationing at her cottage one summer. I've used frozen berries at home with wonderful results. Each time I bake this bread, we're reminded of fun times.

- 1/2 cup butter *or* margarine, softened
- 1-3/4 cups sugar
- 2 eggs
- 2 teaspoons vanilla extract
- 3-1/2 cups all-purpose flour
- 2 tablespoons baking powder
- 1 teaspoon salt
- 1-1/2 cups milk
- 3 cups fresh *or* frozen blueberries*

STREUSEL TOPPING:
- 3/4 cup sugar
- 1/2 teaspoon ground cinnamon
- 1/3 cup cold butter *or* margarine

In a mixing bowl, cream butter and sugar. Beat in eggs and vanilla. Combine the flour, baking powder

and salt; add to creamed mixture alternately with milk. Fold in blueberries. Pour into a greased 13-in. x 9-in. x 2-in. baking pan. For topping, combine sugar and cinnamon. Cut in butter until mixture resembles coarse crumbs. Sprinkle over batter. Bake at 375° for 35-40 minutes or until a toothpick comes out clean. Cool in pan on a wire rack. **Yield:** 12-16 servings. ***Editor's Note:** If using frozen blueberries, do not thaw before adding to the batter.

HOLIDAY BISCUIT BUBBLE RING

Dianna Shimizu, Issaquah, Washington

My family loves this traditional Christmas treat so much that I like to surprise them with it throughout the year. It does takes some time to prepare, but the effort is worth it when I see my family's smiling faces.

- 1 package (8 ounces) cream cheese
- 2 cups all-purpose flour
- 6 tablespoons sugar, *divided*
- 4 teaspoons baking powder
- 1/3 cup shortening
- 2/3 cup milk
- 1/2 teaspoon ground cinnamon
- 5 tablespoons butter *or* margarine, melted, *divided*
- 1/3 cup chopped pecans
- 1/3 cup chopped red candied cherries

GLAZE:
- 1/4 cup light corn syrup
- 2 tablespoons brown sugar
- 2 tablespoons butter *or* margarine

Cut cream cheese into 20 pieces. Roll each into a ball; cover and refrigerate. In a bowl, combine the flour, 2 tablespoons sugar and baking powder. Cut in shortening until mixture resembles coarse crumbs. Stir in milk just until moistened. Turn onto a lightly floured surface and knead 8-10 times. Roll out into a 15-in. x 12-in. rectangle. In a small bowl, combine cinnamon and remaining sugar; mix well. Sprinkle 5 teaspoons cinnamon-sugar over dough; set remaining mixture aside. Cut dough into twenty 3-in. squares. Place one cream cheese ball in center of each. Fold dough around ball; pinch seams to seal. Roll in 2 tablespoons melted butter. Combine pecans, cherries and remaining butter; spoon half into a greased and floured 10-in. fluted tube pan. Sprinkle with half of the remaining cinnamon-sugar. Place 10 balls, seam side up, over topping. Repeat layers. Bake at 375° for 25-30 minutes or until golden brown. Cool for 10 minutes before inverting onto a serving platter. Meanwhile, in a saucepan, combine glaze ingredients. Bring to a boil; cook and stir until sugar is dissolved. Pour over bread. Serve warm. Refrigerate leftovers. **Yield:** 6-8 servings.

ALMOND APRICOT BREAD

Kathy Cary, Wildwood, Missouri

My mother, who is a big apricot and almond fan, inspired me to create this recipe. The teachers at our children's school look forward to me making these pretty loaves each Christmas.

2-1/2 cups all-purpose flour
1/2 cup sugar
1/2 cup packed brown sugar
3 teaspoons baking powder
1 teaspoon salt
2 jars (4 ounces *each*) apricot baby food, *divided*
1 egg
3/4 cup milk
3 tablespoons vegetable oil
1 teaspoon almond extract
2/3 cup sliced almonds, coarsely chopped
1/2 cup diced dried apricots
GLAZE:
1/2 cup confectioners' sugar
1 teaspoon milk
1/8 teaspoon almond extract

In a large bowl, combine the flour, sugars, baking powder and salt. Set aside 1 tablespoon baby food for glaze. In another bowl, beat the egg, milk, oil, extract and remaining baby food. Stir into dry ingredients just until moistened. Fold in almonds and apricots. Pour into a greased 9-in. x 5-in. x 3-in. loaf pan. Bake at 350° for 55-65 minutes or until a toothpick comes out clean. Cool for 10 minutes before removing from pan to a wire rack. For glaze, combine the confectioners' sugar, milk, extract and reserved baby food until smooth. Drizzle over cooled bread. **Yield:** 1 loaf.

CARAWAY CHEESE BREAD

Mrs. Homer Wooten, Ridgetown, Ontario

We enjoy cheese in a variety of ways. In this savory bread, cheddar cheese blends beautifully with just the right amount of caraway.

2-1/2 cups all-purpose flour
2 cups (8 ounces) shredded cheddar cheese

2-1/2 teaspoons baking powder
1-1/2 to 2 teaspoons caraway seeds
3/4 teaspoon baking soda
3/4 teaspoon salt
2 eggs
1 cup (8 ounces) plain yogurt
1/2 cup butter *or* margarine, melted
1 tablespoon Dijon mustard

In a large bowl, combine the flour, cheese, baking powder, caraway, baking soda and salt. In another bowl, beat the eggs, yogurt, butter and mustard. Stir into dry ingredients just until moistened. Pour into a greased 9-in. x 5-in. x 3-in. loaf pan. Bake at 375° for 30-35 minutes or until a toothpick comes out clean. Cool for 10 minutes before removing from pan to a wire rack. Serve warm. Refrigerate leftovers. **Yield:** 1 loaf.

STRAWBERRY RIBBON BREAD

Carol Wilson, Missoula, Montana

My mother, Lois Schmidt, has been making this bread for our family at Christmas for years. It's a big hit with everyone. The cream cheese filling pairs well with the strawberry flavor.

3 cups all-purpose flour
2 cups sugar
1 teaspoon baking soda
1 teaspoon salt
1 teaspoon ground cinnamon
4 eggs, beaten
1/4 cup vegetable oil
2 packages (10 ounces *each*) frozen sliced strawberries, thawed
1 teaspoon red food coloring, optional
FILLING:
2 packages (3 ounces *each*) cream cheese, softened
1 egg
1/3 cup sugar
1 tablespoon all-purpose flour
1/2 teaspoon orange extract

In a large bowl, combine the flour, sugar, baking soda, salt and cinnamon. In another bowl, combine eggs, oil, strawberries and food coloring if desired. Stir into dry ingredients just until moistened. For filling, beat cream cheese. Add the egg, sugar, flour and extract; beat well. Spoon a fourth of the batter into two greased 8-in. x 4-in. x 2-in. loaf pans. Spread half of the filling over each. Top with the remaining batter. Bake at 350° for 70-80 minutes or until a toothpick comes out clean. Cover loosely with foil if top browns too quickly. Cool for 10 minutes before removing from pans to wire racks. Store in the refrigerator. **Yield:** 2 loaves.

PUMPKIN CRANBERRY NUT BREAD

Darlene Conger, Greenville, Texas

(Pictured at left)

This bread has a terrific combination of flavors that's perfect for the holidays. I like to make and freeze loaves to share with friends and neighbors.

      3/4 cup butter *or* margarine, softened
        2 cups sugar
        3 eggs
        1 can (15 ounces) solid-pack pumpkin
  1-1/2 teaspoons grated orange peel
  3-1/2 cups all-purpose flour
        2 teaspoons ground cinnamon
        1 teaspoon salt
        1 teaspoon baking soda
      1/2 teaspoon baking powder
        1 cup chopped walnuts
        1 cup chopped fresh *or* frozen cranberries

In a mixing bowl, cream butter and sugar. Add eggs, one at a time, beating well after each addition. Add pumpkin and orange peel; mix well (mixture will appear curdled). Combine the flour, cinnamon, salt, baking soda and baking powder; add to pumpkin mixture, beating on low speed just until moistened. Fold in walnuts and cranberries. Pour into two greased 8-in. x 4-in. x 2-in. loaf pans. Bake at 350° for 65-75 minutes or until a toothpick comes out clean. Cool for 10 minutes before removing from pans to wire racks. **Yield:** 2 loaves.

CHOCOLATE MINI LOAVES

Elizabeth Downey, Evart, Michigan

(Pictured at left)

The moist texture of these mini loaves resembles a pound cake. Each bite is rich and succulent, making this perfect for dessert as well as snacking.

      1/2 cup butter (no substitutes), softened
      2/3 cup packed brown sugar
        1 cup (6 ounces) semisweet chocolate chips, melted
        2 eggs
        2 teaspoons vanilla extract
  2-1/2 cups all-purpose flour
        1 teaspoon baking powder

SWEET BREADS. Pictured at left, top to bottom: Pumpkin Cranberry Nut Bread and Chocolate Mini Loaves (recipes on this page).

        1 teaspoon baking soda
  1-1/2 cups applesauce
      1/2 cup miniature semisweet chocolate chips
GLAZE:
      1/2 cup semisweet chocolate chips
        1 tablespoon butter (no substitutes)
        5 teaspoons water
      1/2 cup confectioners' sugar
      1/4 teaspoon vanilla extract
Dash salt

In a mixing bowl, cream butter and brown sugar. Add melted chocolate chips, eggs and vanilla; mix well. Combine the flour, baking powder and baking soda; add to creamed mixture alternately with applesauce. Fold in miniature chocolate chips. Divide batter among five greased 5-3/4-in. x 3-in. x 2-in. loaf pans, about 1 cup in each. Bake at 350° for 30-40 minutes or until a toothpick comes out clean. Cool for 10 minutes before removing from pans to wire racks. For glaze, combine chocolate chips, butter and water in a saucepan; cook and stir over low heat until chocolate is melted. Remove from the heat; stir in confectioners' sugar, vanilla and salt. Drizzle over cooled loaves. **Yield:** 5 mini loaves. **Editor's Note:** Two 8-in. x 4-in. x 2-in. loaf pans may be used; bake for 50-55 minutes.

RASPBERRY BANANA BREAD

Nancy Ross, Cape Girardeau, Missouri

A patient at the doctor's office where I work brought in this bread one morning while it was still warm. It was so good I made sure to get the recipe.

  1-3/4 cups all-purpose flour
  1-1/2 cups sugar
        1 teaspoon baking soda
        1 teaspoon salt
        2 eggs
        1 cup mashed ripe bananas (about 2 medium)
      1/2 cup vegetable oil
      1/3 cup water
        1 cup fresh *or* frozen unsweetened raspberries*
      1/2 cup chopped walnuts

In a large bowl, combine the flour, sugar, baking soda and salt. In another bowl, combine the eggs, bananas, oil and water. Stir into the dry ingredients just until moistened. Fold in raspberries and walnuts. Pour into two greased 8-in. x 4-in. x 2-in. loaf pans. Bake at 350° for 55-65 minutes or until a toothpick comes out clean. Cool for 10 minutes before removing from pans to wire racks. **Yield:** 2 loaves. ***Editor's Note:** If using frozen raspberries, do not thaw before adding to the batter.

ORANGE YOGURT BREAD

Nancy Juntunen, Prattville, Alabama

My mother made this often when I was growing up. Now I make it for my husband and two girls. The slightly tangy glaze complements the moist bread.

- 2/3 cup butter *or* margarine, softened
- 1-1/4 cups sugar
- 2 eggs
- 1/2 cup plain yogurt
- 1/2 cup orange juice
- 1 tablespoon grated orange peel
- 2-1/2 cups all-purpose flour
- 1/2 teaspoon baking powder
- 1/2 teaspoon baking soda
- 1/2 teaspoon salt
- GLAZE:
- 1/2 cup confectioners' sugar
- 2 to 3 teaspoons orange juice

In a mixing bowl, cream butter and sugar. Add eggs, one at a time, beating well after each addition. Add yogurt, orange juice and peel. Combine the flour, baking powder, baking soda and salt; add to creamed mixture. Pour into a greased 9-in. x 5-in. x 3-in. loaf pan. Bake at 350° for 55-65 minutes or until a toothpick comes out clean. Cover loosely with foil if top browns too quickly. Cool for 10 minutes before removing from pan to a wire rack. For glaze, combine confectioners' sugar and enough orange juice to achieve desired consistency. Drizzle over cooled bread. **Yield:** 1 loaf.

IRISH SODA BREAD

Sandra Linder, Blue Springs, Nebraska

Each bite of this traditional loaf is dotted with raisins. My family considers this my "best ever" bread recipe. I hope you agree.

- 2 cups all-purpose flour
- 2 tablespoons sugar
- 1 teaspoon baking powder
- 1 teaspoon baking soda
- 1/2 teaspoon salt
- 3 tablespoons cold butter *or* margarine
- 1 cup buttermilk
- 1/2 cup raisins
- Additional butter *or* margarine, melted
- Additional flour

In a bowl, combine the flour, sugar, baking powder, baking soda and salt. Cut in butter until crumbly. Stir in buttermilk just until moistened. Fold in raisins. Knead on a floured surface for 1 minute. Shape into a 7-in. round loaf; place on a greased baking sheet. With a sharp knife, cut a 1/4-in.-deep cross on top of

the loaf. Bake at 375° for 25-35 minutes or until golden brown. Remove from pan to a wire rack. Brush with additional butter. Cool. Dust with additional flour **Yield:** 1 loaf.

ROYAL RHUBARB COFFEE CAKE

Lorraine Robinson, Stony Plain, Alberta

This recipe is a variation of one a close friend and I make for our home baking business. I've used raspberries and blueberries in place of the rhubarb with winning results.

- 1/3 cup butter *or* margarine, softened
- 1 cup sugar
- 1 egg
- 1 teaspoon vanilla extract
- 2 cups all-purpose flour
- 3 teaspoons baking powder
- 1/2 teaspoon salt
- 1 cup milk
- 3-1/2 cups chopped fresh *or* frozen rhubarb, thawed and drained
- TOPPING:
- 3/4 cup packed brown sugar
- 1/4 cup butter *or* margarine, melted
- 1 teaspoon ground cinnamon

In a mixing bowl, cream butter and sugar. Add egg and vanilla. Combine the flour, baking powder and salt add to creamed mixture alternately with milk. Pour into a greased 13-in. x 9-in. x 2-in. baking dish. Spoon rhubarb over top to within 1/2 in. of edges. Combine topping ingredients; sprinkle over rhubarb. Bake at 350° for 45-55 minutes or until a toothpick comes out clean. Cool in pan on a wire rack. **Yield:** 12-16 servings.

ZUCCHINI CHEESE BREAD

Debi Stile, Efland, North Carolina

This recipe came about when I was trying to make a zucchini bread that didn't call for sugar. I use slices of this attractive bread when making sandwiches.

- 3 cups all-purpose flour
- 1 teaspoon baking powder
- 1 teaspoon baking soda
- 1 teaspoon salt
- 3 eggs
- 3/4 cup vegetable oil
- 2-1/2 cups shredded unpeeled zucchini (about 2 medium)
- 1 cup (4 ounces) shredded cheddar cheese
- 1/2 cup chopped onion

PUMPKIN CRANBERRY NUT BREAD

Darlene Conger, Greenville, Texas

(Pictured at left)

This bread has a terrific combination of flavors that's perfect for the holidays. I like to make and freeze loaves to share with friends and neighbors.

    3/4 cup butter *or* margarine, softened
      2 cups sugar
      3 eggs
      1 can (15 ounces) solid-pack pumpkin
1-1/2 teaspoons grated orange peel
3-1/2 cups all-purpose flour
      2 teaspoons ground cinnamon
      1 teaspoon salt
      1 teaspoon baking soda
    1/2 teaspoon baking powder
      1 cup chopped walnuts
      1 cup chopped fresh *or* frozen cranberries

In a mixing bowl, cream butter and sugar. Add eggs, one at a time, beating well after each addition. Add pumpkin and orange peel; mix well (mixture will appear curdled). Combine the flour, cinnamon, salt, baking soda and baking powder; add to pumpkin mixture, beating on low speed just until moistened. Fold in walnuts and cranberries. Pour into two greased 8-in. x 4-in. x 2-in. loaf pans. Bake at 350° for 65-75 minutes or until a toothpick comes out clean. Cool for 10 minutes before removing from pans to wire racks. **Yield:** 2 loaves.

CHOCOLATE MINI LOAVES

Elizabeth Downey, Evart, Michigan

(Pictured at left)

The moist texture of these mini loaves resembles a pound cake. Each bite is rich and succulent, making this perfect for dessert as well as snacking.

    1/2 cup butter (no substitutes), softened
    2/3 cup packed brown sugar
      1 cup (6 ounces) semisweet chocolate chips, melted
      2 eggs
      2 teaspoons vanilla extract
2-1/2 cups all-purpose flour
      1 teaspoon baking powder

      1 teaspoon baking soda
1-1/2 cups applesauce
    1/2 cup miniature semisweet chocolate chips
GLAZE:
    1/2 cup semisweet chocolate chips
      1 tablespoon butter (no substitutes)
      5 teaspoons water
    1/2 cup confectioners' sugar
    1/4 teaspoon vanilla extract
Dash salt

In a mixing bowl, cream butter and brown sugar. Add melted chocolate chips, eggs and vanilla; mix well. Combine the flour, baking powder and baking soda; add to creamed mixture alternately with applesauce. Fold in miniature chocolate chips. Divide batter among five greased 5-3/4-in. x 3-in. x 2-in. loaf pans, about 1 cup in each. Bake at 350° for 30-40 minutes or until a toothpick comes out clean. Cool for 10 minutes before removing from pans to wire racks. For glaze, combine chocolate chips, butter and water in a saucepan; cook and stir over low heat until chocolate is melted. Remove from the heat; stir in confectioners' sugar, vanilla and salt. Drizzle over cooled loaves. **Yield:** 5 mini loaves. **Editor's Note:** Two 8-in. x 4-in. x 2-in. loaf pans may be used; bake for 50-55 minutes.

RASPBERRY BANANA BREAD

Nancy Ross, Cape Girardeau, Missouri

A patient at the doctor's office where I work brought in this bread one morning while it was still warm. It was so good I made sure to get the recipe.

1-3/4 cups all-purpose flour
1-1/2 cups sugar
      1 teaspoon baking soda
      1 teaspoon salt
      2 eggs
      1 cup mashed ripe bananas (about 2 medium)
    1/2 cup vegetable oil
    1/3 cup water
      1 cup fresh *or* frozen unsweetened raspberries*
    1/2 cup chopped walnuts

In a large bowl, combine the flour, sugar, baking soda and salt. In another bowl, combine the eggs, bananas, oil and water. Stir into the dry ingredients just until moistened. Fold in raspberries and walnuts. Pour into two greased 8-in. x 4-in. x 2-in. loaf pans. Bake at 350° for 55-65 minutes or until a toothpick comes out clean. Cool for 10 minutes before removing from pans to wire racks. **Yield:** 2 loaves. ***Editor's Note:** If using frozen raspberries, do not thaw before adding to the batter.

SWEET BREADS. Pictured at left, top to bottom: Pumpkin Cranberry Nut Bread and Chocolate Mini Loaves (recipes on this page).

SKILLET SAUSAGE CORN BREAD

Carolyn Griffin, Macon, Georgia

This unique corn bread is prepared in a skillet. I cut it into wedges and serve it with bacon, eggs and fresh fruit for a hearty breakfast.

> 1 pound bulk pork sausage
> 1-1/2 cups cornmeal
> 1/2 cup all-purpose flour
> 4 teaspoons baking powder
> 1 tablespoon sugar
> 1 egg
> 1 cup milk

In a 9-in. ovenproof skillet, cook sausage over medium heat until no longer pink. Drain, reserving 2 tablespoons drippings. In a large bowl, combine the cornmeal, flour, baking powder and sugar. In another bowl, beat egg and milk. Stir into dry ingredients just until moistened. Fold in sausage and reserved drippings. Return to skillet. Bake at 425° for 20-25 minutes or until a toothpick comes out clean. Serve warm. Refrigerate leftovers. **Yield:** 8 servings.

SWEET POTATO BREAD

Sally Giesbrecht, Orland, California

This recipe originally started from my favorite banana bread recipe. I substituted sweet potatoes and made a few other adjustments to come up with this delicious quick bread.

> 3/4 cup butter *or* margarine, softened
> 1 cup sugar
> 3 eggs
> 1/2 cup honey
> 1-1/2 cups mashed sweet potatoes
> 1 package (3.4 ounces) instant vanilla pudding mix
> 2-1/4 cups all-purpose flour
> 1 teaspoon baking powder
> 1 teaspoon baking soda
> 1/2 teaspoon salt
> 1/2 cup buttermilk
> 1 cup chopped pecans
> 2/3 cup raisins
> ICING:
> 1 cup confectioners' sugar
> 1 tablespoon milk
> 2 teaspoons butter *or* margarine, melted
> 1 teaspoon lemon juice

In a mixing bowl, cream butter and sugar. Add eggs, one at a time, beating well after each addition. Add honey, sweet potatoes and dry pudding mix; mix well. Combine the flour, baking powder, baking soda and

salt; add to creamed mixture alternately with buttermilk. Fold in the pecans and raisins. Pour into two greased 9-in. x 5-in. x 3-in. loaf pans. Bake at 350° for 70-80 minutes or until a toothpick comes out clean. Cool for 10 minutes before removing from pans to wire racks. Combine icing ingredients; drizzle over cooled bread. **Yield:** 2 loaves.

CHERRY CHIP GRANOLA BREAD

Pat Habiger, Spearville, Kansas

Buttermilk makes this colorful bread moist and delicious while granola and almonds add special crunch. We like to snack on slices around the clock.

> 1-1/3 cups all-purpose flour
> 1/3 cup sugar
> 1 teaspoon baking soda
> 1/2 teaspoon salt
> 1 egg
> 1 cup buttermilk
> 1/4 cup vegetable oil
> 1 teaspoon vanilla extract
> 1 cup granola, toasted
> 1/2 cup chopped almonds
> 1/2 cup semisweet chocolate chips
> 1/2 cup chopped red candied cherries

In a large bowl, combine the flour, sugar, baking soda and salt. In another bowl, beat the egg, buttermilk, oil and vanilla. Stir into dry ingredients just until moistened. Fold in the remaining ingredients. Pour into two greased 5-3/4-in. x 3-in. x 2-in. loaf pans. Bake at 350° for 30-35 minutes or until a toothpick comes out clean. Cool for 10 minutes before removing from pans to wire racks. **Yield:** 2 mini loaves.

MOCHA NUT BREAD

Winnie Higgins, Salisbury, Maryland

This rich, dark-colored loaf features the unbeatable combination of coffee and chocolate. Family and friends can't eat just one slice.

> 2 cups all-purpose flour
> 1 cup sugar
> 1/2 cup baking cocoa
> 1/4 cup instant coffee granules
> 1/2 teaspoon baking soda
> 1/4 teaspoon salt
> 2 eggs
> 1-1/4 cups sour cream
> 1/3 cup butter *or* margarine, melted

2 cups (12 ounces) semisweet chocolate chips
1/2 cup chopped pecans

In a large bowl, combine the flour, sugar, cocoa, coffee granules, baking soda and salt. In another bowl, beat eggs, sour cream and butter until smooth. Stir into dry ingredients just until moistened. Fold in chocolate chips and pecans. Pour into a greased 9-in. x 5-in. x 3-in. loaf pan. Bake at 350° for 55-60 minutes or until a toothpick comes out clean. Cool for 10 minutes before removing from pan to a wire rack. **Yield:** 1 loaf.

PEAR BREAD

Janet Lawrence, Grant Park, Illinois

My friends and family thoroughly enjoy this old-fashioned bread. The mellow flavor of pears is a refreshing change of pace from more traditional apples.

3-1/2 cups all-purpose flour
　1 teaspoon baking powder
　1 teaspoon salt
　1 teaspoon ground ginger
1/2 teaspoon baking soda
1/2 teaspoon ground nutmeg
1-1/2 cups sugar
1/2 cup vegetable oil
1/2 cup butter *or* margarine, melted
　4 eggs
　2 teaspoons vanilla extract
　2 cups diced peeled pears

In a large bowl, combine the flour, baking powder, salt, ginger, baking soda and nutmeg; set aside. In a mixing bowl, beat the sugar, oil and butter. Add eggs, one at a time, beating well after each addition. Stir in vanilla. Stir into dry ingredients just until moistened (batter will be stiff). Stir in pears. Pour into two greased 8-in. x 4-in. x 2-in. loaf pans. Bake at 350° for 55-65 minutes or until a toothpick comes out clean. Cool for 10 minutes before removing from pans to wire racks. **Yield:** 2 loaves.

DATE NUT BREAD

Janet Backie, Tracy, California

Many years ago when I was sick, a dear friend stopped with a pot of soup and this beautiful bread. Every cook should have a copy of this traditional quick bread recipe in his or her files.

1-1/2 cups chopped dates
1-1/2 cups hot water
　2 tablespoons butter *or* margarine, softened

2-1/4 cups all-purpose flour
1-1/2 cups sugar
　3/4 cup coarsely chopped walnuts
1-1/2 teaspoons baking soda
1-1/2 teaspoons salt
　2 eggs, beaten
1-1/2 teaspoons vanilla extract

In a bowl, combine the dates, water and butter; let stand for 5 minutes. In a large bowl, combine the flour, sugar, walnuts, baking soda and salt. Stir in the eggs, vanilla and date mixture just until moistened. Pour into two greased 8-in. x 4-in. x 2-in. loaf pans. Bake at 375° for 45-50 minutes or until a toothpick comes out clean. Cover loosely with foil if top browns too quickly. Cool for 10 minutes before removing from pans to wire racks. **Yield:** 2 loaves.

PEACHY PEACH BREAD

Leanne Fried, Bismarck, North Dakota

I've been cooking and baking since I was 6 years old and have become an avid recipe collector. This fruity bread is an appetizing addition to breakfast or brunch.

　2 cups all-purpose flour
　3/4 cup packed brown sugar
　3 teaspoons baking powder
1/2 teaspoon salt
　1 can (15-1/4 ounces) sliced peaches
　2 eggs
　6 tablespoons butter *or* margarine, melted
3/4 cup chopped pecans
Peach preserves

In a large bowl, combine the flour, brown sugar, baking powder and salt. Drain peaches, reserving 1/4 cup syrup (discard remaining syrup or save for another use). Finely chop 1 cup of peaches; set aside. Place remaining peaches and reserved syrup in a blender or food processor; add eggs and butter. Cover and process until smooth. Stir into the dry ingredients just until moistened. Fold in the pecans and chopped peaches. Pour into two greased 5-3/4-in. x 3-in. x 2-in. loaf pans. Bake at 350° for 35-40 minutes or until a toothpick comes out clean. Cool for 10 minutes before removing from pans to wire racks. Serve with peach preserves. **Yield:** 2 mini loaves.

ORANGE YOGURT BREAD

Nancy Juntunen, Prattville, Alabama

My mother made this often when I was growing up. Now I make it for my husband and two girls. The slightly tangy glaze complements the moist bread.

2/3 cup butter *or* margarine, softened
1-1/4 cups sugar
  2 eggs
1/2 cup plain yogurt
1/2 cup orange juice
  1 tablespoon grated orange peel
2-1/2 cups all-purpose flour
1/2 teaspoon baking powder
1/2 teaspoon baking soda
1/2 teaspoon salt
GLAZE:
  1/2 cup confectioners' sugar
  2 to 3 teaspoons orange juice

In a mixing bowl, cream butter and sugar. Add eggs, one at a time, beating well after each addition. Add yogurt, orange juice and peel. Combine the flour, baking powder, baking soda and salt; add to creamed mixture. Pour into a greased 9-in. x 5-in. x 3-in. loaf pan. Bake at 350° for 55-65 minutes or until a toothpick comes out clean. Cover loosely with foil if top browns too quickly. Cool for 10 minutes before removing from pan to a wire rack. For glaze, combine confectioners' sugar and enough orange juice to achieve desired consistency. Drizzle over cooled bread. **Yield:** 1 loaf.

IRISH SODA BREAD

Sandra Linder, Blue Springs, Nebraska

Each bite of this traditional loaf is dotted with raisins. My family considers this my "best ever" bread recipe. I hope you agree.

  2 cups all-purpose flour
  2 tablespoons sugar
  1 teaspoon baking powder
  1 teaspoon baking soda
1/2 teaspoon salt
  3 tablespoons cold butter *or* margarine
  1 cup buttermilk
1/2 cup raisins
Additional butter *or* margarine, melted
Additional flour

In a bowl, combine the flour, sugar, baking powder, baking soda and salt. Cut in butter until crumbly. Stir in buttermilk just until moistened. Fold in raisins. Knead on a floured surface for 1 minute. Shape into a 7-in. round loaf; place on a greased baking sheet. With a sharp knife, cut a 1/4-in.-deep cross on top of the loaf. Bake at 375° for 25-35 minutes or until golden brown. Remove from pan to a wire rack. Brush with additional butter. Cool. Dust with additional flour. **Yield:** 1 loaf.

ROYAL RHUBARB COFFEE CAKE

Lorraine Robinson, Stony Plain, Alberta

This recipe is a variation of one a close friend and I make for our home baking business. I've used raspberries and blueberries in place of the rhubarb with winning results.

1/3 cup butter *or* margarine, softened
  1 cup sugar
  1 egg
  1 teaspoon vanilla extract
  2 cups all-purpose flour
  3 teaspoons baking powder
1/2 teaspoon salt
  1 cup milk
3-1/2 cups chopped fresh *or* frozen rhubarb, thawed and drained
TOPPING:
  3/4 cup packed brown sugar
  1/4 cup butter *or* margarine, melted
  1 teaspoon ground cinnamon

In a mixing bowl, cream butter and sugar. Add egg and vanilla. Combine the flour, baking powder and salt; add to creamed mixture alternately with milk. Pour into a greased 13-in. x 9-in. x 2-in. baking dish. Spoon rhubarb over top to within 1/2 in. of edges. Combine topping ingredients; sprinkle over rhubarb. Bake at 350° for 45-55 minutes or until a toothpick comes out clean. Cool in pan on a wire rack. **Yield:** 12-16 servings.
'

ZUCCHINI CHEESE BREAD

Debi Stile, Efland, North Carolina

This recipe came about when I was trying to make a zucchini bread that didn't call for sugar. I use slices of this attractive bread when making sandwiches.

  3 cups all-purpose flour
  1 teaspoon baking powder
  1 teaspoon baking soda
  1 teaspoon salt
  3 eggs
3/4 cup vegetable oil
2-1/2 cups shredded unpeeled zucchini (about 2 medium)
  1 cup (4 ounces) shredded cheddar cheese
1/2 cup chopped onion

In a large bowl, combine the flour, baking powder, baking soda and salt. In another bowl, beat eggs and oil. Stir into dry ingredients just until moistened. Fold in zucchini, cheese and onion. Pour into a greased 9-in. x 5-in. x 3-in. loaf pan. Bake at 375° for 55-65 minutes or until a toothpick comes out clean. Cool for 10 minutes before removing from pan to a wire rack. Serve warm. Refrigerate leftovers. **Yield:** 1 loaf.

PEANUT BUTTER PUMPKIN BREAD

Anita Chick, Frisco, Texas

My husband brought this recipe home from the office more than 20 years ago. Each fall, I bake several of these lovely loaves to share with family and friends. Pumpkin and peanut butter are a unique, delicious combination.

> 3 cups sugar
> 1 can (15 ounces) solid-pack pumpkin
> 4 eggs
> 1 cup vegetable oil
> 3/4 cup water
> 2/3 cup peanut butter
> 3-1/2 cups all-purpose flour
> 2 teaspoons baking soda
> 1-1/2 teaspoons salt
> 1 teaspoon ground cinnamon
> 1 teaspoon ground nutmeg

In a mixing bowl, combine the sugar, pumpkin, eggs, oil, water and peanut butter; beat well. Combine the flour, baking soda, salt, cinnamon and nutmeg. Gradually add to pumpkin mixture; mix well. Pour into two greased 9-in. x 5-in. x 3-in. loaf pans. Bake at 350° for 60-70 minutes or until a toothpick comes out clean. Cool for 10 minutes before removing from pans to wire racks. **Yield:** 2 loaves. **Editor's Note:** Six 5-3/4-in. x 3-in. x 2-in. loaf pans may be used; bake for 40-45 minutes.

LEMON LOAF

Shelli Aday, Georgetown, Texas

I found this recipe in my files one day when I was looking for a bread that called for ingredients already in my pantry. I gave the loaf to some friends, and it was a hit.

> 1/3 cup shortening
> 1 cup sugar
> 2 eggs
> 1-1/2 cups all-purpose flour
> 1-1/2 teaspoons baking powder
> 1/4 teaspoon salt
> 1/2 cup milk

> 1/2 cup chopped pecans
> 2 teaspoons grated lemon peel
> TOPPING:
> 2/3 cup sugar
> 1/3 cup lemon juice

In a mixing bowl, cream shortening and sugar. Add eggs, one at a time, beating well after each addition. Combine the flour, baking powder and salt; add to creamed mixture alternately with milk. Stir in pecans and lemon peel. Pour into a greased 9-in. x 5-in. x 3-in. loaf pan. Bake at 350° for 55-65 minutes or until a toothpick comes out clean. For topping, combine sugar and lemon juice. Spoon over bread while still in pan. Cool for 10 minutes before removing from pan to a wire rack. **Yield:** 1 loaf.

DUTCH APPLE LOAF

Gladys Meyer, Ottumwa, Iowa

Being of Dutch descent, I knew I had to try this recipe for a moist, fruity quick bread. It freezes well, so I often have a loaf on hand for church bazaars.

> 1/2 cup butter *or* margarine, softened
> 1 cup sugar
> 2 eggs
> 1/4 cup buttermilk
> 1 teaspoon vanilla extract
> 2 cups all-purpose flour
> 1 teaspoon baking soda
> 1/2 teaspoon salt
> 2 cups diced peeled tart apples
> 1/2 cup chopped walnuts
> TOPPING:
> 1/4 cup sugar
> 1/4 cup all-purpose flour
> 2 teaspoons ground cinnamon
> 1/4 cup cold butter *or* margarine

In a mixing bowl, cream butter and sugar. Add eggs, one at a time, beating well after each addition. Beat in buttermilk and vanilla. Combine the flour, baking soda and salt; add to creamed mixture. Fold in apples and walnuts. Pour into a greased 9-in. x 5-in. x 3-in. loaf pan. For topping, combine the sugar, flour and cinnamon in a bowl. Cut in butter until mixture resembles coarse crumbs. Sprinkle over batter. Bake at 350° for 55-60 minutes or until a toothpick comes out clean. Cool for 10 minutes before removing from pan to a wire rack. **Yield:** 1 loaf.

Classic Yeast Breads

"Knead" a basic bread or roll recipe? These traditional white, wheat, rye, oat and sourdough favorites are sure to please.

GOLDEN SESAME BRAID

Barbara Sunberg, Camden, Ohio

(Pictured at left and on front cover)

Our daughter won a blue ribbon at the state fair when she submitted this delicious bread. People always comment on the crisp crust and tender inside.

> 1 package (1/4 ounce) active dry yeast
> 1/2 cup warm water (110° to 115°)
> 1-1/2 cups warm milk (110° to 115°)
> 1/4 cup shortening
> 1/4 cup sugar
> 1 tablespoon salt
> 4 eggs
> 7 to 8 cups all-purpose flour
> 1 tablespoon cold water
> 2 tablespoons sesame seeds

In a mixing bowl, dissolve yeast in warm water. Add the milk, shortening, sugar, salt, 3 eggs and 4 cups flour. Beat until smooth. Stir in enough remaining flour to form a soft dough. Turn onto a floured surface; knead until smooth and elastic, about 6-8 minutes. Place in a greased bowl, turning once to grease top. Cover and let rise in a warm place until doubled, about 1 hour. Punch dough down. Turn onto a lightly floured surface; divide in half. Divide each portion into thirds. Shape each piece into a 12-in. rope. Place three ropes on a greased baking pan; braid. Pinch ends to seal and tuck under. Repeat with remaining dough. Cover and let rise until doubled, about 45 minutes. Beat remaining egg and cold water; brush over braids. Sprinkle with sesame seeds. Bake at 350° for 30-35 minutes or until golden brown. Remove from pans to wire racks to cool. **Yield:** 2 loaves.

SUNFLOWER BREAD

Marianne Segall, Cody, Wyoming

(Pictured at left)

GREAT GRAINS. Pictured at left, top to bottom: Overnight Whole Wheat Rolls (recipe on page 38), Golden Sesame Braid and Sunflower Bread (recipes on this page).

I do the cooking at our family-owned guest ranch. I use thick slices of this nutty bread as an accompaniment to soup in winter and as sandwich bread in summer. Visitors can't resist this bread.

> 4 cups all-purpose flour
> 1 cup salted sunflower kernels, toasted
> 2 packages (1/4 ounce *each*) active dry yeast
> 2 teaspoons salt
> 1-1/4 cups water
> 1/2 cup milk
> 1/3 cup honey
> 3 tablespoons butter *or* margarine
> 1 cup whole wheat flour
> Additional salted sunflower kernels, optional

In a mixing bowl, combine 2 cups all-purpose flour, sunflower kernels, yeast and salt. In a saucepan, heat the water, milk, honey and butter to 120°-130°. Add to dry ingredients; beat until smooth. Beat in whole wheat flour. Stir in enough remaining all-purpose flour to form a soft dough. Turn onto a floured surface; knead until smooth and elastic, about 6-8 minutes. Place in a greased bowl, turning once to grease top. Cover and let rise in a warm place until doubled, about 1 hour. Punch dough down. Turn onto a lightly floured surface; divide in half. Shape into loaves. Roll loaves in additional sunflower kernels if desired. Place in two greased 8-in. x 4-in. x 2-in. loaf pans. Cover and let rise until doubled, about 45 minutes. Bake at 375° for 35-40 minutes or until golden brown. Remove from pans to wire racks to cool. **Yield:** 2 loaves.

YEAST BREAD BASICS

- *Heat liquids to 110° to 115° or 120° to 130° in a saucepan or microwave. Always use a thermometer to check the temperature.*
- *Allow dough to rise in a warm, draft-free area (80° to 85°) until doubled in size. To determine if the dough has doubled, press two fingers 1/2 inch into the dough. If the dents remain, it's ready to punch down.*
- *Test for doneness near the end of the baking time by carefully removing the loaf from the pan and tapping the bottom crust. If it sounds hollow, the bread is done. If the bread is browning too fast and it's not done, tent with aluminum foil and continue baking.*

OVERNIGHT WHOLE WHEAT ROLLS

Denise Fidler
Syracuse, Indiana

**(Pictured at left
and on page 36)**

I love to bake and even have a small business selling bread. Making rolls and bread from scratch is an art easily mastered with practice. The swirled shape of these rolls is very attractive.

> 2 packages (1/4 ounce *each*) active dry yeast
> 1-1/4 cups warm water (110° to 115°)
> 3/4 cup butter *or* margarine, melted, *divided*
> 1/2 cup honey
> 2 teaspoons salt
> 3 eggs
> 2 cups whole wheat flour
> 3 cups all-purpose flour
> **Additional melted butter *or* margarine**

In a mixing bowl, dissolve yeast in warm water. Add 1/2 cup butter, honey, salt, eggs, whole wheat flour and 1/2 cup all-purpose flour. Beat until smooth. Stir in enough remaining all-purpose flour to form a soft dough. Do not knead. Place in a greased bowl, turning once to grease top. Cover and let rise in a warm place until doubled, about 1 hour. Punch dough down. Cover and refrigerate overnight. Punch dough down. Turn onto a lightly floured surface; divide in half. Roll each into a 15-in. x 8-in. rectangle. Brush with remaining butter to within 1/2 in. of edges. Roll up, jelly-roll style, starting with a long side; pinch seam to seal. Cut each into 15 rolls. Place rolls, cut side up, in greased muffin cups. Cover and let rise in a warm place until doubled, about 45 minutes. Bake at 400° for 8-10 minutes or until golden brown. Remove from pans to wire racks. Brush with additional butter. Cool. **Yield:** 2-1/2 dozen.

HEARTY RAISIN BREAD

Maureen Cerza, Wilmington, Illinois

Although I just recently moved to the country, I love from-scratch cooking, and baking bread is a favorite pastime. This rich bread has a delectable cinnamon flavor and is loaded with raisins.

> 2 packages (1/4 ounce *each*) active dry yeast
> 1/2 cup warm water (110° to 115°)
> 1-1/2 cups warm milk (110° to 115°)
> 1/2 cup butter *or* margarine, melted

> 1/4 cup honey
> 2 teaspoons salt
> 1-1/2 teaspoons ground cinnamon
> 2 eggs
> 3 cups whole wheat flour
> 3-1/2 to 4 cups all-purpose flour
> 2 cups raisins
> 1 egg white
> 2 tablespoons cold water

In a mixing bowl, dissolve yeast in warm water. Add the milk, butter, honey, salt, cinnamon, eggs and whole wheat flour. Beat until smooth. Stir in enough all-purpose flour to form a soft dough. Turn onto a floured surface; knead until smooth and elastic, about 8-10 minutes. Place in a greased bowl, turning once to grease top. Cover and let rise in a warm place until doubled, about 1 hour. Punch dough down. Turn onto a lightly floured surface; sprinkle with raisins and knead in. Divide in half. Shape into loaves. Place in two greased 9-in. x 5-in. x 3-in. loaf pans. Cover and let rise until doubled, about 45 minutes. Beat egg white and cold water; brush over dough. Bake at 375° for 35-40 minutes or until golden brown. Cover loosely with foil if top browns too quickly. Remove from pans to wire racks to cool. **Yield:** 2 loaves.

COUNTRY BREAD

Gloria Kaufmann, Orrville, Ohio

Our daughter, Christy, loves baking this pretty braided bread with a hint of ginger. She has entered it in various 4-H competitions and enjoys teaching others how to make it.

> 2 packages (1/4 ounce *each*) active dry yeast
> 1/2 cup warm water (110° to 115°)
> 1 cup warm milk (110° to 115°)
> 1/4 cup butter *or* margarine, softened
> 1/4 cup sugar
> 1 teaspoon salt
> 1/4 teaspoon ground ginger
> 3 eggs
> 5 to 6 cups all-purpose flour
> 2 tablespoons sesame seeds

In a mixing bowl, dissolve yeast in warm water. Add the milk, butter, sugar, salt, ginger, 2 eggs and 3 cups flour. Beat until smooth. Stir in enough remaining flour to form a soft dough. Turn onto a floured surface; knead until smooth and elastic, about 6-8 minutes. Place in a greased bowl, turning once to grease top. Cover and let rise in a warm place until doubled, about 1 hour. Punch dough down. Turn onto a lightly floured surface; divide into six pieces. Shape each into a 12-in. rope. Braid three ropes; pinch ends to seal and tuck under. Repeat with remaining dough. Place in two greased 8-in. x 4-in. x 2-in. loaf pans. Cover and let rise until doubled, about 30 minutes. Beat remaining egg; brush over dough. Sprinkle with sesame seeds. Bake at 350° for 35-40 minutes or until golden brown. Remove from pans to wire racks to cool. **Yield:** 2 loaves.

THREE-GRAIN WILD RICE BREAD

Kim L'Hote, Wausau, Wisconsin

Wild rice really shines in this one-of-a-kind recipe. The first time I made this bread, I knew I'd found a new favorite. Everyone who has tried it since confirms that over and over again!

    1 package (1/4 ounce) active dry yeast
  1/3 cup warm water (110° to 115°)
    2 cups warm milk (110° to 115°)
    2 cups whole wheat flour
  1/2 cup rye flour
  1/2 cup quick-cooking oats
  1/2 cup honey
    2 tablespoons butter *or* margarine, melted
    2 teaspoons salt
    4 to 4-1/2 cups bread *or* all-purpose flour
    1 cup cooked wild rice, cooled to room
      temperature
    1 egg
    1 tablespoon cold water

In a mixing bowl, dissolve yeast in warm water. Add the milk, whole wheat flour, rye flour, oats, honey, butter, salt and 2 cups bread flour. Beat until smooth. Stir in wild rice and enough remaining bread flour to form a stiff dough. Turn onto a floured surface; knead until smooth and elastic, about 8-10 minutes. Place in a greased bowl, turning once to grease top. Cover and let rise in a warm place until doubled, about 1-1/2 hours. Punch dough down. Turn onto a lightly floured surface; divide in half. Shape into loaves. Place in two greased 9-in. x 5-in. x 3-in. loaf pans. Cover and let rise until doubled, about 30 minutes. Beat egg and cold water; brush over loaves. Bake at 375° for 35-40 minutes or until golden brown. Remove from pans to wire racks to cool. **Yield:** 2 loaves.

BASIC PIZZA CRUST

Beverly Anderson, Sinclairville, New York

My aunt shared this recipe quite a few years ago. I like to double the recipe and keep one baked crust in the freezer for a quick snack or meal later.

    1 package (1/4 ounce) active dry yeast
    1 cup warm water (110° to 115°)
    2 tablespoons vegetable oil
    1 teaspoon sugar
  1/4 teaspoon salt
2-1/2 to 2-3/4 cups all-purpose flour
Cornmeal
Pizza toppings of your choice

In a mixing bowl, dissolve yeast in warm water. Add the oil, sugar, salt and 1-1/2 cups flour. Beat until smooth. Stir in enough remaining flour to form a firm dough. Turn onto a floured surface; cover and let rest for 10 minutes. Roll into a 13-in. circle. Grease a 12-in. pizza pan and sprinkle with cornmeal. Transfer dough to prepared pan, building up edges slightly. Do not let rise. Bake at 425° for 12-15 minutes or until browned. Add toppings; bake 10-15 minutes longer. **Yield:** 1 pizza crust.

HONEY WHITE LOAVES

Lois Kamps, Hudsonville, Michigan

When I was searching for a moist bread that wouldn't crumble when thinly sliced, a friend urged me to try her grandmother's age-old recipe. It slices perfectly.

    2 packages (1/4 ounce *each*) active dry yeast
2-1/2 cups warm water (110° to 115°)
  1/2 cup butter *or* margarine, melted
  1/2 cup honey
    2 eggs
    1 tablespoon salt
    8 to 9 cups all-purpose flour

In a mixing bowl, dissolve yeast in warm water. Add the butter, honey, eggs, salt and 4 cups flour. Beat on low speed for 30 seconds. Beat on medium for 3 minutes. Stir in enough remaining flour to form a soft dough. Turn onto a floured surface; knead until smooth and elastic, about 8 minutes. Place in a greased bowl, turning once to grease top. Cover and let rise in a warm place until doubled; about 1 hour. Punch dough down. Divide into thirds. Shape into loaves. Place in three greased 8-in. x 4-in. x 2-in. loaf pans. Cover and let rise until doubled, about 30 minutes. Bake at 375° for 25-30 minutes or until golden brown. Remove from pans to wire racks to cool. **Yield:** 3 loaves.

TASTY WHOLE WHEAT BREAD

Patricia Krueger, Hubbard, Iowa

Because you can bake this bread in loaf pans or on baking sheets, it's perfect for people who don't have four identical loaf pans. I give some loaves as gifts, then freeze the remaining for my family.

>   2 packages (1/4 ounce *each*) active dry yeast
> 1/2 cup warm water (110° to 115°)
>   1 quart warm buttermilk* (110° to 115°)
> 1/2 cup butter *or* margarine, softened
> 2-1/2 cups whole wheat flour
> 1/2 cup packed brown sugar
> 1/3 cup toasted wheat germ
> 2-1/2 teaspoons salt
>   8 to 9 cups all-purpose flour

In a mixing bowl, dissolve the yeast in warm water. Add buttermilk and butter, stirring until butter begins to melt. Add the whole wheat flour, brown sugar, wheat germ, salt and 4 cups all-purpose flour. Beat until smooth. Stir in enough remaining all-purpose flour to form a soft dough. Turn onto a floured surface; knead until smooth and elastic, about 6-8 minutes. Place in a greased bowl, turning once to grease top. Cover and let rise in a warm place until doubled, about 1 hour. Punch dough down. Turn onto a lightly floured surface; divide into four pieces. Shape into loaves. Place in four greased 8-in. x 4-in. x 2-in. loaf pans or on greased baking sheets. Cover and let rise until doubled, about 45 minutes. Bake at 375° for 30-40 minutes or until golden brown. Remove from pans to wire racks to cool. **Yield:** 4 loaves. **Editor's Note:* Warmed buttermilk will appear curdled.

LIGHT RYE SANDWICH LOAVES

Katie Koziolek, Hartland, Minnesota

I'll sometimes shape half of the dough into a round loaf, hollow it out after baking and fill it with dip for parties.

>   4 to 4-1/2 cups all-purpose flour
> 2-1/2 cups rye flour
> 1/3 cup packed brown sugar
>   2 packages (1/4 ounce *each*) active dry yeast
>   1 tablespoon grated orange peel
>   2 teaspoons salt
> 1/2 teaspoon fennel seed *or* aniseed, crushed
> 2-1/4 cups water
> 1/4 cup shortening
> 1-1/2 teaspoons molasses
> Cornmeal
> Melted butter *or* margarine

In a mixing bowl, combine 2 cups all-purpose flour, rye flour, brown sugar, yeast, orange peel, salt and fennel seed. In a saucepan, heat the water, shortening and molasses to 120°-130°. Add to dry ingredients; beat until smooth. Stir in enough remaining all-purpose flour to form a soft dough. Turn onto a floured surface; knead until smooth and elastic, about 6-8 minutes. Place in a greased bowl, turning once to grease top. Cover and let rise in a warm place until doubled, about 1-1/4 hours. Punch dough down. Turn onto a lightly floured surface; divide in half. Shape into loaves. Grease two 8-in. x 4-in. x 2-in. loaf pans and sprinkle with cornmeal. Place loaves in prepared pans. Cover and let rise until doubled, about 45 minutes. With a sharp knife, make three shallow slashes across the top of each loaf. Bake at 375° for 30-35 minutes or until golden brown. Remove from pans to wire racks. Brush with melted butter. Cool. **Yield:** 2 loaves. **Editor's Note:** Bread may also be shaped into two round loaves. Place loaves on two baking sheets that have been greased and sprinkled with cornmeal.

HOT DOG BUNS

Bernice Fenn, Carp, Ontario

This recipe has been in my family for years. Store-bought buns just can't compete with these homemade ones. The dough is made ahead and rises in the refrigerator.

>   1 package (1/4 ounce) active dry yeast
>   1 cup warm water (110° to 115°), *divided*
>   2 teaspoons plus 1/2 cup sugar, *divided*
>   1 cup warm milk (110° to 115°)
> 1/4 cup shortening
>   2 teaspoons salt
>   3 eggs
>   6 to 6-1/2 cups all-purpose flour
>   1 tablespoon cold water
> Caraway, poppy *or* sesame seeds

In a mixing bowl, dissolve yeast in 1/4 cup warm water. Add 2 teaspoons sugar; let stand for 5 minutes. Add the remaining water and sugar, milk, shortening, salt, 2 eggs and 4 cups flour. Beat until smooth. Stir in enough remaining flour to form a soft dough. Do not knead. Cover and refrigerate overnight. Punch dough down. Turn onto a floured surface; divide into 12 pieces. Shape each into a 5-in. x 2-in. roll. Place 4 in. apart on greased baking sheets. Beat remaining egg and cold water; brush over rolls. Sprinkle with caraway, poppy or sesame seeds. Cover and let rise in a warm place until doubled, about 2 hours. Bake at 425° for 8-10 minutes or until golden brown. Remove from pans to wire racks to cool. **Yield:** 1 dozen.

ENGLISH MUFFIN LOAF

Rosemarie Leek, Lake Hopatcong, New Jersey

This simple recipe does not require kneading and calls for just one rising time. Slices are absolutely delicious toasted and topped with butter.

3 cups all-purpose flour
1 package (1/4 ounce) active dry yeast
-1/2 teaspoons sugar
1 teaspoon salt
1/8 teaspoon baking soda
1 cup milk
1/4 cup water
Cornmeal

In a mixing bowl, combine 2 cups flour, yeast, sugar, salt and baking soda. In a saucepan, heat milk and water to 120°-130°. Add to dry ingredients; beat until smooth. Stir in remaining flour (batter will be stiff). Do not knead. Grease a 8-in. x 4-in. x 2-in. loaf pan and sprinkle with cornmeal. Spoon batter into prepared pan. Cover and let rise in a warm place until doubled, about 45 minutes. Bake at 400° for 30-35 minutes or until golden brown. Remove from pan to a wire rack to cool. **Yield:** 1 loaf.

GOLDEN DINNER ROLLS

Carolyn Brinkmeyer, Aurora, Colorado

My husband and I were raised on farms, so we agree nothing compares to home cooking. I came across this recipe when working on a cookbook as a fund-raiser for church.

5-1/2 to 6 cups all-purpose flour
1/2 cup sugar
2 packages (1/4 ounce *each*) active dry yeast
1-1/2 teaspoons salt
1 cup milk
2/3 cup water
1/4 cup butter *or* margarine, softened
2 eggs
Melted butter *or* margarine

In a mixing bowl, combine 2 cups flour, sugar, yeast and salt. In a saucepan, heat the milk, water and butter to 120°-130°. Add to dry ingredients; beat on medium speed for 2 minutes. Add eggs and 3/4 cup flour. Beat on high for 2 minutes. Stir in enough remaining flour to form a stiff dough. Turn onto a floured surface; knead until smooth and elastic, about 6-8 minutes. Place in a greased bowl, turning once to grease top. Cover and let rest for 20 minutes. Punch dough down. Turn onto a lightly floured surface; divide into 24 pieces. Shape each into a ball. Place 3 in. apart on greased baking sheets. Brush with melted butter. Cov-

er and refrigerate for 2 to 24 hours. Remove from the refrigerator 15 minutes before baking. Bake at 350° for 15-20 minutes or until golden brown. Remove from pans to wire racks to cool. **Yield:** 2 dozen.

SKILLET ROLLS

Susan Baughman, Houston, Pennsylvania

Baking these rolls in a skillet makes them soft and tender. My family requests them for most holiday dinners and other special occasions. I like them best split and spread with butter and black raspberry jelly.

1 package (1/4 ounce) active dry yeast
1/4 cup warm water (110° to 115°)
1 cup warm buttermilk* (110° to 115°)
1/4 cup butter *or* margarine, softened
1/4 cup sugar
1 teaspoon salt
1/4 teaspoon baking soda
1 egg
4 to 4-1/2 cups all-purpose flour
1 tablespoon cornmeal
1 tablespoon butter *or* margarine, melted

In a mixing bowl, dissolve yeast in warm water. Add the buttermilk, butter, sugar, salt, baking soda and egg. Beat until blended. Stir in enough flour to form a soft dough. Turn onto a floured surface; knead until smooth and elastic, about 6-8 minutes. Place in a greased bowl, turning once to grease top. Cover and let rise in a warm place until doubled, about 1 hour. Punch dough down. Turn onto a lightly floured surface; knead for 5 minutes. Divide into 24 pieces. Shape each into a ball. Grease a 12-in. ovenproof skillet and sprinkle with cornmeal. Place rolls in prepared pan. Cover and let rise until doubled, about 40 minutes. Drizzle butter over rolls. Bake at 375° for 18-20 minutes or until golden brown. Remove from skillet to a wire rack to cool. **Yield:** 2 dozen. ***Editor's Note:** Warmed buttermilk will appear curdled.

SHAPING ROLLS

You can shape dough for rolls in a variety of ways. Instead of just making a traditional round dinner roll, try one of these techniques:
- *For crescent rolls, roll a portion of dough into a 12-in. circle. Cut into wedges. Roll up from the wide end.*
- *For knot-shaped rolls, shape dough into 3-in. balls. Roll each ball into a rope. Tie a knot; tuck and pinch ends.*
- *For cloverleaf rolls, shape dough into 1-1/2-in. balls. Place three balls in each greased muffin cup.*

EASY BREAD SQUARES

Elsie Harms, Nokomis, Illinois

There's no kneading or rolling out dough in this extra-easy yeast recipe. I like to serve generous slices alongside spaghetti.

3-1/2 cups all-purpose flour
   1 tablespoon sugar
   1 package (1/4 ounce) active dry yeast
   1 teaspoon salt
1-1/2 cups warm water (120° to 130°)
   2 tablespoons shortening
Melted butter *or* margarine

In a mixing bowl, combine 1-1/2 cups flour, sugar, yeast and salt. Add water and shortening; beat on low speed for 30 seconds. Beat on high for 3 minutes. Stir in remaining flour (batter will be thick). Do not knead. Cover and let rise in a warm place for 30 minutes. Stir dough down. Spread evenly into a greased 13-in. x 9-in. x 2-in. baking pan. Cover and let rise until doubled, about 40 minutes. Bake at 375° for 30-35 minutes or until golden brown. Cool for 10 minutes before removing from pan to a wire rack. Brush with melted butter. Cut into squares. **Yield:** 12-15 servings.

WHOLESOME GRAIN LOAVES

Nancy Knapp, Sedro Woolley, Washington

This recipe began as a basic wheat bread. I added wholesome graham flour, raisins and sunflower kernels. Now my family begs me to make this for them.

   1 package (1/4 ounce) active dry yeast
2-3/4 cups warm water (110° to 115°)
   1/2 cup packed brown sugar
   1/4 cup butter *or* margarine, melted
1-1/2 teaspoons salt
   1 teaspoon ground cinnamon
   1 egg
   4 cups whole wheat flour
   1 cup graham flour *or* additional whole wheat flour
   3 to 3-1/2 cups all-purpose flour
   1 cup golden raisins
   1 cup unsalted sunflower kernels

In a mixing bowl, dissolve yeast in warm water. Add the brown sugar, butter, salt, cinnamon, egg, 3 cups whole wheat flour and graham flour. Beat until smooth. Stir in remaining whole wheat flour and enough all-purpose flour to form a soft dough. Turn onto a floured surface. Sprinkle with raisins and sunflower kernels. Knead until smooth and elastic, about 8-10 minutes. Place in a greased bowl, turning once to grease top. Cover and let rise in a warm place

until doubled, about 1 hour. Punch dough down. Turn onto a lightly floured surface; divide in half. Shape into loaves. Place in two greased 9-in. x 5-in. x 3-in. loaf pans. Cover and let rise until doubled, about 1 hour. Bake at 350° for 40-45 minutes or until golden brown. Remove from pans to wire racks to cool. **Yield:** 2 loaves.

BRAN BUNS

Julie Eblen, Belgrade, Montana

I grew up on a ranch with 20 brothers and sisters, so I learned to cook at an early age. After college, I went to work on a farm. My employer's wife shared this recipe with me.

   1 cup All-Bran cereal
   2 cups water, *divided*
   2 tablespoons active dry yeast
   8 tablespoons sugar, *divided*
   2 eggs
   3/4 cup vegetable oil
   2 teaspoons salt
5-1/2 to 6 cups all-purpose flour

Place cereal in a bowl. Heat 1 cup water to 120-130°; pour over cereal to soften. Set aside. Place yeast in a mixing bowl. Heat remaining water to 110-115°; pour over yeast to dissolve. Add 2 tablespoons sugar; let stand for 5 minutes. Add the eggs, oil, salt, bran mixture and remaining sugar; mix well. Stir in enough flour to form a soft dough. Turn onto a floured surface; knead until smooth and elastic, about 6-8 minutes. Place in a greased bowl, turning once to grease top. Cover and let rise in a warm place until doubled, about 1-1/2 hours. Punch dough down. Turn onto a lightly floured surface; divide into 24 pieces. Shape each into a ball. Place 2 in. apart on greased baking sheets. Cover and let rise until doubled, about 30 minutes. Bake at 350° for 15-20 minutes or until golden brown. Remove from pans to wire racks to cool. **Yield:** 2 dozen.

CLASSIC WHOLE WHEAT BREAD

Verna Lofberg, Bemidji, Minnesota

A lot of wheat is produced in this area, so I use it often in my baking. Buttermilk makes this bread a little lighter.

and less dense than other wheat breads. The aroma while it bakes is terrific.

3 cups whole wheat flour
1-1/2 cups quick-cooking oats
2 packages (1/4 ounce *each*) active dry yeast
1 tablespoon salt
2-1/2 cups buttermilk
1/3 cup butter *or* margarine, softened
1/4 cup honey
1/4 cup molasses
2 eggs
5 to 6 cups all-purpose flour
Melted butter *or* margarine

In a mixing bowl, combine the whole wheat flour, oats, yeast and salt. In a saucepan, heat the buttermilk, butter, honey and molasses to 120°-130°. Add to dry ingredients just until moistened. Beat in eggs until smooth. Stir in enough all-purpose flour to form a medium stiff dough. Turn onto a floured surface; knead until smooth and elastic, about 8-10 minutes. Place in a greased bowl, turning once to grease top. Cover and let rise in a warm place until doubled, about 1 hour. Punch dough down; let rest for 20 minutes. Punch dough down. Turn onto a lightly floured surface; divide in half. Shape into loaves. Place in two greased 9-in. x 5-in. x 3-in. loaf pans. Cover and let rise until doubled, about 45 minutes. Bake at 375° for 35-40 minutes or until golden brown. Remove from pans to wire racks. Brush with melted butter. Cool. **Yield:** 2 loaves. **Editor's Note:** Warmed buttermilk will appear curdled.

TWICE-BAKED ROLLS

Mary Jane Henderson, Salem, New Jersey

Everyone appreciates being offered home-baked rolls at dinner, but time doesn't always allow…especially on busy weeknights. These rolls can be conveniently partially baked and frozen. Then you can remove and bake as many rolls as needed.

2 packages (1/4 ounce *each*) active dry yeast
1 cup warm water (110° to 115°)
1 teaspoon plus 1/4 cup sugar, *divided*
2 cups warm milk (110° to 115°)
1/2 cup shortening
5 teaspoons salt
10 cups all-purpose flour

In a mixing bowl, dissolve yeast in warm water. Add 1 teaspoon sugar; let stand for 5 minutes. Add the milk,

shortening, salt, 2 cups flour and remaining sugar. Beat until smooth. Stir in enough remaining flour to form a stiff dough. Turn onto a floured surface; knead until smooth and elastic, about 6-8 minutes. Place in a greased bowl, turning once to grease top. Cover and let rise in a warm place until doubled, about 1-1/2 hours. Punch dough down. Turn onto a lightly floured surface; divide into four pieces. Cover three with plastic wrap. Divide remaining piece into 12 balls. Shape into balls. Place 2 in. apart on greased baking sheets. Repeat with remaining dough. Cover and let rise until doubled, about 20 minutes. To serve immediately, bake at 375° for 12-15 minutes or until golden brown. To freeze for later use, partially bake at 300° for 15 minutes. Allow to cool; freeze. Reheat frozen rolls at 375° for 12-15 minutes or until golden brown. **Yield:** 4 dozen.

GRAHAM ROLLS

Sandra Gates, Denham Springs, Louisiana

In the course of catching up with a friend I hadn't seen for well over 10 years, she requested this recipe that she had remembered me making. That's a true testament to the appeal of these rolls. Graham crackers are an unusual ingredient that add terrific taste and texture.

1/2 cup shortening
1/2 cup sugar
1 tablespoon salt
1 cup boiling water
2 packages (1/4 ounce *each*) active dry yeast
1 cup warm water (110° to 115°)
1 egg
3 cups graham cracker crumbs (about 48 squares), *divided*
2 cups whole wheat flour
3 cups all-purpose flour
1/3 cup butter *or* margarine, melted

In a mixing bowl, combine the shortening, sugar and salt. Stir in boiling water. Cool to 110°-115°. Dissolve yeast in warm water. Add yeast mixture, egg, 1 cup cracker crumbs and whole wheat flour to shortening mixture; mix well. Stir in enough all-purpose flour to form a soft dough. Turn onto a floured surface; knead until smooth and elastic, about 6-8 minutes. Place in a greased bowl, turning once to grease top. Cover and let rise in a warm place until doubled, about 1 hour. Punch dough down. Turn onto a lightly floured surface; divide into 48 pieces. Shape each into a ball. Dip into melted butter, then roll in remaining cracker crumbs. Place in greased muffin cups. Cover and let rise until doubled, about 30 minutes. Bake at 350° for 18-20 minutes or until golden brown. Remove from pans to wire racks to cool. **Yield:** 4 dozen.

KAISER ROLLS

Loraine Meyer, Bend, Oregon

(Pictured at left)

These rolls can be enjoyed plain with soup or used for sandwiches. I make them at least once a month. This recipe earned me a blue ribbon at the county fair.

- **2 packages (1/4 ounce *each*) active dry yeast**
- **2 cups warm water (110° to 115°), *divided***
- **4 tablespoons sugar, *divided***
- **1/3 cup vegetable oil**
- **2 teaspoons salt**
- **6 to 6-1/2 cups all-purpose flour**
- **1 egg white**
- **2 teaspoons cold water**
- **Poppy *and/or* sesame seeds**

In a mixing bowl, dissolve yeast in 1/2 cup warm water. Add 1 tablespoon sugar; let stand for 5 minutes. Add the remaining warm water and sugar. Beat in oil, salt and 4 cups flour until smooth. Stir in enough remaining flour to form a soft dough. Turn onto a floured surface; knead until smooth and elastic, about 6-8 minutes. Place in a greased bowl, turning once to grease top. Cover and let rise in a warm place until doubled, about 1 hour. Punch dough down. Turn onto a lightly floured surface; divide into 16 pieces. Shape each into a ball. Place 2 in. apart on greased baking sheets. Cover and let rise until doubled, about 30 minutes. Beat egg white and cold water; brush over rolls. Sprinkle with poppy and/or sesame seeds. With scissors, cut a 1/4-in.-deep cross on tops of rolls. Bake at 400° for 15-20 minutes or until golden brown. Remove from pans to wire racks to cool. **Yield:** 16 rolls.

POTATO BREAD

Martha Clayton, Utopia, Texas

(Pictured at left)

This bread's firm crust is reminiscent of the old-fashioned breads my grandmother used to make. I let my stand mixer with dough hook do most of the work for me.

- **1 medium potato, peeled and diced**
- **1-1/2 cups water**
- **2 packages (1/4 ounce *each*) active dry yeast**
- **1/2 cup warm water (110° to 115°)**
- **1 cup warm milk (110° to 115°)**
- **2 tablespoons butter *or* margarine, softened**
- **2 tablespoons sugar**

- **1 tablespoon salt**
- **6-1/2 to 7-1/2 cups all-purpose flour**
- **Additional all-purpose flour**

In a saucepan, cook potato in 1-1/2 cups water until very tender; drain, reserving 1/2 cup liquid. Mash potatoes (without added milk or butter); set aside. In a mixing bowl, dissolve yeast in warm water. Add the milk, butter, sugar, salt, 4 cups flour, potatoes and reserved cooking liquid. Beat until smooth. Stir in enough remaining flour to form a stiff dough. Turn onto a floured surface; knead until smooth and elastic, about 6-8 minutes. Place in a greased bowl, turning once to grease top. Cover and let rise in a warm place until doubled, about 1 hour. Punch dough down. Turn onto a lightly floured surface; divide in half. Shape into loaves. Place in two greased 9-in. x 5-in. x 3-in. loaf pans. Cover and let rise until doubled, about 30 minutes. Sprinkle lightly with additional flour. Bake at 375° for 35-40 minutes or until golden brown. Remove from pans to wire racks to cool. **Yield:** 2 loaves.

40-MINUTE HAMBURGER BUNS

Jessie McKenney, Twodot, Montana

Here on our ranch, I cook for three men, who love hamburgers. These fluffy yet hearty buns are just right for their big appetites. I also serve the buns plain with a meal.

- **2 tablespoons active dry yeast**
- **1 cup plus 2 tablespoons warm water (110° to 115°)**
- **1/3 cup vegetable oil**
- **1/4 cup sugar**
- **1 egg**
- **1 teaspoon salt**
- **3 to 3-1/2 cups all-purpose flour**

In a mixing bowl, dissolve yeast in warm water. Add oil and sugar; let stand for 5 minutes. Add the egg, salt and enough flour to form a soft dough. Turn onto a floured surface; knead until smooth and elastic, about 3-5 minutes. Do not let rise. Divide into 12 pieces; shape each into a ball. Place 3 in. apart on greased baking sheets. Cover and let rest for 10 minutes. Bake at 425° for 8-12 minutes or until golden brown. Remove from pans to wire racks to cool. **Yield:** 1 dozen.

ONE AT A TIME

If you're making several loaves of bread or a large batch of rolls at once and they don't all fit on one baking sheet, put one sheet in the oven and the other in the refrigerator. If you bake two sheets at the same time, not enough air will circulate and the bread or rolls will bake unevenly.

OLD-WORLD RYE BREAD

Perlene Hoekema, Lynden, Washington

(Pictured above and on page 44)

Rye and caraway lend to this bread's wonderful flavor, while the surprise ingredient of baking cocoa gives it a rich, dark color. I sometimes stir in a cup each of raisins and walnuts.

> **2 packages (1/4 ounce *each*) active dry yeast**
> **1-1/2 cups warm water (110° to 115°)**
> **1/2 cup molasses**
> **6 tablespoons butter *or* margarine, softened**
> **2 cups rye flour**
> **1/4 cup baking cocoa**
> **2 tablespoons caraway seeds**
> **2 teaspoons salt**
> **3-1/2 to 4 cups all-purpose flour**
> **Cornmeal**

In a mixing bowl, dissolve yeast in warm water. Beat in the molasses, butter, rye flour, cocoa, caraway seeds, salt and 2 cups all-purpose flour until smooth. Stir in enough remaining all-purpose flour to form a stiff dough. Turn onto a floured surface; knead until smooth and elastic, about 6-8 minutes. Place in a greased bowl, turning once to grease top. Cover and let rise in a warm place until doubled, about 1-1/2 hours. Punch dough down. Turn onto a lightly floured surface; divide in half. Shape into loaves, about 10 in. long. Grease two baking sheets and sprinkle with cornmeal. Place loaves on prepared pans. Cover and let rise until doubled, about 1 hour. Bake at 350° for 35-40 minutes or until bread tests done. Remove from pans to wire racks to cool. **Yield:** 2 loaves.

GRAMMY'S OAT ROLLS

Kathy Bungard, Ione, Washington

I make almost all of my own breads and rolls, and everyone in the family is a very eager tester. This is the recipe they request most often. Leftovers can be wrapped in foil and frozen.

> **1/2 cup quick-cooking oats**
> **1/2 cup whole wheat flour**

> **1/4 cup butter *or* margarine**
> **2 tablespoons plus 1 teaspoon honey, *divided***
> **2 tablespoons molasses**
> **2 teaspoons salt**
> **1 cup boiling water**
> **2 packages (1/4 ounce *each*) active dry yeast**
> **1/2 cup warm water (110° to 115°)**
> **1 egg**
> **3 to 3-1/2 cups all-purpose flour**

In a mixing bowl, combine the oats, whole wheat flour, butter, 2 tablespoons honey, molasses and salt. Stir in boiling water; cool to 110°-115°. Dissolve yeast in warm water; add remaining honey and let stand for [ ] minutes. Stir yeast mixture into oat mixture with egg and enough all-purpose flour to form a soft dough. Turn onto a floured surface; knead until smooth and elastic, about 6-8 minutes. Place in a greased bowl, turning once to grease top. Cover and let rise in a warm place until doubled, about 1 hour. Punch dough down. Turn onto a lightly floured surface; divide into 1[ ] pieces. Shape each into a ball. Place in two greased 8-in. round baking pans. Cover and let rise until doubled, about 45 minutes. Bake at 350° for 25-30 minutes or until golden brown. Remove from pans to wire racks to cool. **Yield:** 16 rolls.

MOM'S SWEDISH RYE

Kathy Ponton, Delphos, Kansas

My mom baked this bread in coffee cans, but I prefer to use regular loaf pans. I usually double the recipe so I have extra loaves available in the freezer.

> **1 package (1/4 ounce) active dry yeast**
> **2 cups warm water (110° to 115°)**
> **1/4 cup sugar**
> **1/4 cup shortening**
> **1/4 cup molasses**
> **2 teaspoons salt**
> **3/4 cup rye flour**
> **5 to 6 cups all-purpose flour**
> **Melted butter *or* margarine, optional**

In a mixing bowl, dissolve yeast in warm water. Add the sugar, shortening, molasses, salt, rye flour and 3 cups all-purpose flour. Beat until smooth. Stir in enough remaining all-purpose flour to form a soft dough. Turn onto a floured surface; knead until smooth and elastic, about 6-8 minutes. Place in a greased bowl, turning once to grease top. Cover and let rise in a warm place until doubled, about 1-1/2 hours. Punch dough down. Turn onto a lightly floured surface; divide in half. Shape into loaves. Place in two greased 9-in. x 5-in. x 3-in. loaf pans. Cover and let rise until doubled, about 1 hour. Bake at 350° for 40-45 minutes or until

olden brown. Remove from pans to wire racks. Brush
ith melted butter if desired. Cool. **Yield:** 2 loaves.

BLUE RIBBON WHITE BREAD

Pam Goodlet, Washington Island, Wisconsin

*This recipe took first-place honors 7 consecutive years at
ur local fair. My relatives rave about this bread and its
leasant subtle ginger flavor.*

    1 package (1/4 ounce) active dry yeast
-1/2 cups warm water (110° to 115°)
    1 cup instant nonfat dry milk powder
    3 tablespoons shortening
    2 tablespoons sugar
    2 teaspoons salt
 1/4 teaspoon ground ginger
    6 to 7 cups all-purpose flour

n a mixing bowl, dissolve yeast in warm water. Add the
ilk powder, shortening, sugar, salt, ginger and 3-1/2
ups flour. Beat until smooth. Stir in enough remain-
g flour to form a soft dough. Turn onto a floured sur-
ace; knead until smooth and elastic, about 6-8 min-
tes. Place in a greased bowl, turning once to grease
op. Cover and let rise in a warm place until doubled,
bout 1 hour. Punch dough down. Turn onto a lightly
oured surface; divide in half. Shape into loaves.
lace in two greased 8-in. x 4-in. x 2-in. loaf pans. Cov-
r and let rise until doubled, about 45 minutes. Bake at
50° for 40-45 minutes or until golden brown. Remove
om pans to wire racks to cool. **Yield:** 2 loaves.

HONEY WHOLE WHEAT BRAIDS

Pat Young, Backus, Minnesota

*his hearty, wholesome bread has a slightly sweet taste
om honey. I grind my own whole wheat to use in this
ecipe.*

    1 package (1/4 ounce) active dry yeast
-1/4 cups warm water (110° to 115°), *divided*
    1 tablespoon sugar
 1/3 cup honey
    3 tablespoons vegetable oil
-1/2 teaspoons salt
 1/2 cup instant nonfat dry milk powder
    6 to 6-1/2 cups whole wheat flour
ll-purpose flour
Melted butter *or* margarine

n a mixing bowl, dissolve yeast in 1/4 cup warm water.
dd sugar; let stand for 5 minutes. Add the honey, oil,
alt, milk powder, 3 cups whole wheat flour and re-
aining water. Beat for 5 minutes. Let stand for 5 min-

utes. Stir in enough remaining whole wheat flour to form
a soft dough. Turn onto a surface dusted with all-purpose flour; knead until smooth and elastic, about 8-10
minutes. Place in a greased bowl, turning once to grease
top. Cover and let rise in a warm place until doubled,
about 2 hours. Punch dough down. Turn onto a lightly
floured surface; divide into six pieces. Shape each into a
15-in. rope. Braid three ropes; pinch ends to seal and tuck
under. Repeat with remaining dough. Place in two
greased 8-in. x 4-in. x 2-in. loaf pans. Cover and let rise
until doubled, about 1 hour. Bake at 350° for 30-35 minutes or until golden brown. Remove from pans to wire
racks. Brush with melted butter. Cool. **Yield:** 2 loaves.

SHREDDED WHEAT BREAD

Carol Eastman, Chillicothe, Ohio

*The recipe for this low-fat bread came from my grand-
mother. It's now my husband's favorite. Nothing makes
the house smell better than the aroma of molasses as
this bread bakes.*

    2 cups boiling water
    1 cup crushed Shredded Wheat cereal
 1/2 cup molasses
    2 tablespoons shortening
1-1/2 teaspoons salt
    1 package (1/4 ounce) active dry yeast
 1/4 cup warm water (110° to 115°)
5-1/2 to 6-1/2 cups all-purpose flour
Melted butter *or* margarine, optional

In a bowl, pour boiling water over cereal. Add the
molasses, shortening and salt. Let stand until mixture
cools to 110°-115°, stirring occasionally. In a mixing
bowl, dissolve yeast in warm water. Add cereal mixture
and 3 cups flour. Beat until smooth. Stir in enough
remaining flour to form a soft dough (dough will be
sticky). Turn onto a floured surface; knead until
smooth and elastic, about 6-8 minutes. Place in a
greased bowl, turning once to grease top. Cover and let
rise in a warm place until doubled, about 1 hour.
Punch dough down. Turn onto a lightly floured surface; divide in half. Shape into loaves. Place in two
greased 9-in. x 5-in. x 3-in. loaf pans. Cover and let rise
until doubled, about 1 hour. Bake at 375° for 30-35
minutes or until golden brown. Remove from pans to
wire racks. Brush with melted butter if desired. Cool.
Yield: 2 loaves.

FLAKY CROISSANTS

Pam Butler, Branson, Missouri

These croissants may be a little time-consuming, but for holidays and other special occasions, it's worth the extra effort—and calories!

2-1/2 to 3 cups all-purpose flour
    1 tablespoon sugar
    1 package (1/4 ounce) active dry yeast
    3/4 teaspoon salt
    1 cup warm water (120° to 130°)
    1 tablespoon shortening
    1 cup cold butter (no substitutes), cubed
    1 egg, beaten

In a mixing bowl, combine 1 cup flour, sugar, yeast and salt. Add warm water and shortening. Beat on medium speed for 2 minutes. Add 1/2 cup flour; beat 2 minutes longer. Stir in enough remaining flour to form a soft dough. Turn onto a floured surface; knead until smooth and elastic, about 6-8 minutes. Place in a greased bowl, turning once to grease top. Cover and let rise in a warm place until doubled, about 45 minutes. Punch dough down. Cover and refrigerate for 2 hours. Turn dough onto a floured surface; roll into a 15-in. x 10-in. rectangle. In a small mixing bowl, beat cold butter until softened but still cold. Spread dough with a fourth of the butter. Fold dough into thirds, starting with a short side. Turn dough a quarter turn. Repeat rolling, buttering and folding three times. Wrap in plastic wrap. Refrigerate overnight. On a floured surface, roll dough into a 14-in. square. With a sharp knife, cut into quarters. Cut each quarter diagonally in half, forming two triangles. Roll up triangles from the wide end; place with pointed end down 2 in. apart on a greased baking sheet. Curve ends to form a crescent shape. Cover and refrigerate for 20 minutes. Brush with egg. Bake at 450° for 18-22 minutes or until golden brown. Remove from pan to a wire rack to cool. **Yield: 8 croissants.**

OATMEAL MINI LOAVES

Doris Kosmicki, Pinckney, Michigan

I first came across this recipe in an old cookbook. As I became more brave with bread baking, I decided to redo this recipe, changing and adding ingredients to enhance flavor and nutrition.

1-1/2 cups old-fashioned oats
    3/4 cup whole wheat flour
    1/2 cup packed brown sugar
    1/4 cup toasted wheat germ
    1 tablespoon salt
    1 package (1/4 ounce) active dry yeast
2-1/2 cups water

    2 tablespoons butter *or* margarine
5-1/2 to 6 cups all-purpose flour
Melted butter *or* margarine, optional
Additional old-fashioned oats, optional

In a mixing bowl, combine the oats, whole wheat flour, brown sugar, wheat germ, salt and yeast. In a saucepan, heat water and butter to 120°-130°. Add to dry ingredients; beat on medium speed for 3 minutes. Add cups all-purpose flour; beat until smooth. Stir in enough remaining all-purpose flour to form a soft dough. Turn onto a floured surface; knead until smooth and elastic, about 6-8 minutes. Place in greased bowl, turning once to grease top. Cover and let rise in a warm place until doubled, about 1 hour. Punch dough down. Turn onto a lightly floured surface; divide into five pieces. Shape each into a loaf. Place in five greased 5-3/4-in. x 3-in. x 2-in. loaf pans. Cover and let rise until doubled, about 30 minutes. Bake at 350° for 30-35 minutes or until golden brown. Remove from pans to wire racks. Brush with melted butter and sprinkle with additional oats if desired. Cool. **Yield:** 5 mini loaves. **Editor's Note:** Two greased 9-in. x 5-in. x 3-in. loaf pans may be used; bake for 35-40 minutes.

RUSTIC MULTI-GRAIN BREAD

Dorothy Daniel, Fremont, Nebraska

Milk gives this bread a soft tender crust that appeals to all. All-purpose, whole wheat and rye flours blend beautifully in this family-favorite recipe.

4 cups all-purpose flour
1-1/2 cups whole wheat flour
    1/2 cup rye flour
    1/2 cup packed brown sugar
    2 tablespoons sugar
    2 packages (1/4 ounce *each*) active dry yeast
    2 teaspoons salt
    2 cups milk
    1/2 cup water
    3 tablespoons vegetable oil

In a mixing bowl, combine 2 cups all-purpose flour, whole wheat flour, rye flour, sugars, yeast and salt. In saucepan, heat the milk, water and oil to 120°-130°. Add to dry ingredients; beat until smooth. Stir in enough remaining all-purpose flour to form a soft dough. Turn onto a floured surface; knead until smooth and elastic, about 6-8 minutes. Place in greased bowl, turning once to grease top. Cover and let rise in a warm place until doubled, about 1 hour.

Punch dough down. Turn onto a lightly floured surface; divide into four pieces. Roll each into a 15-in. rope. Twist two ropes together; pinch ends to seal. Repeat with remaining dough. Place in two greased 9-in. x 5-in. x 3-in. loaf pans. Cover and let rise until doubled, about 45 minutes. Bake at 375° for 30-35 minutes or until golden brown. Remove from pans to wire racks to cool. **Yield:** 2 loaves.

NO-FUSS DINNER ROLLS

Laurie Rice, Butler, Pennsylvania

I really enjoy making these rolls for our son because he loves them and the recipe is so easy. In a little over an hour, you can offer your family oven-fresh rolls.

1 package (1/4 ounce) active dry yeast
1-1/2 cups warm milk (110° to 115°)
1 egg
2 tablespoons butter *or* margarine, softened
2 tablespoons sugar
1 teaspoon salt
4 cups all-purpose flour
Melted butter *or* margarine

In a mixing bowl, dissolve yeast in warm milk. Add the egg, butter, sugar, salt and 2 cups flour. Beat on low speed for 30 seconds. Beat on high for 3 minutes. Stir in remaining flour (batter will be thick). Do not knead. Cover and let rest for 15 minutes. Stir dough down. Fill greased muffin cups three-fourths full. Cover and let rise in a warm place until doubled, about 20 minutes. Bake at 400° for 12-15 minutes or until golden brown. Brush with melted butter. Cool for 1 minute before removing from pans to wire racks. **Yield:** about 15 rolls.

FOUR-GRAIN BREAD

Rita Reese, Huntsburg, Ohio

My family usually gobbles up these loaves before I have a chance to get them in the freezer. But I'm pleased they like this original recipe of mine.

1 cup quick-cooking oats
2 cups boiling water
2 tablespoons butter *or* margarine, softened
2 packages (1/4 ounce *each*) active dry yeast
1/3 cup warm water (110° to 115°)
1/2 cup cornmeal
1/2 cup whole wheat flour
1/2 cup honey
2 teaspoons salt

5 to 6 cups all-purpose flour
Melted butter *or* margarine

In a mixing bowl, combine the oats, boiling water and butter; cool to 110°-115°, stirring occasionally. In a small bowl, dissolve yeast in warm water. Add to oat mixture. Add the cornmeal, whole wheat flour, honey, salt and 3 cups all-purpose flour. Beat until smooth. Stir in enough remaining all-purpose flour to form a soft dough. Turn onto a floured surface; knead until smooth and elastic, about 6-8 minutes. Place in a greased bowl, turning once to grease top. Cover and let rise in a warm place until doubled, about 1 hour. Punch dough down. Turn onto a lightly floured surface; divide in half. Shape into loaves. Place in two greased 9-in. x 5-in. x 3-in. loaf pans. Cover and let rise until doubled, about 45 minutes. Bake at 350° for 40-45 minutes or until golden brown. Remove from pans to wire racks. Brush with melted butter. Cool. **Yield:** 2 loaves.

SOFT OAT ROLLS

Judiann McNulty, Laramie, Wyoming

An old friend served these rolls when my family went to her house for Sunday dinner several years ago. I made sure I had a copy of the recipe before leaving.

2/3 cup quick-cooking oats
1/2 cup sugar
1/4 cup butter *or* margarine, softened
1/2 teaspoon salt
3/4 cup boiling water
1 package (1/4 ounce) active dry yeast
1/2 cup warm water (110° to 115°)
1 egg, beaten
3-1/2 to 4 cups all-purpose flour

In a mixing bowl, combine the oats, sugar, butter and salt. Stir in boiling water; cool to 110°-115°. Dissolve yeast in warm water. Stir into oat mixture with egg and enough flour to form a soft dough. Turn onto a floured surface; knead until smooth and elastic, about 5 minutes. Cover and let rest for 10 minutes. Roll to 1/2-in. thickness. Cut with a floured 2-1/2-in. biscuit cutter. Place 2 in. apart on lightly greased baking sheets. Cover and let rise in a warm place until doubled, about 1 hour. Bake at 375° for 15-20 minutes or until golden brown. Remove from pans to wire racks. Serve warm. **Yield:** about 1-1/2 dozen.

EASY CRESCENT ROLLS

Ruth Sanford, Wasilla, Alaska

I learned to cook and bake under my mother's fantastic guidance. She always treated the family to home-baked bread and I've learned to do the same.

- **1 package (1/4 ounce) active dry yeast**
- **1 cup warm water (110° to 115°)**
- **3 eggs**
- **4 to 4-1/2 cups all-purpose flour**
- **1/2 cup sugar**
- **1 teaspoon salt**
- **1/2 cup shortening**

In a small bowl, dissolve yeast in warm water. In a mixing bowl, beat eggs until light. Add to yeast mixture; set aside. In a large mixing bowl, combine 1 cup flour, sugar and salt. Cut in shortening until mixture resembles coarse crumbs. Stir in yeast mixture. Stir in enough remaining flour until dough leaves the side of the bowl and is soft (dough will be sticky). Do not knead. Cover and refrigerate overnight. Punch dough down. Turn onto a well-floured surface; divide into thirds. Roll each into a 12-in. circle; cut each circle into 12 wedges. Roll up wedges from the wide end and place with pointed end down 2 in. apart on greased baking sheets. Curve ends to form a crescent shape. Cover and let rise in a warm place until doubled, about 45 minutes. Bake at 375° for 8-12 minutes or until light golden brown. Remove from pans to wire racks. **Yield:** 3 dozen.

CRUSTY FRENCH BREAD

Deanna Naivar, Temple, Texas

A delicate texture makes this bread absolutely wonderful. I sometimes use the dough to make breadsticks, which I brush with melted butter and sprinkle with garlic powder.

- **1 package (1/4 ounce) active dry yeast**
- **1 cup warm water (110° to 115°)**
- **2 tablespoons sugar**
- **2 tablespoons vegetable oil**
- **1-1/2 teaspoons salt**
- **3 to 3-1/4 cups all-purpose flour**
- **Cornmeal**
- **1 egg white**
- **1 teaspoon cold water**

In a mixing bowl, dissolve yeast in warm water. Add the sugar, oil and salt. Beat until blended. Stir in enough flour to form a stiff dough. Turn onto a floured surface; knead until smooth and elastic, about 6-8 minutes. Place in a greased bowl, turning once to grease top. Cover and let rise in a warm place until doubled, about 1 hour. Punch dough down; return to bowl. Cover and let rise for 30 minutes. Punch dough down. Turn on-

to a lightly floured surface. Shape into a loaf 16 in. long x 2-1/2 in. wide with tapered ends. Sprinkle a greased baking sheet with cornmeal; place loaf on baking sheet. Cover and let rise until doubled, about 25 minutes. Beat egg white and cold water; brush over dough. With a sharp knife, make diagonal slashes 2 in. apart across top of loaf. Bake at 375° for 25-30 minutes or until golden brown. Remove from pan to a wire rack to cool. **Yield:** 1 loaf.

60-MINUTE MINI BREADS

Holly Hill, Franklin, Texas

When I was 11 years old, I entered this bread at our county fair. It beat out more than 90 food entries to win Junior Grand Champion and Best of Show! Sometimes make one large loaf instead of two mini loaves.

- **3 cups all-purpose flour**
- **1 tablespoon sugar**
- **1 teaspoon salt**
- **1 package (1/4 ounce) quick-rise yeast**
- **3/4 cup water**
- **1/4 cup milk**
- **2 tablespoons butter *or* margarine**

In a mixing bowl, combine 2 cups flour, sugar, salt and yeast. In a saucepan, heat the water, milk and butter to 120°-130°. Add to dry ingredients; beat until smooth. Stir in enough remaining flour to form a soft dough. Turn onto a floured surface; knead until smooth and elastic, about 4 minutes. Do not let rise. Divide in half. Roll each portion into an 8-in. x 5-in. rectangle. Roll up, jelly-roll style, starting with a short side; pinch seam to seal. Place, seam side down, in two greased 5-3/4-in. x 3-in. x 2-in. loaf pans. Fill a 13-in. x 9-in. x 2-in. baking pan with 1 in. of hot water. Set loaf pans in water. Cover and let rise for 15 minutes. Remove loaf pans from the water bath. Bake at 400° for 20-25 minutes or until golden brown. Remove from pans to wire racks to cool. **Yield:** 2 mini loaves.

KANSAS WHOLE WHEAT BREAD

Linda Pauls, Buhler, Kansas

We harvested wheat for 36 years, and I was the chief cook for the crew. This lightly textured wheat bread won an award at the Celebrate Kansas Wheat Bake-Off several years ago.

- **2-1/2 cups whole wheat flour**
- **1/2 cup quick-cooking oats**
- **1/4 cup toasted wheat germ**
- **2 packages (1/4 ounce *each*) active dry yeast**
- **2 teaspoons salt**

1 cup water
1 cup small-curd cottage cheese
1/2 cup mashed potatoes (without added milk or
    butter)
1/4 cup butter *or* margarine, softened
1/4 cup milk
1/4 cup honey
2 tablespoons molasses
2 eggs
3 to 4 cups all-purpose flour

In a mixing bowl, combine the whole wheat flour, oats, wheat germ, yeast and salt. In a saucepan, heat the water, cottage cheese, potatoes, butter, milk, honey and molasses to 120°-130°. Add to dry ingredients; beat until blended. Beat in the eggs until smooth. Stir in enough all-purpose flour to form a soft dough. Turn onto a floured surface; knead until smooth and elastic, about 8-10 minutes. Place in a greased bowl, turning once to grease top. Cover and let rise in a warm place until doubled, about 1 hour. Punch dough down. Turn onto a lightly floured surface; divide in half. Shape into two flattened balls. Place on two greased baking sheets. Cover and let rise until doubled, about 45 minutes. With a sharp knife, make a shallow X-shaped cut in the top of each loaf. Bake at 350° for 35-40 minutes. Cover loosely with foil if top browns too quickly. Remove from pans to wire racks to cool. **Yield:** 2 loaves.

COLONIAL OAT BREAD

Marge Kriner, Bloomsburg, Pennsylvania

My mother baked bread several times a week when I was young, and this was one of our favorites. Now my family enjoys it, especially with homemade soup.

4 cups whole wheat flour
1 cup quick-cooking oats
2 packages (1/4 ounce *each*) active dry yeast
1 tablespoon salt
-1/4 cups water
1/2 cup honey
1/4 cup butter *or* margarine, softened
1 egg
3 to 3-1/2 cups all-purpose flour
Additional quick-cooking oats, optional

In a mixing bowl, combine the whole wheat flour, oats, yeast and salt. In a saucepan, heat the water, honey and butter to 120°-130°. Add to dry ingredients; beat until blended. Beat in egg until smooth. Stir in enough all-purpose flour to form a stiff dough. Turn onto a floured surface; knead until smooth and elastic, about 6-8 minutes. Place in a greased bowl, turning once to grease top. Cover and let rise in a warm place until doubled, about 1 hour. Punch dough down. Turn onto a lightly floured surface; divide in half. Shape into

loaves. Place on two greased baking sheets. Cover and let rise until doubled, about 30 minutes. With a sharp knife, make several shallow X-shaped cuts across top of each loaf. Sprinkle with additional oats if desired. Bake at 350° for 35-40 minutes or until browned. Remove from pans to wire racks to cool. **Yield:** 2 loaves.

CORNMEAL MINI LOAVES

Ellen Govertsen, Wheaton, Illinois

This recipe makes six miniature loaves that can be baked, cooled and tucked into your freezer. To reheat, wrap in foil and bake at 400° for 15-20 minutes.

2 packages (1/4 ounce *each*) active dry yeast
1 cup warm water (110° to 115°)
1 cup warm milk (110° to 115°)
1/2 cup shortening
1/2 cup sugar
2 eggs
2 teaspoons salt
1 cup cornmeal
6 to 6-1/2 cups all-purpose flour
Additional cornmeal

In a mixing bowl, dissolve yeast in warm water. Add the milk, shortening, sugar, eggs, salt, cornmeal and 4 cups flour. Beat until smooth. Stir in enough remaining flour to form a soft dough. Turn onto a floured surface; knead until smooth and elastic, about 6-8 minutes. Place in a greased bowl, turning once to grease top. Cover and let rise in a warm place until doubled, about 1 hour. Punch dough down. Turn onto a lightly floured surface; divide into six pieces. Shape each into a 6-in. oval loaf. Grease two baking sheets; sprinkle with cornmeal. Place three loaves 3 in. apart on each prepared pan. Cover and let rise until doubled, about 30 minutes. With a sharp knife, make three shallow diagonal slashes across the top of each loaf. Bake at 400° for 15-20 minutes or until golden brown. Remove from pans to wire racks to cool. **Yield:** 6 mini loaves.

KNEADING DOUGH

- *To knead dough, turn it out onto a floured surface and shape into a ball. Fold the top of the dough toward you. With palms, push with a rolling motion. Turn dough a quarter turn; repeat motion until dough is smooth and elastic. Add flour to surface only as needed.*
- *If you're kneading the dough on a pastry board, place a damp dishcloth underneath the board to prevent it from sliding. When working with a sticky dough, oil your hands lightly so the dough won't cling.*

SOURDOUGH STARTER

Delila George, Junction City, Oregon

Some 25 years ago, I received this recipe and some starter from a good friend, who is now a neighbor. I use it to make many loaves of the Sourdough French Bread (recipe below).

1 package (1/4 ounce) active dry yeast
2 cups warm water (110° to 115°)
2 cups all-purpose flour

In a 4-qt. non-metallic bowl, dissolve yeast in warm water; let stand for 5 minutes. Add flour; stir until smooth. Cover loosely with a clean towel. Let stand in a warm place (80°-90°) to ferment for 48 hours; stir several times daily (the mixture will become bubbly and rise, have a "yeasty" sour aroma and a transparent yellow liquid will form on the top). Use starter for your favorite sourdough recipes. The starter will keep in the refrigerator for up to 2 weeks. Use and replenish or nourish at least every 2 weeks. Refer to the Sourdough Starter Secrets on page 54. **Yield:** about 3 cups.

SOURDOUGH FRENCH BREAD

Delila George, Junction City, Oregon

(Pictured at left)

Since receiving the recipe for the Sourdough Starter, I've made this French bread countless times. In fact, one year I donated 2 dozen loaves for a benefit dinner! These loaves rival any found in stores and can be made with relative ease.

1 package (1/4 ounce) active dry yeast
1-3/4 cups warm water (110° to 115°)
4-1/4 cups all-purpose flour
1/4 cup Sourdough Starter (recipe on this page)
2 tablespoons vegetable oil
2 tablespoons sugar
2 teaspoons salt
CORNSTARCH WASH:
1/2 cup water
1-1/2 teaspoons cornstarch

In a mixing bowl, dissolve yeast in warm water. Add the flour, Sourdough Starter, oil, sugar and salt; mix well. Turn onto a floured surface; gently knead 20-30 times (dough will be slightly sticky). Place in a greased bowl, turning once to grease top. Cover and let rise in a warm place until doubled, about 1 to 1-1/2 hours. Punch dough down. Turn onto a lightly floured surface; divide in half. Roll each into a 12-in. x 8-in. rectangle. Roll up, jelly-roll style, starting with a long side; pinch ends to seal. Place, seam side down, on two greased baking sheets; tuck ends under. Cover and let rise until doubled, about 30 minutes. With a sharp knife, make four shallow diagonal slashes across top of loaves. Meanwhile, combine water and cornstarch in a small saucepan. Cook and stir over medium heat until thickened. Brush some over loaves. Bake at 400° for 15 minutes. Brush loaves with the remaining cornstarch wash. Bake 5-10 minutes longer or until lightly browned. Remove from pans to wire racks to cool. **Yield:** 2 loaves.

HONEY WHEAT SOURDOUGH BREAD

Evelyn Newlands, Sun Lakes, Arizona

(Pictured at left)

We've been enjoying this slightly sweet bread on a daily basis for more than 10 years. A fellow teacher shared the recipe with me when my family lived in New York. I was sure to pack up the recipe when we headed west.

1 tablespoon active dry yeast
1 cup warm milk (110° to 115°)
3 tablespoons butter *or* margarine, softened
2 tablespoons honey
2 tablespoons molasses
2 cups Sourdough Starter (recipe on this page)
3 tablespoons wheat germ
1 tablespoon sugar
1 teaspoon baking soda
1 teaspoon salt
1 cup whole wheat flour
3-1/4 to 3-3/4 cups all-purpose flour
Vegetable oil

In a mixing bowl, dissolve yeast in warm milk. Add the butter, honey, molasses, Sourdough Starter, wheat germ, sugar, baking soda, salt, whole wheat flour and 2 cups all-purpose flour. Beat until smooth. Stir in enough remaining all-purpose flour to form a soft dough. Turn onto a floured surface; knead until smooth and elastic, about 6-8 minutes. Place in a greased bowl, turning once to grease top. Cover and let rise in a warm place until doubled, about 1 hour. Punch dough down. Turn onto a lightly floured surface; divide in half. Shape into loaves. Place in two greased 8-in. x 4-in. x 2-in. loaf pans. Cover and let rise until doubled, about 1 hour. Brush with oil. Bake at 375° for 25-30 minutes or until browned. Remove from pans to wire racks to cool. **Yield:** 2 loaves.

> **SOURDOUGH SUCCESS.** Pictured at left, top to bottom: Sourdough French Bread and Honey Wheat Sourdough Bread (recipes on this page) and Sourdough Ham Crescent Rolls (recipe on page 54).

SOURDOUGH HAM CRESCENT ROLLS

Jean Graf, Albany, Oregon

(Pictured above and on page 52)

These eye-appealing crescent rolls are loaded with ham and hard-cooked eggs. They're a terrific main course for a ladies' luncheon.

> 2 packages (1/4 ounce *each*) active dry yeast
> 1/2 cup warm water (110° to 115°)
> 1 cup warm milk (110° to 115°)
> 1 cup Sourdough Starter (recipe on page 53)
> 1/2 cup vegetable oil
> 1/4 cup sugar
> 2 teaspoons salt
> 5 to 5-1/2 cups all-purpose flour

FILLING:

> 2 cups finely chopped fully cooked ham
> 2 hard-cooked eggs, chopped
> 1 small onion, chopped
> 1/2 cup condensed cream of mushroom soup, undiluted

In a mixing bowl, dissolve yeast in warm water. Add the milk, Sourdough Starter, oil, sugar, salt and 2 cups flour. Beat until smooth. Stir in enough remaining flour to form a medium stiff dough. Turn onto a floured surface; knead until smooth and elastic, about 6-8 minutes. Place in a greased bowl, turning once to grease top. Cover and let rise in a warm place until doubled, about 1 hour. Punch dough down. Turn onto a lightly floured surface; divide into four pieces. Roll each into a 12-in. circle; cut into eight wedges. Combine the filling ingredients; spread over wedges. Roll up from the wide end and place with pointed end down 2 in. apart on greased baking sheets. Curve ends to form a crescent shape. Cover and let rise until doubled, about 45 minutes. Bake at 375° for 12-15 minutes or until golden brown. Serve immediately. Refrigerate leftovers. **Yield:** 32 rolls.

GOLDEN SOURDOUGH BISCUITS

Stephanie Church, Delaware, Ohio

I obtained this recipe from a friend when we were exchanging sourdough recipes a few years ago. These soft biscuits are best enjoyed straight from the oven.

> 2 cups all-purpose flour
> 1 teaspoon baking powder
> 1 teaspoon salt
> 1/2 teaspoon baking soda
> 1/2 cup cold butter *or* margarine
> 1 cup Sourdough Starter (recipe on page 53)
> 1/2 cup buttermilk

Melted butter *or* margarine

In a bowl, combine the flour, baking powder, salt and baking soda; cut in butter until mixture resembles

oarse crumbs. Combine Sourdough Starter and but-
ermilk; stir into flour mixture with a fork. Turn onto a
well-floured surface; knead 10-12 times. Roll to 1/2-in.
hickness. Cut with a floured 2-1/2-in. biscuit cutter.
Place 2 in. apart on a greased baking sheet. Bake at
-25° for 12-15 minutes or until golden brown. Brush
with melted butter. Remove from pan to a wire rack to
ool. **Yield:** 1 dozen.

COUNTRY CRUST SOURDOUGH BREAD

Beverley Whaley, Camano Island, Washington

*For many years, I've been making 45 loaves of this
bread for an annual Christmas bazaar, where we feed
bread and soup to over 300 folks.*

   2 packages (1/4 ounce *each*) active dry yeast
-1/4 cups warm water (110° to 115°)
   1 cup Sourdough Starter (recipe on page 53)
   2 eggs
1/4 cup sugar
1/4 cup vegetable oil
   1 teaspoon salt
   6 to 6-1/2 cups all-purpose flour
Melted butter *or* margarine

In a mixing bowl, dissolve yeast in warm water. Add the
Sourdough Starter, eggs, sugar, oil, salt and 3 cups
lour. Beat until smooth. Stir in enough remaining
lour to form a soft dough. Turn onto a floured surface;
knead until smooth and elastic, about 6-8 minutes.
Place in a greased bowl, turning once to grease top.
Cover and let rise in a warm place until doubled, about
 hour. Punch dough down. Turn onto a lightly floured
urface; divide in half. Shape into loaves. Place in two
reased 8-in. x 4-in. x 2-in. loaf pans. Cover and let rise
ntil doubled, about 45 minutes. Bake at 375° for 30-
5 minutes or until golden brown. Remove from pans
o wire racks to cool. Brush with butter. **Yield:** 2 loaves.

SOURDOUGH ENGLISH MUFFINS

Jean Graf, Albany, Oregon

*This recipe was a winner in a local newspaper contest
ears ago and has become a family favorite. The muffins
re fun to make on a griddle and delicious to eat.*

-3/4 to 3 cups all-purpose flour
   1 cup water
1/2 cup Sourdough Starter (recipe on page 53)
1/3 cup instant nonfat dry milk powder
   1 tablespoon sugar
3/4 teaspoon salt

1/4 cup cornmeal, *divided*
Butter, jam *or* honey

In a mixing bowl, combine 2 cups flour, water and
Sourdough Starter. Cover and let stand overnight.
Combine the milk powder, sugar, salt and 1/2 cup
flour. Add to sourdough mixture; mix well. Turn onto
a floured surface; knead until smooth and no longer
sticky, about 2-3 minutes, adding more flour if needed.
Roll to 1/2-in. thickness. Cut with a 3-in. round cookie cutter. Grease baking sheets and sprinkle with 2 tablespoons cornmeal. Place muffins 2 in. apart on prepared baking sheets. Sprinkle remaining cornmeal over
muffin tops. Cover and let rise in a warm place until
doubled, about 45 minutes. In a lightly greased griddle
or electric skillet, cook muffins at 275° for 10 minutes. Turn and cook 10-15 minutes longer or until
golden brown. Split with a sharp knife or a fork and
toast if desired. Serve with butter, jam or honey. **Yield:**
1 dozen.

CRANBERRY SOURDOUGH COFFEE CAKE

Paula Zsiray, Logan, Utah

*This is an adaptation of a friendship bread. The original
recipe called for raisins, but I started using cranberries to
suit my family's taste. If you have Sourdough Starter on
hand, you can quickly prepare the coffee cake.*

   2 cups all-purpose flour
   1 cup packed brown sugar
   1 cup vegetable oil
   1 cup Sourdough Starter (recipe on page 53)
   2 packages (3.4 ounces *each*) instant French
      vanilla pudding mix
1/2 cup buttermilk
   3 eggs
   2 tablespoons sugar
   1 tablespoon ground cinnamon
1-1/2 teaspoons baking powder
1/2 to 1 teaspoon ground nutmeg
   1 teaspoon vanilla extract
1/2 teaspoon salt
1/2 teaspoon baking soda
3/4 cup dried cranberries
TOPPING:
1/4 cup sugar
1/2 teaspoon ground cinnamon

In a mixing bowl, combine the first 14 ingredients; mix
well. Fold in dried cranberries. Pour into a greased and
sugared 10-in. tube or fluted tube pan. Combine topping ingredients; sprinkle over batter. Bake at 325° for
65-75 minutes or until a toothpick comes out clean.
Cool for 10 minutes before removing from pan to a
wire rack to cool completely. **Yield:** 12-16 servings.

Savory Yeast Breads

These yeast breads and rolls showcasing cheese, herbs, vegetables and meats can be served alongside any meal or used to hold your favorite sandwich fillings.

CHEDDAR BATTER BREAD

Debbie Keslar, Seward, Nebraska

(Pictured at left)

I love batter breads because I can offer my family delicious homemade bread without the hassle of kneading and shaping the dough. This is terrific with chili.

- 2 cups all-purpose flour
- 2 tablespoons sugar
- 1 package (1/4 ounce) active dry yeast
- 1/4 teaspoon onion powder
- 1/4 teaspoon salt
- 1/4 teaspoon pepper
- 1 cup milk
- 2 tablespoons butter *or* margarine, softened
- 1 egg
- 1/2 cup cornmeal
- 3/4 cup shredded cheddar cheese
- Additional cornmeal

In a mixing bowl, combine 1-1/2 cups flour, sugar, yeast, onion powder, salt and pepper. In a saucepan, heat milk and butter to 120°-130°. Add to dry ingredients; beat until moistened. Add egg; beat on low speed for 30 seconds. Beat on high for 3 minutes. Stir in cornmeal and remaining flour. Stir in cheese (batter will be thick). Do not knead. Cover and let rise in a warm place until doubled, about 20 minutes. Stir dough down. Grease an 8-in. x 4-in. x 2-in. loaf pan and sprinkle with additional cornmeal. Spoon batter into prepared pan. Cover and let rise in a warm place until doubled, about 30 minutes. Bake at 350° for 35-40 minutes or until golden brown. Cool in pan for 10 minutes before removing to a wire rack. Store in the refrigerator. **Yield:** 1 loaf.

BRAIDED PEPPERY CHEESE ROLLS

Deborah Amrine, Grand Haven, Michigan

(Pictured at left)

These eye-catching braided rolls are a wonderful accompaniment to any meal. The coarsely ground pepper isn't overpowering. I sometimes like to use the dough when making hamburger buns.

- 4-1/4 to 4-3/4 cups all-purpose flour
- 3 tablespoons sugar
- 2 packages (1/4 ounce *each*) active dry yeast
- 1-1/2 teaspoons salt
- 1 teaspoon coarsely ground pepper
- 1-1/2 cups milk
- 1/4 cup butter *or* margarine
- 2 eggs
- 1/2 cup shredded cheddar cheese

In a mixing bowl, combine 2 cups flour, sugar, yeast, salt and pepper. In a saucepan, heat milk and butter to 120°-130°. Add to dry ingredients; beat on medium speed for 2 minutes. Add 1 egg and 1/2 cup flour; beat 2 minutes longer. Stir in cheese and enough remaining flour to form a soft dough. Turn onto a floured surface; knead until smooth and elastic, about 6-8 minutes. Place in a greased bowl, turning once to grease top. Cover and let rise in a warm place until doubled, about 30 minutes. Punch dough down. Turn onto a floured surface; cover and let rest for 15 minutes. Divide into 36 pieces. Shape each into a 6-in. rope. Braid three ropes together. Pinch ends to seal. Repeat with remaining dough. Place on greased baking sheets. Cover and let rise in a warm place until doubled, about 30 minutes. Beat remaining egg; brush over braids. Bake at 375° for 15-17 minutes or until golden brown. Remove from pan to a wire rack to cool. Store in the refrigerator. **Yield:** 1 dozen.

BREAD AND BUTTER

For special occasions, try serving butter for your homemade bread in fun ways with little work.

- *To create butter cutouts, slice a chilled stick of butter 1/4 inch thick. Cut out shapes with small cookie cutters (simple shapes work best).*
- *To make balls of butter, cut balls from a chilled 1-pound block of butter using a large melon baller that's been dipped in hot water.*
- *Arrange butter cutouts or balls on crushed ice in a small decorative bowl, on a lettuce-lined butter serving plate or on individual bread and butter plates.*

CHEESE REALLY PLEASES. Pictured at left, top to bottom: Braided Peppery Cheese Rolls and Cheddar Batter Bread (both recipes on this page).

HAM-STUFFED BREAD

Lilburne Flohr-Svendsen, Barra Bonita, Brazil

I made this hearty bread at our daughter's wedding years ago. It caught on so well that I now serve it at all of our special-occasion events.

    1 tablespoon active dry yeast
    1 cup warm milk (110° to 115°)
    1 egg
  1/2 cup vegetable oil
  1/2 teaspoon salt
2-3/4 to 3-1/4 cups all-purpose flour
FILLING:
    1 small onion, chopped
  1/3 cup vegetable oil
    2 medium tomatoes, chopped
    1 garlic clove, minced
Salt and pepper to taste
  1/2 pound fully cooked ham, chopped
    1 teaspoon vinegar
  1/2 teaspoon dried oregano

In a mixing bowl, dissolve yeast in warm milk. Add the egg, oil and salt; beat until smooth. Stir in enough flour to form a stiff dough. Place in a greased bowl, turning once to grease top. Cover and let rise in a warm place until doubled, about 1 hour. Meanwhile, in a skillet, saute onion in oil until tender. Add tomatoes, garlic, salt and pepper. Cook over medium heat until liquid is absorbed, about 30 minutes. Remove from the heat. Add ham, vinegar and oregano; mix well. Cool. Punch dough down. Turn onto a lightly floured surface; roll into a 14-in. x 12-in. rectangle. Spread filling over dough to within 1/2 in. of edges. Roll up, jelly-roll style, starting with a long side; pinch seam to seal and tuck ends under. Place, seam side down, on a greased baking sheet. Do not let rise. Bake at 375° for 18-22 minutes or until golden brown. Remove from pan to a wire rack. Serve warm. Refrigerate leftovers. **Yield:** 1 loaf.

DILL RYE ROUNDS

Betty Pittman, Letts, Iowa

This herb bread has always been a success when I've made it for family and friends. But I was really proud when it became a prize-winning recipe in a local newspaper contest!

3-1/2 to 4 cups all-purpose flour
1-1/2 cups rye flour
  1/2 cup instant nonfat dry milk powder
    2 packages (1/4 ounce *each*) active dry yeast
    2 teaspoons sugar
    1 teaspoon salt
    1 teaspoon caraway seeds
    1 teaspoon dill seed
    1 teaspoon dill weed
1-3/4 cups water
    2 teaspoons shortening

In a mixing bowl, combine 2 cups all-purpose flour, rye flour, milk powder, yeast, sugar, salt and seasonings. In a saucepan, heat water and shortening to 120°-130°. Add to dry ingredients; beat until smooth. Stir in enough remaining all-purpose flour to form a soft dough. Turn onto a floured surface; knead until smooth and elastic, about 6-8 minutes. Place in a greased bowl, turning once to grease top. Cover and let rise in a warm place until doubled, about 45 minutes. Punch dough down. Turn onto a lightly floured surface; divide in half. Shape into two balls. Place on two greased baking sheets. Cover and let rise in a warm place until doubled, about 35 minutes. With a sharp knife, make several shallow slashes across the top of each loaf. Bake at 375° for 30-35 minutes or until golden brown. Remove from pans to wire racks to cool. **Yield:** 2 loaves.

RYE HORNS

Marvine Koliha, Howells, Nebraska

We live on a farm, so filling, flavorful meals are a must. No one can resist these tender rye rolls brushed with melted butter.

    6 to 6-1/2 cups all-purpose flour
    1 package (1/4 ounce) active dry yeast
    2 cups warm milk (120° to 130°)
    2 eggs
  1/4 cup butter *or* margarine, melted
  1/4 cup packed brown sugar
    2 tablespoons dark molasses
    2 teaspoons caraway seeds
    2 teaspoons salt
  1/2 teaspoon baking soda
1-1/2 cups rye flour
Additional melted butter *or* margarine

In a mixing bowl, combine 2 cups all-purpose flour and yeast. Add milk; mix well. Let stand for 30 minutes. Add eggs, butter, brown sugar, molasses, caraway seeds, salt and baking soda; mix well. Stir in rye flour and enough remaining all-purpose flour to form a soft dough. Turn onto a floured surface; knead until smooth and elastic, about 6-8 minutes. Place in a greased bowl, turning once to grease top. Cover and let rise in a warm place until doubled, about 1 hour. Punch dough down. Turn onto a lightly floured surface; divide into 16 pieces. Shape each into a ball. Cover and let rise in a warm place until doubled, about 30 minutes. Roll each ball into a 6-in. x 3-in. oval. Roll up, jelly-roll style, starting with a long side;

stretching and pinching ends while rolling to taper ends. Place on greased baking sheets. Curve rolls to form a crescent shape. Cover and let rise in a warm place until doubled, about 30 minutes. Bake at 375° for 8-12 minutes or until lightly browned. Remove from pans to wire racks. Brush with melted butter. Cool. **Yield:** 16 rolls.

CARAWAY PUFFS

Glennis Endrud, Buxton, North Dakota

Our daughter took these light-as-a-feather rolls to a 4-H event and came home with a Grand Champion ribbon! We think they're especially delectable served straight from the oven.

>   1 package (1/4 ounce) active dry yeast
> 1/4 cup warm water (110° to 115°)
>   1 cup warm cottage cheese (110° to 115°)
>   1 egg
>   2 tablespoons sugar
>   1 tablespoon butter *or* margarine, softened
>   2 teaspoons caraway seeds
>   1 teaspoon salt
> 1/4 teaspoon baking soda
> 2-1/3 cups all-purpose flour

In a mixing bowl, dissolve yeast in warm water. Add the cottage cheese, egg, sugar, butter, caraway seeds, salt, baking soda and 1-1/3 cups flour; beat on low speed for 30 seconds. Beat on high for 3 minutes. Stir in the remaining flour (batter will be stiff). Do not knead. Cover and let rise in a warm place until doubled, about 45 minutes. Stir dough down. Spoon into greased muffin cups. Cover and let rise in a warm place until doubled, about 35 minutes. Bake at 400° for 12-14 minutes or until golden brown. Cool in pan for 1 minute. Serve immediately. **Yield:** 1 dozen.

HARVEST SQUASH ROLLS

Ellen Govertsen, Wheaton, Illinois

A pretty golden color makes these great to serve alongside a hearty fall dinner. This recipe is a wonderful way to use up your remaining garden squash.

>   1 cup mashed cooked acorn *or* butternut squash
>   1 cup sugar
>   2 tablespoons butter *or* margarine, melted
>   1 teaspoon salt
>   1 cup warm milk (120° to 130°)
>   1 package (1/4 ounce) active dry yeast
> 1/2 cup warm water (110° to 115°)
> 4-1/2 to 5 cups all-purpose flour

In a mixing bowl, combine the squash, sugar, butter and salt; mix well. Stir in milk; cool to 110°-115°. Dissolve yeast in warm water. Add to squash mixture; mix well. Stir in enough flour to form a soft dough. Turn onto a floured surface; knead until smooth and elastic, about 6-8 minutes. Place in a greased bowl, turning once to grease top. Cover and let rise in a warm place until doubled, about 1 hour. Punch dough down. Turn onto a floured surface; divide into 24 pieces. Shape each into a ball. Place 2 in. apart on greased baking sheets. Cover and let rise in a warm place until doubled, about 45 minutes. Bake at 400° for 15-18 minutes or until golden. Remove from pans to wire racks to cool. **Yield:** 2 dozen.

TOMATO BREAD

Dolores Skrout, Summerhill, Pennsylvania

With tomato juice and Parmesan cheese, this bread tastes like a grilled cheese and tomato sandwich. I often top slices with our favorite pizza toppings for a unique snack.

>   1 package (1/4 ounce) active dry yeast
> 1/4 cup warm water (110° to 115°)
>   2 cups warm tomato juice (110° to 115°)
> 1/4 cup ketchup
> 1/4 cup grated Parmesan cheese
>   3 tablespoons sugar
>   2 tablespoons butter *or* margarine, melted
>   1 teaspoon salt
> 1/2 teaspoon dried basil
> 1/2 teaspoon dried oregano
> 6-3/4 to 7-1/4 cups all-purpose flour

In a mixing bowl, dissolve yeast in warm water. Add the tomato juice, ketchup, Parmesan cheese, sugar, butter, salt, basil, oregano and 3 cups flour. Beat until smooth. Stir in enough remaining flour to form a soft dough. Turn onto a floured surface; knead until smooth and elastic, about 6-8 minutes. Place in a greased bowl, turning once to grease top. Cover and let rise in a warm place until doubled, about 1-1/4 hours. Punch dough down. Divide in half. Cover and let rest for 10 minutes. Shape into loaves. Place in two greased 9-in. x 5-in. x 3-in. loaf pans. Cover and let rise in a warm place until doubled, about 1 hour. Bake at 375° for 25-30 minutes or until golden brown. Remove from pans to wire racks to cool. **Yield:** 2 loaves.

Herbed Oat Pan Bread

Robbin Thomas, Grouse Creek, Utah

The Parmesan cheese and herb topping on this rich pan bread is too tempting to resist. Eating just one piece isn't an option around our house!

> 2 cups water
> 1 cup quick-cooking oats
> 3 tablespoons butter *or* margarine, softened
> 3-3/4 to 4-3/4 cups all-purpose flour
> 1/4 cup sugar
> 2 packages (1/4 ounce *each*) active dry yeast
> 2 teaspoons salt
> 1 egg
> TOPPING:
> 6 tablespoons butter *or* margarine, melted, *divided*
> 1 tablespoon grated Parmesan cheese
> 1/2 teaspoon dried basil
> 1/4 teaspoon garlic powder
> 1/4 teaspoon dried oregano

In a saucepan, bring water to a boil; stir in oats. Remove from the heat. Stir in butter; cool to 120°-130°. In a mixing bowl, combine 1-1/2 cups flour, sugar, yeast and salt; set aside. Beat in oat mixture until moistened. Add egg. Beat on medium speed for 3 minutes. Stir in enough remaining flour to form a stiff dough. Turn onto a floured surface; knead until smooth and elastic, about 6-8 minutes. Cover and let rest for 15 minutes. Punch dough down. Press dough into a greased 13-in. x 9-in. x 2-in. baking pan. Cover and let rise in a warm place until doubled, about 45 minutes. Brush with 4 tablespoons melted butter. Bake at 375° for 15 minutes. Brush with remaining butter. Combine the Parmesan cheese, basil, garlic powder and oregano; sprinkle over bread. Bake 10-15 minutes longer or until golden brown. **Yield:** 16-20 servings.

Pumpkin Cloverleaf Rolls

Donna Bucher, Tirane, Albania

I came up with this recipe when I was looking for something festive to take to a fall covered-dish dinner. These rolls were a big hit.

> 1 package (1/4 ounce) active dry yeast
> 1/4 cup warm water (110° to 115°)
> 10 teaspoons brown sugar, *divided*
> 1 cup warm milk (110° to 115°)
> 1 cup cooked *or* canned pumpkin
> 6 tablespoons butter *or* margarine, melted
> 4-1/2 teaspoons grated orange peel
> 1 tablespoon salt
> 4-1/4 to 4-3/4 cups all-purpose flour
> 1 egg, beaten

In a mixing bowl, dissolve yeast in warm water. Add 1 teaspoon brown sugar; let stand for 5 minutes. Add milk, pumpkin, butter, orange peel, salt and remaining sugar; mix well. Add 2 cups flour. Beat on medium speed for 2 minutes. Stir in enough remaining flour to form a soft dough. Turn onto a floured surface; knead until smooth and elastic, about 10 minutes. Place in a greased bowl, turning once to grease top. Cover and let rise in a warm place until doubled, about 1 hour. Punch dough down. Turn onto a lightly floured surface; knead until smooth and elastic, about 1 minute. Divide into six portions. Divide each into 12 pieces. Shape each into a ball; place three balls in each greased muffin cup. Cover and let rise until doubled, about 30 minutes. Brush rolls with egg. Bake at 400° for 20-25 minutes or until browned. Remove from pans to wire racks to cool. **Yield:** 2 dozen.

Italian Dinner Rolls

Marie Elaine Basinger, Connellsville, Pennsylvania

Over the years, I've added a pinch of this and a dash of that to this recipe until my family agreed it was just right. These rolls are especially good served warm with spaghetti and lasagna.

> 3-1/2 to 4 cups all-purpose flour
> 2 tablespoons sugar
> 2 packages (1/4 ounce *each*) active dry yeast
> 2 teaspoons garlic salt
> 1 teaspoon Italian seasoning
> 1 teaspoon dried parsley flakes
> 1 teaspoon onion powder
> 1 cup milk
> 1/2 cup water
> 4 tablespoons butter *or* margarine, *divided*
> 1 egg
> 3/4 cup grated Parmesan cheese, *divided*

In a mixing bowl, combine 1-1/2 cups flour, sugar, yeast and seasonings. In a saucepan, heat the milk, water and 2 tablespoons butter to 120°-130°. Add to dry ingredients; beat until moistened. Add egg; beat on medium speed for 3 minutes. Stir in 1/2 cup Parmesan cheese and enough remaining flour to form a soft dough. Turn onto a floured surface; knead until smooth and elastic, about 3-5 minutes. Place in a greased bowl, turning once to grease top. Cover and let rest for 15 minutes. Punch dough down. Turn onto a lightly floured surface; divide into 16 pieces. Shape each into a ball. Melt remaining butter; dip tops of balls in butter and remaining Parmesan cheese. Place in a greased 13-in. x 9-in. x 2-in. baking pan or two 8-in. round baking pans. Cover and let rest for 10 minutes. Bake at 375° for 20-25 minutes or until golden brown. Remove from pans to wire racks to cool. **Yield:** 16 rolls.

PULL-APART GARLIC BUNS

Carolina Hofeldt, Lloyd, Montana

My Italian neighbor has passed along many mouth-watering recipes, including this one. The soft, tender buns are easy to pull apart.

2-1/2 to 3 cups all-purpose flour
 1 tablespoon sugar
 1 package (1/4 ounce)
  active dry yeast
 1 teaspoon salt
 1/2 cup milk
 1/2 cup water
 2 tablespoons
  shortening
 1 egg
 1 teaspoon paprika
 1/2 teaspoon garlic powder
 1/4 cup butter *or* margarine, melted
 1 tablespoon sesame seeds

In a mixing bowl, combine 1-1/2 cups flour, sugar, yeast and salt. In a saucepan, heat the milk, water and shortening to 120°-130°. Add to dry ingredients; beat until moistened. Add egg; beat on medium speed for 3 minutes. Stir in enough remaining flour to form a soft dough. Turn onto a floured surface; knead until smooth and elastic, about 6-8 minutes. Do not let rise. Divide into 12 pieces. Shape each into a bun. Combine paprika and garlic powder. Dip each bun in melted butter, then in paprika mixture. Place six buns in a greased 9-in. x 5-in. x 3-in. loaf pan; sprinkle with half of the sesame seeds. Top with remaining buns and sesame seeds. Cover and let rise in a warm place until doubled, about 45 minutes. Bake at 375° for 30-35 minutes or until golden brown. Remove from pan to a wire rack to cool. **Yield:** 1 loaf.

CHEDDAR FLAT BREAD

Joan Lucia, Gilboa, New York

I work full-time and don't get to spend as much time in the kitchen as I'd like. So I often make an entire meal from scratch on Sunday. This tantalizing bread is usually on the menu.

 1 package (1/4 ounce) active dry yeast
 1/4 cup warm water (110° to 115°)
 3/4 cup warm milk (110° to 115°)
 2 tablespoons butter *or* margarine, softened
 1 tablespoon sugar
1-1/2 teaspoons salt
2-1/2 to 3 cups all-purpose flour
 1/4 cup butter *or* margarine, melted
 2 tablespoons dried minced onion
 1/2 teaspoon dried oregano

 1/2 teaspoon paprika
 1/4 teaspoon celery seed
 1/4 teaspoon garlic salt
 1 cup (4 ounces) shredded cheddar cheese

In a mixing bowl, dissolve yeast in warm water. Add the milk, butter, sugar and salt. Stir in enough flour to form a stiff dough. Turn onto a floured surface; knead until smooth and elastic, about 4 minutes. Place in a greased bowl, turning once to grease top. Cover and let rise in a warm place until doubled, about 45 minutes. Punch dough down. Divide in half. Press each into a greased 9-in. pie plate. In a small bowl, combine melted butter and seasonings; brush over dough. Sprinkle with cheese. Prick dough several times with a fork. Cover and let rise until doubled, about 30 minutes. Bake at 350° for 20-25 minutes or until golden brown. Remove from pans to wire racks to cool. Store in the refrigerator. **Yield:** 2 loaves.

POTATO CASSEROLE BREAD

Lisa Powers, Leadore, Idaho

This bread features delicious russet potatoes produced in our state. We often enjoy one loaf right away and freeze the other to have later.

 2 packages (1/4 ounce *each*) active dry yeast
 1/2 cup warm water (110° to 115°)
 1 can (12 ounces) evaporated milk
 2 cups mashed potatoes (without added milk or butter)
 1/2 cup crumbled cooked bacon
 1/4 cup butter *or* margarine, softened
 2 eggs
 3 tablespoons sugar
 2 tablespoons dried minced onion
 1 tablespoon caraway seeds
 2 teaspoons garlic salt
 1 teaspoon salt
6-1/4 to 6-3/4 cups all-purpose flour

In a mixing bowl, dissolve yeast in warm water. Add the milk, potatoes, bacon, butter, eggs, sugar, onion, caraway seeds, garlic salt, salt and 3 cups flour. Beat until smooth. Stir in enough remaining flour to form a soft dough. Turn onto a floured surface; knead until smooth and elastic, about 8-10 minutes. Place in a greased bowl, turning once to grease top. Cover and let rise in a warm place until doubled, about 1 hour. Punch dough down. Turn onto a lightly floured surface; divide in half. Shape each into a round loaf. Place in two greased 2-qt. baking dishes with straight sides. Cover and let rise in a warm place until doubled, about 40 minutes. Bake at 350° for 40-50 minutes or until golden brown. Remove from baking dishes to wire racks to cool. **Yield:** 2 loaves.

BROCCOLI CHEESE FAN

Jo Groth, Plainfield, Iowa

(Pictured at left)

*With broccoli, bacon and cheese, this delectable bread has
the taste of a stuffed baked potato. Brunches at our house
wouldn't be complete without this pretty bread. Even
beginner bakers will soon master this attractive loaf.*

3-1/4 to 3-1/2 cups all-purpose flour
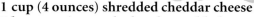
1 tablespoon sugar
1 package (1/4 ounce)
    quick-rise yeast
1 teaspoon salt
1 cup water
1 tablespoon butter *or*
    margarine, softened
1-1/2 cups finely chopped
    broccoli, cooked and
    drained
1 cup (4 ounces) shredded cheddar cheese
5 bacon strips, cooked and crumbled
1 egg
1/2 teaspoon dried minced onion
1/2 teaspoon dried oregano
1 egg white
1 tablespoon cold water

In a mixing bowl, combine 2-1/4 cups flour, sugar,
yeast and salt. In a saucepan, heat water and butter to
120°-130°. Add to dry ingredients; beat until smooth.
Stir in enough remaining flour to form a soft dough.
Turn onto a floured surface; knead until smooth and
elastic, about 4 minutes. Cover and let rest for 10
minutes. Meanwhile, in a bowl, combine broccoli,
cheese, bacon, egg, onion and oregano. On a lightly
floured surface, roll dough into a 16-in. x 9-in. rectangle with a 16-in. side facing you. Spoon broccoli
mixture lengthwise over top two-thirds of dough to
within 1 in. of edges. Starting at the plain long side, fold
dough over half of filling; fold over again. Pinch seams
to seal and tuck ends under. Place, seam side down,
in a greased baking sheet. With a sharp knife, cut into eight strips to within 1 in. of pinched edge. Separate
strips slightly; twist to allow filling to show. Place a
large shallow pan on the counter; fill half full with boiling water. Place baking sheet containing bread over the
water-filled pan. Cover and let rise until doubled,
about 15 minutes. Beat egg white and cold water; brush
over dough. Bake at 400° for 25 minutes or until gold-
en brown. Remove from pan to a wire rack. Serve
warm. Refrigerate leftovers. **Yield:** 1 loaf.

YEAST BREADS RISE TO THE OCCASION. Pictured at left, top to bottom: Ranch Rolls (recipe on
page 64), Country Herb Bread and Broccoli Cheese
Fan (recipes on this page).

COUNTRY HERB BREAD

Sandy Neukam, Huntingburg, Indiana

(Pictured at left)

*I've relied on this traditional recipe for years. Everyone in
the family loves the perfectly flavored herb loaves, especially our little boy, who always asks for "more brown
bread".*

2 cups all-purpose flour
2 cups whole wheat flour
1 cup rye flour
2 packages (1/4 ounce *each*) active dry yeast
1 tablespoon sugar
2 teaspoons salt
1/4 cup dried parsley flakes
1/4 to 1/2 teaspoon dried marjoram
1/4 to 1/2 teaspoon dried rosemary, crushed
1-1/2 cups water
3 tablespoons butter *or* margarine
1 egg white
1 tablespoon cold water

Combine the flours. Place 1-1/2 cups in a mixing bowl;
add yeast, sugar, salt and herbs. In a saucepan, heat water and butter to 120°-130°. Add to dry ingredients;
beat until moistened. Beat on medium speed for 2
minutes. Add 3/4 cup flour mixture; beat 2 minutes
longer. Stir in enough remaining flour mixture to form
a stiff dough. Turn onto a floured surface; knead until
smooth and elastic, about 8-10 minutes. Place in a
greased bowl, turning once to grease top. Cover and let
rise in a warm place until doubled, about 1 hour.
Punch dough down. Let rest for 15 minutes. Turn onto a lightly floured surface; divide in half. Shape into
two loaves. Place on two greased baking sheets or in
two greased 9-in. x 5-in. x 3-in. loaf pans. With a
sharp knife, make four to five diagonal slashes across
the top of each loaf. Cover and let rise in a warm
place until doubled, about 1 hour. Beat egg white and
cold water; brush over loaves. Bake at 375° for 30-35
minutes or until golden brown. Remove from pans to
wire racks to cool. **Yield:** 2 loaves.

BROCCOLI CHEESE FAN HINTS

*Don't be afraid to try your hand at making the Broccoli
Cheese Fan on this page. With the two simple secrets de-
scribed below, you can serve this attractive filled bread to
your family with ease.*

- *After filling and shaping the dough, use a sharp knife
to cut eight strips, leaving about 1 inch attached at
the bottom. Slightly separate the strips.*
- *Gently grasp a strip and twist it to one side so one
of the cut sides is down. Repeat with remaining
strips, making sure not to tear the dough or spill the
filling.*

RANCH ROLLS

Larry Miller, Ashland, Kentucky

(Pictured above and on page 62)

After sampling some homemade crackers from friends a few years ago, I was inspired to add some ranch salad dressing mix to my basic roll recipe. This recipe was the mouth-watering result.

    1 package (1/4 ounce) active dry yeast
1-1/4 cups warm water (110° to 115°), *divided*
    1 teaspoon honey
    1/2 cup vegetable oil
    1/3 cup sugar
    2 eggs
    2 envelopes ranch salad dressing mix
    2 teaspoons salt
    1 teaspoon dill weed
4-1/2 to 5-1/2 cups all-purpose flour
CHEESE TOPPING:
    2 tablespoons sesame seeds
    2 tablespoons grated Parmesan cheese
    2 tablespoons finely chopped pecans
    1/4 teaspoon dill weed

In a mixing bowl, dissolve yeast in 1/4 cup warm water. Add honey; let stand for 5 minutes. Add the oil, sugar, 1 egg, salad dressing mix, salt, dill, 1 cup flour and remaining water. Beat until smooth. Stir in enough remaining flour to form a soft dough. Turn onto a lightly floured surface; knead until smooth and elastic, about 6-8 minutes. Place in a greased bowl, turning once to grease top. Cover and let rise in a warm place until doubled, about 1 hour. Punch dough down. Turn onto a lightly floured surface; divide into 12 pieces. Place in greased muffin cups. Beat the remaining egg; brush over dough. Combine topping ingredients; sprinkle over rolls. Cover and let rise in a warm place until doubled, about 45 minutes. Bake at 400° for 15-20 minutes or until golden brown. Remove from pans to wire racks to cool. **Yield:** 2 dozen.

BUBBLE HERB RING

Lori Gindlesperger, Berlin, Pennsylvania

Whenever I prepare an Italian meal, my family expec it to be accompanied by this savory pull-apart bread Everyone has fun nibbling on the soft seasoned squares

3-1/4 to 3-3/4 cups all-purpose flour
    1/3 cup sugar
    2 packages (1/4 ounce *each***) quick-rise yeast**
    2 tablespoons grated Parmesan cheese
    1 teaspoon salt
    1 tablespoon dried parsley flakes
    1 teaspoon dried thyme
    1/2 teaspoon *each* **dill weed, dried basil and rosemary, crushed**
    1 cup water
    6 tablespoons butter *or* **margarine,** *divided*
    1 egg

In a mixing bowl, combine 2-1/2 cups flour, sugar, yeas cheese, salt and herbs. In a saucepan, heat water and tablespoons butter to 120°-130°. Add to dry ingredient beat until smooth. Stir in egg and enough remainin flour to form a soft dough. Turn onto a floured surfac knead until smooth and elastic, about 4 minutes. Cov er and let rest for 10 minutes. Roll into a 12-in. squar Melt remaining butter and brush over dough. Cut int 25 squares. Place, butter side down, in a greased 10-ir fluted tube pan, overlapping slightly. Cover and let ris in a warm place until doubled, about 30 minutes. Bak at 375° for 20-25 minutes or until golden brown. Inve onto a serving platter. Serve warm. **Yield:** 25 rolls.

PARMESAN BUTTERHORNS

Mrs. Bruce Shidler, Plymouth, Indiana

Our youngest daughter, Stephanie, has won sever awards with this recipe. These buttery rolls with subt Parmesan flavor are wonderful served warm or at roor temperature.

    1 package (1/4 ounce) active dry yeast
    1 cup warm milk (110° to 115°)
3-3/4 cups all-purpose flour
    1 teaspoon salt
    1 cup cold butter (no substitutes)
    1 egg
    1/4 cup sugar
    1/2 cup grated Parmesan cheese
Melted butter

Dissolve yeast in warm milk. In a mixing bowl, com bine flour and salt. Cut in butter until crumbly. In ar other bowl, beat egg and sugar. Add egg mixture an yeast mixture to flour mixture; mix well. Do not knea Cover and refrigerate overnight. Punch dough dow

Turn onto a lightly floured surface; divide into thirds. Roll each into a 12-in. circle. Sprinkle with Parmesan cheese. Cut each circle into 12 wedges. Roll up wedges from the wide end and place with pointed end down 2 in. apart on ungreased baking sheets. Curve ends to form a crescent shape. Cover and let rise in a warm place until doubled, about 30 minutes. Bake at 375° for 10-15 minutes or until golden brown. Brush with melted butter. Remove from pans to wire racks to cool. **Yield:** 3 dozen.

TENDER HERB DINNER ROLLS

Ruth Campbell, Staunton, Virginia

A blend of herbs makes these mouth-watering rolls stand out from all others. They're especially tasty with poultry and fish dishes.

    3-1/2 to 4 cups all-purpose flour
        3 tablespoons sugar
        1 package (1/4 ounce) active dry yeast
        2 teaspoons dried basil
        1 teaspoon salt
        1 teaspoon celery seed
        1 teaspoon rubbed sage
        1 teaspoon dried thyme
    Pinch dried ginger
    1-1/4 cups milk
        1/4 cup shortening
        1 egg

In a mixing bowl, combine 1-1/2 cups flour, sugar, yeast and seasonings. In a saucepan, heat milk and shortening to 120°-130°. Add to dry ingredients; beat until moistened. Beat in egg until smooth. Stir in enough remaining flour to form a soft dough. Do not knead. Cover and refrigerate for 2 hours. Punch dough down. Turn onto a floured surface; divide into 24 pieces. Shape each into a ball. Place 2 in. apart on greased baking sheets. Cover and let rise in a warm place until doubled, about 1 hour. Bake at 400° for 12-14 minutes or until golden brown. Remove from pans to wire racks to cool. **Yield:** 2 dozen.

COUNTRY SAGE BREAD

Norma Round, Sparks, Nevada

This recipe was given to me more than 15 years ago by a friend. The unique combination of sage, celery seed and nutmeg makes this bread deliciously different.

        1 package (1/4 ounce) active dry yeast
        1/4 cup warm water (110° to 115°)

        3/4 cup warm milk (110° to 115°)
        2 tablespoons sugar
        2 tablespoons shortening
        2 teaspoons celery seed
    1-1/2 teaspoons salt
        1 teaspoon rubbed sage
        1/4 to 1/2 teaspoon ground nutmeg
        1 egg
        3 to 3-1/2 cups all-purpose flour

In a mixing bowl, dissolve yeast in warm water. Add the milk, sugar, shortening, celery seed, salt, sage, nutmeg, egg and 2 cups flour. Beat until smooth. Stir in enough remaining flour to form a soft dough. Turn onto a floured surface; knead until smooth and elastic, about 6-8 minutes. Place in a greased bowl, turning once to grease top. Cover and let rise in a warm place until doubled, about 1-1/2 hours. Punch dough down. Shape into a round loaf. Place in a greased 8-in. or 9-in. pie plate. Cover and let rise in a warm place until doubled, about 45 minutes. Bake at 400° for 35-40 minutes or until golden brown. Remove from pie plate to a wire rack to cool. **Yield:** 1 loaf.

ITALIAN CHEESE LOAVES

Tina Molitor, New Market, Minnesota

This quick-and-easy yeast bread is a favorite of my daughter and my best friend. They could sit down and eat an entire loaf!

        2 packages (1/4 ounce *each*) active dry yeast
        3 cups warm water (110° to 115°)
        3 tablespoons shortening
        3 tablespoons sugar
        1/2 teaspoon salt
        7 to 8 cups all-purpose flour
        1/2 cup shredded mozzarella cheese
        1/4 cup shredded cheddar cheese
        1/4 teaspoon garlic powder
        1/4 teaspoon onion powder

In a mixing bowl, dissolve yeast in warm water. Add the shortening, sugar, salt and 4 cups flour. Beat until smooth. Add the cheeses, garlic powder and onion powder. Stir in enough remaining flour to form a soft dough. Turn onto a floured surface; knead until smooth and elastic, about 6-8 minutes. Do not let rise. Divide in half; shape into two loaves. Place in two greased 9-in. x 5-in. x 3-in. loaf pans. Do not let rise. Bake at 350° for 25-30 minutes or until golden brown. Remove from pans to wire racks to cool. Store in the refrigerator. **Yield:** 2 loaves.

HERBED WHOLE WHEAT BREAD

Barbara Glover, Port St. Lucie, Florida

I'm a serious bread baker, and this is my most prized recipe. My husband jokes that the real reason he married me was so that he could enjoy this herb bread forever!

>   1 medium onion, chopped
>   3 tablespoons vegetable oil
>   2 packages (1/4 ounce *each*) active dry yeast
> 1/2 cup warm water (110° to 115°)
>   1 can (12 ounces) evaporated milk
> 1/2 cup minced fresh parsley
>   3 tablespoons sugar
>   1 teaspoon salt
> 1/2 teaspoon dill weed
> 1/4 teaspoon rubbed sage
> 3/4 cup cornmeal
>   2 cups whole wheat flour
> 1-3/4 to 2-1/4 cups all-purpose flour

In a skillet, saute onion in oil until tender; cool. In a mixing bowl, dissolve yeast in warm water. Add the milk, parsley, sugar, salt, dill, sage and onion mixture; mix well. Add cornmeal; mix well. Stir in whole wheat flour and enough all-purpose flour to form a soft dough. Turn onto a floured surface; knead until smooth and elastic, about 3-5 minutes. Place in a greased bowl, turning once to grease top. Cover and let rise in a warm place until doubled, about 1 hour. Punch dough down. Turn onto a lightly floured surface; divide in half. Shape into two loaves. Place in two greased 9-in. x 5-in. x 3-in. loaf pans. Cover and let rise in a warm place until doubled, about 30-45 minutes. Bake at 350° for 30 minutes. Cover with foil. Bake 15-20 minutes longer or until golden brown. Remove from pans to wire racks to cool. **Yield:** 2 loaves.

KRAUTBURGERS

Naomi Dyer, Eaton, Colorado

Even after more than 50 years of marriage, I love to bake and cook for family and friends. The recipe for these rolls stuffed with cabbage and ground beef has been in my files for years.

>   1 package (1/4 ounce) active dry yeast
> 1-1/4 cups warm water (110° to 115°)
>   1 cup warm milk (110° to 115°)
> 1/4 cup sugar
>   2 tablespoons shortening
>   2 teaspoons salt
> 5-3/4 to 6-1/4 cups all-purpose flour
> 1-1/2 pounds ground beef

>   1 medium cabbage, shredded
>   1 medium onion, chopped
> Salt, pepper and seasoned salt to taste
> Melted butter *or* margarine

In a mixing bowl, dissolve yeast in warm water. Add the milk, sugar, shortening and salt; mix well. Stir in enough flour to form a soft dough. Turn onto a floured surface; knead until smooth and elastic, about 6-8 minutes. Place in a greased bowl, turning once to grease top. Cover and let rise in a warm place until doubled, about 1 hour. Meanwhile, in a skillet over medium heat, cook beef until no longer pink; drain. In a large saucepan, cook cabbage and onion until tender. In a large bowl, combine meat, cabbage mixture, salt, pepper and seasoned salt. Punch dough down. Turn onto a lightly floured surface; divide in half. Roll each into a 16-in. square. Cut into 4-in. squares. Place 1/4 cup filling in the center of each. Bring corners over filling; pinch to seal. Place, seam side down, on greased baking sheets. Do not let rise. Bake at 425° for 10 minutes. Reduce heat to 350°; bake 15-20 minutes longer or until golden brown. Remove from pans to wire racks. Brush with melted butter. Serve warm. Refrigerate leftovers. **Yield:** 32 buns.

RICH CHEESE BREAD

Linda Bamber, Bolivar, Missouri

Our two sons always request this cheesy bread during the holidays. It's a favorite to serve with soup or to use for making sandwiches.

>   2 cups water
> 1/2 cup cornmeal
> 1/2 teaspoon salt
> 1/2 cup molasses
>   2 tablespoons butter *or* margarine, softened
>   5 to 6 cups bread flour
>   1 package (1/4 ounce) active dry yeast
> All-purpose flour
>   8 ounces process American cheese, cut into
>   1/2-inch cubes
> Additional cornmeal

In a saucepan, bring water, cornmeal and salt to a boil. Cook and stir until thickened. Remove from the heat. Add molasses and butter; cool to 120°-130°. In a mixing bowl, combine 2 cups bread flour and yeast. Add cornmeal mixture; beat until smooth. Stir in enough remaining bread flour to form a soft dough. Turn onto a surface dusted with all-purpose flour; knead until smooth and elastic, about 6-8 minutes. Cover and let rise in a warm place until doubled, about 1 hour. Punch dough

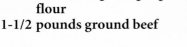

own. Turn onto a lightly floured surface; divide in half. Work half of the cheese cubes into each portion of dough. Shape into round loaves. Place in two greased 8-in. or 9-in. round baking pans. Sprinkle with additional cornmeal. Cover and let rise in a warm place until doubled, about 1 hour. Bake at 350° for 45-50 minutes or until golden brown. Remove from pans to wire racks to cool. Store in the refrigerator. **Yield:** 2 loaves.

ONION POPPY SEED TWIST

Florence Leitgeb, Medford, New York

This buttery bread is fancy enough to share with company but easy enough to make every day. Savory slices are great served with stews and soups.

        1 package (1/4 ounce) active dry yeast
    1/4 cup warm water (110° to 115°)
        1 cup warm milk (110° to 115°)
    1/2 cup butter *or* margarine, softened
        1 egg
    1/4 cup sugar
    1-3/4 teaspoons salt
    4-1/2 to 5 cups
            all-purpose
            flour
FILLING:
        1 cup chopped
            onion
    1/4 cup butter *or*
            margarine,
            melted
        3 tablespoons poppy
            seeds
    1/4 teaspoon salt
        1 egg, beaten
    Additional poppy seeds

In a mixing bowl, dissolve yeast in warm water. Add the milk, butter, egg, sugar, salt and 2 cups flour. Beat on medium speed for 2 minutes. Stir in enough remaining flour to form a soft dough. Turn onto a floured surface; knead until smooth and elastic, about 6-8 minutes. Place in a greased bowl, turning once to grease top. Cover and let rise in a warm place until doubled, about 1 hour. Punch dough down. Turn onto a floured surface; roll into a 20-in. x 8-in. rectangle. Cut in half lengthwise, forming two 20-in. x 4-in. rectangles. For filling, combine onion, butter, poppy seeds and salt. Spread over dough to within 1/2 in. of edges. Fold rectangles in half lengthwise. Pinch seams to seal, forming two ropes. Place ropes, side by side, on a greased baking sheet. Twist together and shape into a ring. Pinch ends together. Cover and let rise in a warm place until doubled, about 1 hour.

Brush with egg. Sprinkle with additional poppy seeds. Bake at 350° for 40-45 minutes or until golden brown. Remove from pan to a wire rack to cool. **Yield:** 1 loaf.

SAVORY WHEAT CRESCENTS

Martha Larson, Great Falls, Montana

Parmesan cheese and garlic salt give these hearty crescent rolls a scrumptious, savory flavor. Living in wheat country has prompted me to experiment with many whole wheat recipes.

        1 package (1/4 ounce) active dry yeast
    1/2 cup warm water (110° to 115°)
    8-1/2 teaspoons honey, *divided*
    3/4 cup warm milk (110° to 115°)
        6 tablespoons butter *or* margarine, softened,
            divided
        1 teaspoon salt
        1 egg
        2 cups whole wheat flour
    1-3/4 to 2-1/4 cups all-purpose flour
    1/4 cup grated Parmesan cheese
    1/4 teaspoon garlic salt

In a mixing bowl, dissolve yeast in warm water. Stir in 2 teaspoons honey; let stand for 5 minutes. Add milk, 2 tablespoons butter, salt and remaining honey; mix well. Add egg and whole wheat flour; beat on medium speed for 2 minutes. Stir in enough all-purpose flour to form a soft dough. Turn onto a floured surface; knead until smooth and elastic, about 6-8 minutes. Place in a greased bowl, turning once to grease top. Cover and let rise in a warm place until doubled, about 1 hour. Punch dough down. Knead on a floured surface for 30 seconds. Roll into a 12-in. circle. Melt remaining butter; brush over dough. Combine Parmesan cheese and garlic salt; sprinkle over dough. Cut into 16 wedges. Roll up wedges from the wide end and place with pointed end down on greased baking sheets. Curve ends to form a crescent shape. Cover and let rise in a warm place until doubled, about 20 minutes. Bake at 400° for 12-15 minutes or until golden brown. Remove from pans to wire racks to cool. **Yield:** 16 rolls.

STORING YEAST BREADS

- *When baked yeast breads and rolls are completely cool, store in an airtight plastic bag or container in a cool dry place for 2 to 3 days. If the bread contains meat or cheese, eat what you can the day it's baked, then freeze the rest.*
- *To freeze yeast breads, place the cooled bread in a freezer-safe plastic bag or container for up to 3 months. Thaw wrapped bread at room temperature for several hours. Reheat if desired.*

Honey Mustard Loaf

Dorine Arvidson, Eudora, Kansas

(Pictured at left)

Rave reviews will come your way when you present this golden bread. For a flavorful variation, I sometimes add 1/2 teaspoon dried oregano and thyme to the dough.

2 packages (1/4 ounce *each*) active dry yeast
3/4 cup warm water (110° to 115°)
2 eggs
3 tablespoons honey
3 tablespoons Dijon mustard
2 tablespoons butter *or* margarine, softened
1 teaspoon salt
1/8 teaspoon ground turmeric, optional
3 to 3-3/4 cups all-purpose flour

In a mixing bowl, dissolve yeast in warm water. Add 1 egg, honey, mustard, butter, salt, turmeric if desired and 2 cups flour. Beat until smooth. Stir in enough remaining flour to form a soft dough. Turn onto a floured surface; knead until smooth and elastic, about 6-8 minutes. Place in a greased bowl, turning once to grease top. Cover and let rise in a warm place until doubled, about 1 hour. Punch dough down; shape into a loaf. Place in a greased 9-in. x 5-in. x 3-in. loaf pan. Cover and let rise in a warm place until doubled, about 1 hour. Beat remaining egg; brush over top. Bake at 400° for 20 minutes. Cover with foil. Bake 25 minutes longer or until golden brown. Remove from pan to a wire rack to cool. **Yield:** 1 loaf.

Dilly Onion Braid

Gail Bailey, Edgewood, Illinois

(Pictured at left)

This delicious bread recipe, given to me by a neighbor, pairs very well with spaghetti and a crisp salad. Top it off with a fresh fruit bowl for a well-balanced meal.

1 cup (8 ounces) sour cream
1 package (1/4 ounce) active dry yeast
1/4 cup warm water (110° to 115°)
1 egg
2 tablespoons butter *or* margarine, softened
2 tablespoons sugar
1-1/2 teaspoons salt
2-1/2 to 3 cups all-purpose flour
1/3 cup finely chopped onion

HERB GARDEN. Pictured at left, top to bottom: Honey Mustard Loaf (recipe on this page), Rosemary Focaccia (recipe on page 70) and Dilly Onion Braid (recipe on this page).

1 tablespoon dill seed
1 to 2 teaspoons dill weed
1 egg yolk
2 teaspoons cold water

Let sour cream stand at room temperature for 1 hour. In a mixing bowl, dissolve yeast in warm water. Add the sour cream, egg, butter, sugar, salt and 1 cup flour. Beat on medium speed for 2 minutes. Add the onion, dill seed and dill weed; mix well. Stir in enough remaining flour to form a soft dough. Turn onto a floured surface; knead until smooth and elastic, about 6-8 minutes. Place in a greased bowl, turning once to grease top. Cover and let rise in a warm place until doubled, about 1-1/2 hours. Punch dough down. Turn onto a lightly floured surface; divide into thirds. Cover and let rest for 10 minutes. Shape each into an 18-in. rope. Place ropes on a greased baking sheet and braid; pinch seams to seal and tuck ends under. Cover and let rise in a warm place until doubled, about 30 minutes. Beat egg yolk and cold water; brush over braid. Bake at 350° for 30-40 minutes or until golden brown. Remove from pan to a wire rack to cool. **Yield:** 1 loaf.

Veggie Loaves

Judiann McNulty, Laramie, Wyoming

A vegetable puree lends to this bread's lovely light texture. Made with egg whites, this bread is lower in fat and cholesterol than other breads.

2 tablespoons active dry yeast
1/2 cup warm water (110° to 115°)
2 cups milk
1/3 cup vegetable oil
2 egg whites
3 tablespoons honey
2 cups chopped cabbage
2 large carrots, sliced
1 large celery rib, cut into chunks
1/2 cup cornmeal
1 tablespoon salt
5 to 6 cups whole wheat flour

In a mixing bowl, dissolve yeast in warm water. In a blender or food processor, combine the milk, oil, egg whites, honey and vegetables. Cover and process until smooth. Add cornmeal, salt and vegetable mixture to yeast mixture; mix well. Stir in enough flour to form a stiff dough. Turn onto a floured surface; knead until smooth and elastic, about 8-10 minutes. Do not let rise. Divide in half. Shape into two loaves. Place in two greased 9-in. x 5-in. x 3-in. loaf pans. Cover and let rise in a warm place until doubled, about 1 hour. Bake at 350° for 35-40 minutes or until browned. Remove from pans to wire racks to cool. Store in the refrigerator. **Yield:** 2 loaves.

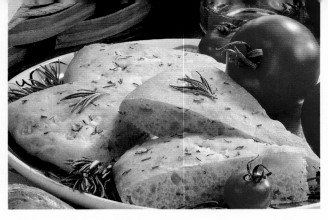

ROSEMARY FOCACCIA

Debra Peoples, Calgary, Alberta

(Pictured above and on page 68)

The savory aroma of rosemary as this classic bread bakes is simply irresistible. This bread tastes great as a side dish with any meal, as a snack or as a pizza crust.

> **2 medium onions, chopped**
> **1/4 cup plus 3 tablespoons olive *or* vegetable oil, *divided***
> **1-1/2 teaspoons active dry yeast**
> **1-1/2 cups warm water (110° to 115°), *divided***
> **1/2 teaspoon sugar**
> **1/2 teaspoon salt**
> **3 to 4 cups all-purpose flour**
> **2 tablespoons snipped fresh rosemary *or* 2 teaspoons dried rosemary, crushed, *divided***

Cornmeal
Coarse salt

In a skillet, saute onions in 1/4 cup oil until tender; cool. In a mixing bowl, dissolve yeast in 1/4 cup warm water. Add sugar; let stand for 5 minutes. Add 2 tablespoons oil, salt, 2 cups flour and remaining water. Beat until smooth. Stir in enough remaining flour to form a soft dough. Turn onto a floured surface; knead until smooth and elastic, about 6-8 minutes. Add onions and half of the rosemary. Knead 1 minute longer. Place in a greased bowl, turning once to grease top. Cover and let rise in a warm place until doubled, about 40 minutes. Punch dough down. Turn onto a lightly floured surface; divide in half. Pat each flat. Let rest for 5 minutes. Grease two baking sheets and sprinkle with cornmeal. Stretch each portion of dough into a 10-in. circle on prepared pans. Cover and let rise until doubled, about 40 minutes. Brush with remaining oil. Sprinkle with coarse salt and remaining rosemary. Bake at 375° for 25-30 minutes or until golden brown. Remove from pans to wire racks to cool. **Yield:** 2 loaves.

PARMESAN LOAVES

Sue Trotter, Coweta, Oklahoma

I've been making this bread since my college days, whe[n] I shared an apartment with five home economics major[s]. My family likes this best fresh out of the oven, but it als[o] freezes and reheats well.

> **1 package (1/4 ounce) active dry yeast**
> **1/4 cup warm water (110° to 115°)**
> **2 cups warm milk (110° to 115°)**
> **1 cup grated Parmesan cheese**
> **2 tablespoons sugar**
> **2 tablespoons vegetable oil**
> **2 teaspoons salt**
> **1/8 teaspoon cayenne pepper**
> **5-1/2 to 6 cups all-purpose flour**
> **1/4 cup butter *or* margarine, melted**
> **2 teaspoons garlic salt**

In a mixing bowl, dissolve yeast in warm water. Add th[e] milk, cheese, sugar, oil, salt, cayenne and 2 cups flou[r]. Beat until smooth. Stir in enough remaining flour t[o] form a soft dough. Turn onto a floured surface; knea[d] until smooth and elastic, about 6-8 minutes. Place i[n] a greased bowl, turning once to grease top. Cover an[d] let rise in a warm place until doubled, about 1-1/[2] hours. Punch dough down. Turn onto a floured sur[-] face; divide in half. Cover and let rest for 10 minute[s]. Roll each into a 16-in. x 10-in. rectangle. Brush wit[h] butter; sprinkle with garlic salt. Cut into four 10-in. [x] 4-in. rectangles. Stack with butter side up. Cut eac[h] stack into five 4-in. x 2-in. strips. Place five strips, cu[t] side down, in a greased 8-in. x 4-in. x 2-in. loaf pan. Re[-] peat with remaining dough. Cover and let rise in [a] warm place until doubled, about 1 hour. Bake at 350[°] for 40-45 minutes or until golden brown. Remov[e] from pans to wire racks to cool. **Yield:** 2 loaves.

BASIL TOMATO ROLLS

Betty Jane Custer, Fishertown, Pennsylvania

I made these rolls from my Aunt Ethel's recipe. The toma[-] to herb filling rises and spills over the top of the crusty ro[ll] tops. Folks have a hard time eating just one.

> **1 package (1/4 ounce) active dry yeast**
> **1-1/3 cups warm water (110° to 115°)**
> **1 tablespoon sugar**
> **1 tablespoon olive *or* vegetable oil**
> **1 teaspoon salt**
> **3-1/2 to 4 cups all-purpose flour**

FILLING:

> **1 small onion, finely chopped**
> **1 tablespoon olive *or* vegetable oil**
> **1 medium tomato, peeled and chopped**

1 can (8 ounces) tomato sauce
1 garlic clove, minced
-1/4 teaspoons salt
1 teaspoon dried basil
Dash pepper
1/4 cup grated Parmesan cheese

In a mixing bowl, dissolve yeast in warm water. Add the sugar, oil, salt and 2-1/2 cups flour. Beat until smooth. Stir in enough remaining flour to form a stiff dough. Turn onto a floured surface; knead until smooth and elastic, about 6-8 minutes. Place in a greased bowl, turning once to grease top. Cover and let rise in a warm place until doubled, about 1 hour. Meanwhile, in a skillet, saute onion in oil until tender. Add tomato, tomato sauce, garlic, salt, basil and pepper. Bring to a boil; cook and stir until thickened. Cool to 110°-115°. Punch dough down. Turn onto a lightly floured surface; divide into 12 pieces. Shape each into a ball. Place 3 in. apart on a greased baking sheet. Make an indentation in center of rolls. Fill with 1 tablespoon filling. Sprinkle with Parmesan cheese. Cover and let rise in a warm place until doubled, about 20 minutes. Bake at 375° for 25-30 minutes or until golden brown. Remove from pan to a wire rack. Serve warm. **Yield:** 1 dozen.

SWISS ONION BREAD

Martha Smith, Canton, Ohio

Our granddaughter, Lena, used this recipe as part of her -H project, and it was very well received. The slight runch from poppy seeds pairs well with the creamy Swiss heese.

2 packages (1/4 ounce *each*) active dry yeast
-1/2 cups warm water (110° to 115°), *divided*
1 teaspoon plus 1/4 cup sugar, *divided*
1/2 cup butter *or* margarine, melted
1 medium onion, finely chopped
1 egg
2 teaspoons salt
1/4 teaspoon ground mustard
-3/4 to 7-1/4 cups bread *or* all-purpose flour
3/4 cup shredded Swiss cheese
ILLING:
3/4 cup finely chopped onion
1/4 cup shredded Swiss cheese
3 tablespoons butter *or* margarine
1 tablespoon poppy seeds
1 teaspoon paprika
1/2 teaspoon salt
GG WASH:
1 egg yolk
2 teaspoons water
dditional poppy seeds, optional

In a mixing bowl, dissolve yeast in 1/2 cup warm water. Add 1 teaspoon sugar; let stand for 5 minutes. Add butter, onion, egg, salt, mustard, 3 cups flour and remaining water and sugar. Beat until smooth. Stir in cheese and enough remaining flour to form a soft dough. Turn onto a floured surface; knead until smooth and elastic, about 8-10 minutes. Place in a greased bowl, turning once to grease top. Cover and let rise in a warm place until doubled, about 45 minutes. Punch dough down. Turn onto a lightly floured surface; divide in half. Roll each into an 18-in. x 10-in. rectangle. Cut in half lengthwise. Combine filling ingredients; spread to within 1/2 in. of edges. Roll up, jelly-roll style, starting with a long side; pinch seams to seal. Place two rolls, side by side, on a greased baking sheet. Twist rolls together; pinch ends to seal and tuck under. Repeat with remaining dough. Cover and let rise in a warm place until doubled, about 45 minutes. Beat egg yolk and water; brush over twists. Sprinkle with additional poppy seeds if desired. Bake at 375° for 25-35 minutes or until golden brown. Remove from pans to wire racks to cool. Store in the refrigerator. **Yield:** 2 loaves.

GRANDPA'S PIZZA BREAD

Barbara Schimke, Etna, New Hampshire

My grandmother made this pan bread often but never wrote down the recipe. Eventually, my dad experimented until he came up with precise measurements. Our kids love Grandpa's Pizza Bread.

1 package (1/4 ounce) active dry yeast
1-1/2 cups warm water (110° to 115°), *divided*
4 teaspoons sugar
4 teaspoons plus 2 tablespoons olive *or*
vegetable oil, *divided*
1-1/2 teaspoons salt
3-1/2 to 4 cups all-purpose flour
Salt and coarsely ground pepper to taste

In a mixing bowl, dissolve the yeast in 1/2 cup warm water. Add sugar; let stand for 5 minutes. Add 4 teaspoons of oil, salt, remaining water and enough flour to form a soft dough. Turn onto a floured surface; knead until smooth and elastic, about 6-8 minutes. Place in a greased bowl, turning once to grease top. Cover and let rise in a warm place until doubled, about 1 hour. Punch dough down. Brush a 13-in. x 9-in. x 2-in. baking pan with 1 tablespoon oil. Press dough into pan. Brush with the remaining oil and sprinkle with salt and pepper. Cover and let rise in a warm place until doubled, about 45 minutes. Bake at 375° for 20-25 minutes or until lightly browned. Cut into squares; serve warm or at room temperature. **Yield:** 16-20 servings.

BUTTERY HERB LOAVES

Rhoda Coffey, Oklahoma City, Oklahoma

A succulent herb butter is the secret to this bread's irresistible richness. These lovely loaves disappear quickly.

    2 packages (1/4 ounce *each*) active dry yeast
1/4 cup warm water (110° to 115°)
    1 cup warm milk (110° to 115°)
    2 eggs
1/3 cup shortening
1/4 cup sugar
    1 tablespoon salt
4-1/2 to 5 cups all-purpose flour
HERB BUTTER:
    1/2 cup butter (no substitutes) softened
    1 garlic clove, minced
    1/2 teaspoon dried basil
    1/2 teaspoon dried minced onion
    1/2 teaspoon caraway seeds
    1/4 teaspoon dried oregano
    1/8 teaspoon cayenne pepper
Poppy *or* sesame seeds

In a mixing bowl, dissolve yeast in warm water. Add the milk, eggs, shortening, sugar, salt and 1 cup flour. Beat until smooth. Stir in enough remaining flour to form a soft dough. Turn onto a floured surface; knead until smooth and elastic, about 2-3 minutes. Place in a greased bowl, turning once to grease top. Cover and let rise in a warm place until doubled, about 1-1/2 hours. Punch dough down. Turn onto a lightly floured surface; divide in half. Roll each to 1/16-in. thickness; cut into 5-in. circles. Combine the butter, garlic, basil, onion, caraway seeds, oregano and cayenne; spread over dough. Fold circles in half; set half aside. For each loaf, start with one folded circle on a greased baking sheet with folded edge toward the right. Working from right to left, add another piece with folded edge on right side, overlapping three-fourths of the previous piece. Repeat. Form a second rectangular loaf from the reserved folded circles. Sprinkle with poppy seeds. Cover and let rise in a warm place until doubled, about 30 minutes. Bake at 350° for 20-25 minutes or until golden brown. Remove from pans to wire racks. Serve warm. **Yield:** 2 loaves.

FINNISH WHEAT ROLLS

Tarya Mannonen-Cameron, Seattle, Washington

When I came to the United States from Finland for college, I missed the breads from back home. So I came up with this recipe to recapture those fabulous flavors.

    2 packages (1/4 ounce *each*) active dry yeast
    2 cups warm water (110° to 115°)
    1 cup butter *or* margarine, melted
1/4 cup dried parsley flakes

    1 tablespoon dried rosemary, crushed
    2 teaspoons salt
    1 teaspoon rubbed sage
    1 teaspoon dried thyme
2-3/4 cups whole wheat flour
    3 to 3-1/2 cups all-purpose flour
Additional melted butter *or* margarine

In a mixing bowl, dissolve yeast in warm water. Add the butter, parsley, rosemary, salt, sage, thyme and whole wheat flour. Beat until smooth. Stir in enough all-purpose flour to form a soft dough. Turn onto a floured surface; knead until smooth and elastic, about 6-8 minutes. Place in a greased bowl, turning once to grease top. Cover and let rise in a warm place until doubled, about 30 minutes. Punch dough down. Turn onto a lightly floured surface; divide into 24 pieces. Shape each into a ball. Place 2 in. apart on greased baking sheets. Cover and let rise in a warm place until doubled, about 30 minutes. Brush with additional melted butter. Bake at 425° for 25-30 minutes or until golden brown. Remove from pans to wire racks to cool. **Yield:** 2 dozen.

MOM'S DINNER ROLLS

Patricia Collins, Imbler, Oregon

My mother was always experimenting with recipes. She had a knack for combining the right ingredients. This is one of my most treasured recipes she shared with me.

    1/4 cup finely chopped onion
    4 garlic cloves, minced
    1/4 cup butter *or* margarine
    1 teaspoon dried basil
    1 teaspoon dried oregano
    1/2 teaspoon *each* dried marjoram, parsley flakes
        and tarragon
    1 package (1/4 ounce) active dry yeast
3/4 cup warm water (110° to 115°)
    1 teaspoon sugar
    1 teaspoon salt
    2 cups all-purpose flour
    1 egg, beaten

In a skillet, saute onion and garlic in butter until tender. Stir in herbs; cool. In a food processor, dissolve yeast in warm water. Add the sugar, salt and onion mixture. Add flour; cover and process until dough forms a smooth ball. Turn onto a floured surface; knead until smooth and elastic, about 6-8 minutes. Place in a greased bowl, turning once to grease top. Cover and let rise in a warm place until doubled, about 1 hour. Punch dough down. Turn onto a floured surface; divide into 24 pieces. Shape each into a ball. Place 2 in. apart on greased baking sheets. Cover and let rise in a warm place until doubled, about 30 minutes. Brush with egg. Bake at 350° for 20-25 minutes or until golden brown. Remove from pans to wire racks. Serve warm. **Yield:** 2 dozen.

Taco Bread

Twilla Eisele, Wellsville, Kansas

Taco seasoning and green chilies are the secrets to this bread's slightly spicy flavor. A friend gave me the recipe.

3-1/2 to 4 cups all-purpose flour
    1 cup cornmeal
    1 envelope taco seasoning
    3 tablespoons sugar
    2 packages (1/4 ounce *each*) active dry yeast
    1 tablespoon dried minced onion
    1 teaspoon salt
    1 can (10-3/4 ounces) condensed tomato soup, undiluted
    3/4 cup water
    2 tablespoons butter *or* margarine
    1 can (4 ounces) chopped green chilies, drained

In a mixing bowl, combine 1-1/2 cups flour, cornmeal, taco seasoning, sugar, yeast, onion and salt. In a saucepan, heat the soup, water and butter to 120°-130°. Add to dry ingredients; beat on medium speed for 3 minutes. Stir in chilies and enough remaining flour to form a soft dough. Turn onto a floured surface; knead until smooth and elastic, about 6-8 minutes. Place in a greased bowl, turning once to grease top. Cover and let rise in a warm place until doubled, about 1 hour. Punch dough down. Shape into a loaf. Place in a greased 9-in. x 5-in. x 3-in. loaf pan. Cover and let rise in a warm place until doubled, about 45 minutes. Bake at 350° for 45-50 minutes or until golden brown. Remove from pan to a wire rack. Serve warm. **Yield:** 1 loaf.

Easy Stromboli

Katie Troyer, Meadville, Pennsylvania

My family prefers this stromboli instead of ordinary pizza. Experiment with different filling ingredients to suit your family's tastes.

    1 tablespoon active dry yeast
    1 cup warm water (110° to 115°)
    3 tablespoons vegetable oil
    1/2 teaspoon salt
2-3/4 to 3-1/4 cups all-purpose flour
    1 cup pizza sauce
    1 pound bulk pork sausage, cooked and drained
    1 can (4 ounces) mushrooms stems and pieces, drained
    1 package (3-1/2 ounces) sliced pepperoni

    1 cup (4 ounces) shredded mozzarella cheese

In a mixing bowl, dissolve yeast in warm water. Add oil, salt and 2 cups flour. Beat until smooth. Stir in enough remaining flour to form a soft dough. Turn onto a floured surface; knead until smooth and elastic, about 6-8 minutes. Cover and let rest for 10 minutes. Turn onto a lightly floured surface; roll into a 14-in. x 12-in. rectangle. Transfer to a greased 15-in. x 10-in. x 1-in. baking pan. Spoon pizza sauce to within 1/2 in. of edges. Top with sausage, mushrooms, pepperoni and cheese. Roll up, jelly-roll style, starting with a long side; pinch seam to seal and tuck ends under. Bake at 400° for 30-35 minutes or until golden brown. Serve warm. Refrigerate leftovers. **Yield:** 1 loaf.

Green Onion Potato Rolls

Louise Beaulieu, Monticello, Maine

The mild green onion flavor of these tender rolls appeals to all. I keep the ingredients on hand so I can bake up a batch on a moment's notice.

4-1/2 to 5-1/2 cups bread flour
1-1/4 cups mashed potato flakes, *divided*
    3 tablespoons sugar
    2 packages (1/4 ounce *each*) active dry yeast
    2 teaspoons salt
    2 cups milk
    1/2 cup butter *or* margarine
    4 to 6 green onions, sliced
    2 eggs
All-purpose flour

In a mixing bowl, combine 1-1/2 cups flour, 1 cup potato flakes, sugar, yeast and salt. In a saucepan, heat the milk, butter and onions to 120°-130°. Add to dry ingredients; beat until moistened. Add eggs; beat on medium speed for 3 minutes. Stir in enough remaining flour to form a soft dough. Turn onto a surface; knead until smooth and elastic, about 8-10 minutes. Place in a greased bowl, turning once to grease top. Cover and let rise in a warm place until doubled, about 45 minutes. Punch dough down. Cover and let rest for 15 minutes. Turn onto a floured surface; divide into 24 pieces. Shape each into a ball. Dip each ball into remaining potato flakes. Place in a greased 13-in. x 9-in. x 2-in. baking pan. Cover and let rise in a warm place until doubled, about 30 minutes. Bake at 375° for 25-35 minutes or until golden brown. Remove from pan to a wire rack to cool. **Yield:** 2 dozen.

Sweet Yeast Breads

From cinnamon rolls, pastries and kringles to braids, stollens and coffee cakes, these yummy yeast breads add a sweet touch to any table.

DANISH KRINGLE

Lorna Jacobsen, Arrowwood, Alberta

(Pictured at left)

This traditional yeast bread wonderfully reflects my Scandinavian heritage. Flaky layers of tender dough are flavored with almond paste. The unique sugar cookie crumb coating adds the perfect amount of sweetness.

8 tablespoons butter (no substitutes), softened,
   divided
1-1/2 to 2 cups all-purpose flour, *divided*
1 package (1/4 ounce) active dry yeast
2 tablespoons warm water (110° to 115°)
1/4 cup warm half-and-half cream (110° to 115°)
2 tablespoons sugar
1/4 teaspoon salt
1 egg, beaten
1/2 cup almond paste
1 egg white, beaten
1/4 cup sugar cookie crumbs
2 tablespoons sliced almonds

In a small mixing bowl, cream 6 tablespoons butter and 2 tablespoons flour. Spread into an 8-in. x 4-in. rectangle on a piece of waxed paper. Cover with waxed paper; refrigerate. In a mixing bowl, dissolve yeast in warm water. Add the cream, sugar, salt and egg; beat until smooth. Stir in enough remaining flour to form a soft dough. Turn onto a floured surface; knead until smooth and elastic, about 6-8 minutes. Do not let rise. Roll into an 8-in. square. Remove top sheet of waxed paper from butter mixture; invert onto center of dough. Peel off waxed paper. Fold plain dough over butter layer. Fold widthwise into thirds. Roll out into a 12-in. x 6-in. rectangle. Fold into thirds. Repeat rolling and folding twice. Wrap in waxed paper; refrigerate for 30 minutes. Roll into a 24-in. x 5-in. rectangle. In a mixing bowl, combine almond paste and remaining butter; beat until smooth. Spread lengthwise down the center of dough. Fold dough over filling to cover; pinch to seal. Place on a greased baking sheet. Shape into a pretzel. Flatten lightly with a rolling pin. Cover and let rise in a warm place until doubled, about 1 hour. Brush with egg white. Sprinkle with cookie crumbs and almonds. Bake at 350° for 20-25 minutes or until golden brown. Carefully remove from pan to a wire rack to cool. **Yield:** 16-20 servings.

ROSE ROLLS

Mary Wolfe, LaCrete, Alberta

(Pictured at left)

These eye-catching cherry-filled rolls make any breakfast or coffee break special. They freeze very well...just thaw and reheat a few minutes before serving.

1 cup cubed peeled potatoes
1 cup water
1 package (1/4 ounce) active dry yeast
1 cup warm milk (110° to 115°)
1/2 cup sugar
1/2 cup butter *or* margarine, softened
2 teaspoons salt
1 egg
5-1/4 to 5-3/4 cups all-purpose flour
1 cup cherry pie filling
Vanilla Glaze (recipe on page 89)

In a saucepan, bring potatoes and water to a boil. Reduce heat; cover and simmer for 15-20 minutes or until tender. Drain potatoes, reserving 1/2 cup cooking liquid; cool liquid to 110°-115°. Mash potatoes; set aside to cool to 110°-115°. In a mixing bowl, dissolve yeast in warm milk. Add the mashed potatoes, cooking liquid, sugar, butter, salt, egg and 1-1/2 cups flour; beat until smooth. Stir in enough remaining flour to form a soft dough. Do not knead. Cover and let rise in a warm place until doubled, about 1 hour. Punch dough down. Turn onto a lightly floured surface; divide into 24 pieces. Gently roll each into a 12-in. rope. Holding one end of rope, loosely wrap dough, forming a coil. Tuck end under; pinch to seal. Place 2 in. apart on greased baking sheets. Cover and let rise until doubled, about 30 minutes. With thumb, make a 1-in. indentation in center of each coil. Fill with cherry pie filling. Bake at 400° for 12-15 minutes or until golden brown. Remove from pans to wire racks to cool. Drizzle with Vanilla Glaze. **Yield:** 2 dozen.

RISE 'N' SHINE TREATS. Pictured at left, top to bottom: Danish Kringle (recipe on this page), Giant Upside-Down Pecan Rolls (recipe on page 76) and Rose Rolls (recipe on this page).

GIANT UPSIDE-DOWN PECAN ROLLS

Janet Miller, Lafayette, Indiana

(Pictured above and on page 74)

I like to keep a baked batch of these extra-large sweet rolls in the freezer to surprise my family on weekends. To re-heat, thaw in the refrigerator overnight, wrap in foil and bake at 350° for 20 to 30 minutes or until heated through.

>   2 packages (1/4 ounce *each*) active dry yeast
> 1/2 cup warm water (110° to 115°)
> 1-3/4 cups sugar, *divided*
>   2/3 cup warm milk (110° to 115°)
>   3/4 cup butter *or* margarine, softened, *divided*
>   1 teaspoon salt
>   1 egg
>   1 egg yolk
> 4-3/4 to 5-1/4 cups all-purpose flour
>   1 tablespoon ground cinnamon
>   1 cup chopped pecans
> **BROWN SUGAR-NUT SYRUP:**
>   1 cup packed dark brown sugar
> 1/4 cup butter *or* margarine
>   2 tablespoons water
>   1 cup pecan halves
> **EGG WASH:**
>   1 egg white
>   1 teaspoon water

In a mixing bowl, dissolve yeast in warm water. Add 3/4 cup sugar, milk, 1/2 cup butter, salt, egg, egg yolk and 3 cups flour. Beat on medium speed for 5 minutes. Stir in enough remaining flour to form a soft dough. Turn onto a floured surface; knead until smooth and elastic, about 6-8 minutes. Place in a greased bowl, turning once to grease top. Cover and let rise in a warm place until doubled, about 1-1/2 hours. Punch dough down. Turn onto a lightly floured surface. Roll into a 24-in. x 18-in. rectangle. Melt remaining butter; brush over dough. Combine cinnamon and remaining sugar; sprinkle to within 1/2 in. of edges. Sprinkle with pecans. Roll up, jelly-roll style, starting with a short side; pinch seam to seal. Cut into six slices. For syrup, combine brown sugar, butter and water in a saucepan.

Bring to a boil; boil and stir for 1 minute. Pour into a greased 13-in. x 9-in. x 2-in. baking pan. Arrange pecan halves, flat side up, over syrup. Place rolls, cut side down, over pecans. Press down gently. Cover and let rise until doubled, about 1 hour. Beat egg white and water; brush over rolls. Bake at 350° for 35-40 minutes or until golden brown. Immediately invert onto a serving platter. **Yield:** 6 rolls.

CORNMEAL CINNAMON ROLLS

Sonna Lea Hunsley, Phoenix, Arizona

I always loved the aroma of Mom's kitchen, especially when these sweet, tender rolls were in the oven. When I take them to a potluck, people always snitch before serving time.

>   2 cups milk
> 1/2 cup cornmeal
> 1/2 cup sugar
> 1/2 cup butter *or* margarine
>   1 tablespoon salt
>   2 packages (1/4 ounce *each*) active dry yeast
> 1/2 cup warm water (110° to 115°)
>   3 eggs, beaten
> 6-1/2 to 7 cups all-purpose flour
> **FILLING:**
> 1-1/4 cups raisins
>   2 tablespoons butter *or* margarine, melted
>   3/4 cup sugar
>   2 teaspoons ground cinnamon
> **Pinch ground nutmeg, optional**
> **FROSTING:**
> 3-1/2 cups confectioners' sugar
>   2 tablespoons butter *or* margarine, softened
>   2 tablespoons cream cheese, softened
> 1/2 teaspoon almond extract
>   4 to 5 tablespoons milk

In a saucepan, combine milk and cornmeal. Bring to a boil over medium heat, stirring constantly. Add the sugar, butter and salt; cool to 110°-115°. In a mixing bowl, dissolve yeast in warm water. Add the eggs, cornmeal mixture and 2 cups flour; beat until smooth. Stir in enough remaining flour to form a soft dough. Turn onto a floured surface; knead until smooth and elastic, about 6-8 minutes. Place in a greased bowl, turning once to grease top. Cover and let rise in a warm place until doubled, about 1 hour. Meanwhile, place raisins in a saucepan and cover with water. Bring to a boil; remove from the heat. Cover and let stand for 15 minutes. Drain; set aside. Punch dough down. Turn onto a lightly floured surface; divide in half. Roll each into a 12-in. x 10-in. rectangle; brush with melted butter. Combine sugar, cinnamon and nutmeg if desired; sprinkle over dough to within 1/2 in. of edges. Sprin le with raisins. Roll up, jelly-roll style, starting with a long side; pinch seam to seal. Cut each into 12 slices. Place, cut side down, in two greased 13-in. x 9-in. x 2-in. baking pans. Cover and let rise until doubled, about 1 hour. Bake at 375° for 20-25 minutes or until golden brown. Cool in pans on wire racks. For frosting, combine sugar, butter, cream cheese, extract and enough milk to achieve desired consistency. Spread or drizzle over rolls. Refrigerate leftovers. **Yield:** 2 dozen.

TANGY LEMON CLOVERS

Judy Jack, Holt, Missouri

Lemon extract and lemon peel lend to the refreshingly different flavor of these rolls. My family can barely wait for them to cool slightly before eating one.

2 packages (1/4 ounce *each*) active dry yeast
1-1/2 cups warm water (110° to 115°)
1/2 cup sugar
1/2 cup instant nonfat dry milk powder
1/2 cup butter-flavored shortening
3 eggs
1 teaspoon salt
1 teaspoon lemon extract
1/2 teaspoon ground cinnamon
1/2 teaspoon ground nutmeg
1/4 teaspoon ground ginger
5 to 5-1/2 cups all-purpose flour
TOPPING:
1 cup sugar
1 teaspoon grated lemon peel
1/2 teaspoon ground nutmeg
1/4 cup butter *or* margarine, melted

In a mixing bowl, dissolve yeast in warm water. Add the sugar, milk powder, shortening, eggs, salt, extract, spices and 2 cups flour. Beat until smooth. Stir in enough remaining flour to form a soft dough. Turn onto a lightly floured surface; knead until smooth and elastic, about 6-8 minutes. Place in a greased bowl, turning once to grease top. Cover and let rise in a warm place until doubled, about 1 hour. Punch dough down. Turn onto a floured surface; divide in half. Cover and let rest for 15 minutes. For topping, combine the sugar, lemon peel and nutmeg; set aside. Shape each portion of dough into a 16-in. log. Cut each log into 12 pieces; shape each into a ball. Dip top in melted butter, then in topping mixture. Place topping side up in well-greased muffin cups. Set aside remaining melted butter and topping. Using greased scissors, cut rolls in half and then in quarters, almost to the bottom. Cover and let rise until doubled, about 45 minutes. Brush with remaining melted butter; sprinkle with remaining topping. Bake at 375° for 15-20 minutes or until

golden brown. Remove from pans to wire racks. Serve warm. **Yield:** 2 dozen.

CHRISTMAS STOLLEN RING

Dee Beyer, East Bernard, Texas

It's common for German families to gather on Christmas Eve to eat this traditional sweet bread. I've been cooking and baking for more than 35 years and especially enjoy doing so during the holidays.

5-1/4 cups all-purpose flour
1/4 cup sugar
2 packages (1/4 ounce *each*) active dry yeast
1 teaspoon salt
1 cup milk
1 cup butter *or* margarine, softened
1/2 cup water
2 eggs
1/2 cup golden raisins
1/2 cup chopped candied fruit
1/2 cup chopped walnuts
1/2 teaspoon grated lemon peel
1/2 teaspoon grated orange peel
FILLING:
3 tablespoons butter *or* margarine, softened
1/2 cup sugar
1 tablespoon ground cinnamon
GLAZE:
1 cup confectioners' sugar
1/4 teaspoon vanilla extract
2 to 3 tablespoons milk
Red and green candied cherries, halved

In a mixing bowl, combine the flour, sugar, yeast and salt. In a saucepan, heat the milk, butter and water to 120°-130°. Add to dry ingredients; beat until moistened. Beat in eggs until smooth. Stir in the raisins, candied fruit, walnuts, and lemon and orange peel. Cover and refrigerate overnight. Punch dough down. Turn onto a lightly floured surface. Roll into an 18-in. x 12-in. rectangle; spread butter to within 1/2 in. of edges. Combine sugar and cinnamon; sprinkle over dough. Roll up, jelly-roll style, starting with a long side; pinch seam to seal. Place, seam side down, on a greased baking sheet; pinch ends together to form a ring. With a scissors, cut from outside edge two-thirds of the way toward center of the ring at 1-in. intervals. Separate strips slightly; twist to allow filling to show, slightly overlapping with the previous piece. Cover and let rise in a warm place until doubled, about 1 hour. Bake at 350° for 25-30 minutes or until golden brown. Remove from pan to a wire rack to cool. For glaze, combine the sugar, vanilla and enough milk to achieve desired consistency. Drizzle over warm stollen. Decorate with candied cherries. **Yield:** 1 loaf.

Orange Oatmeal Raisin Bread

Doris Heath, Bryson City, North Carolina

For a delicious breakfast, spread slices of this hearty bread with marmalade. The orange juice, molasses and oats are a palate-pleasing combination.

    2 cups quick-cooking oats
    1/2 cup raisins
2-1/2 cups water, *divided*
    1 package (1/4 ounce) active dry yeast
    1/2 cup orange juice
    1/2 cup molasses
    1/3 cup vegetable oil
    1 tablespoon salt
    6 to 6-1/2 cups all-purpose flour
    1 egg
    1 tablespoon milk

Place oats and raisins in a bowl. Heat 2 cups water to 120°-130°; pour over oats and raisins. Cool to 110°-115°, about 10 minutes. Place yeast in a small bowl. Heat remaining water to 110°-115°; pour over yeast to dissolve. Add to oat mixture. Add the orange juice, molasses, oil, salt and 3 cups flour; beat until smooth. Stir in enough remaining flour to form a soft dough. Turn onto a floured surface; knead until smooth and elastic, about 6-8 minutes. Place in a greased bowl, turning once to grease top. Cover and let rise in a warm place until doubled, about 1-1/2 hours. Punch dough down. Turn onto a lightly floured surface; divide into thirds. Shape each into a round or oval loaf. Place on greased baking sheets. Cover and let rise until doubled, about 45 minutes. With a sharp knife, make three to five shallow slashes across the top of each loaf. Beat egg and milk; lightly brush over loaves. Bake at 350° for 35-40 minutes or until golden brown. Remove from pans to wire racks to cool. **Yield:** 3 loaves.

Brioche

Wanda Kristoffersen, Owatonna, Minnesota

At 10 o'clock each morning, it's coffee time at our house. Friends, neighbors and relatives stop by just to see what's baking in my oven. These rolls always satisfy.

3-1/2 cups all-purpose flour
    1/2 cup sugar
    2 packages (1/4 ounce *each*) active dry yeast
    1 teaspoon grated lemon peel
    1/2 teaspoon salt
    2/3 cup butter *or* margarine
    1/2 cup milk
    5 eggs

In a mixing bowl, combine 1-1/2 cups flour, sugar, yeast, lemon peel and salt. In a saucepan, heat butter and milk to 120°-130°. Add to dry ingredients; beat until moistened. Add 4 eggs. Beat on medium speed for 2 minutes. Add 1 cup of flour. Beat until smooth. Stir in the remaining flour. Do not knead. Spoon into greased bowl. Cover and let rise in a warm place until doubled, about 1 hour. Stir dough down. Cover and refrigerate overnight. Punch dough down. Turn onto lightly floured surface. Cover with a bowl; let rest for 15 minutes. Cut one-sixth from the dough; set aside. Shape remaining dough into 12 balls and place in well-greased muffin cups. Divide reserved dough into 12 small balls. Make an indentation in the top of each large ball; place a small ball in each indentation. Cover and let rise in a warm place until doubled, about 1 hour. Beat remaining egg; brush over rolls. Bake at 375° for 15-20 minutes or until golden brown. Remove from pan to wire racks to cool. **Yield:** 1 dozen.

Orange Bow Knots

Daphne Blandford, Gander, Newfoundland

Baking is my favorite pastime, and I normally have my freezer well-stocked with breads, muffins and cookies. This recipe for rolls with a refreshing orange flavor has been in the family as long as I can remember. We especially enjoy them for breakfast and brunch.

    1 package (1/4 ounce) active dry yeast
    1/4 cup warm water (110° to 115°)
    1 cup warm milk (110° to 115°)
    1/2 cup shortening
    1/3 cup sugar
    1/4 cup orange juice
    2 tablespoons grated orange peel
    1 teaspoon salt
    2 eggs
5-1/4 to 5-3/4 cups all-purpose flour
ICING:
    1 cup confectioners' sugar
    2 tablespoons orange juice
    1 teaspoon grated orange peel

In a mixing bowl, dissolve yeast in warm water. Add the milk, shortening, sugar, orange juice and peel, salt, eggs and 3 cups flour. Beat until smooth. Stir in enough remaining flour to form a soft dough. Turn onto a lightly floured surface; knead until smooth and elastic, about 6-8 minutes. Place in a greased bowl, turning once to grease top. Cover and let rise in a warm place until doubled, about 1-1/4 hours. Punch dough down. Turn onto a lightly floured surface; divide in half. Shape each into 12 balls. Roll each into a 10-in. rope. Tie into a knot and tuck ends under. Place 2 in. apart on greased baking sheets. Cover and let rise until doubled, about 45 minutes. Bake at 375° for 12-15 minutes or until golden brown. Remove from pans to

wire racks. Combine icing ingredients; drizzle over
rolls. **Yield:** 2 dozen.

CINNAMON-APRICOT DAISY RING

Sherri Rush, Converse, Indiana

I submitted this pretty bread to a 4-H competition
more than 12 years ago and was named Grand Champion. Since then, it's earned honors for my Grandma
Catherine and six of my cousins. We consider this a
true family recipe!

3-1/2 cups all-purpose flour
   2 tablespoons sugar
   1 package (1/4 ounce) active dry yeast
   1 teaspoon salt
3/4 cup milk
1/4 cup butter *or* margarine
   2 eggs
FILLING:
   2 tablespoons butter *or* margarine, melted
1/4 cup sugar
   2 teaspoons ground cinnamon
   1 egg yolk
   2 tablespoons water
1/2 cup apricot preserves
Vanilla Glaze (recipe on page 89)
Slivered almonds, toasted

In a mixing bowl, combine 1-1/2 cups flour, sugar,
yeast and salt. In a saucepan, heat milk and butter to
120°-130°. Add to dry ingredients; beat until moistened. Add eggs; beat on low speed for 30 seconds. Beat
on high for 3 minutes. Stir in remaining flour; beat
well. Turn onto a floured surface; knead until smooth
and elastic, about 6-8 minutes. Place in a greased bowl,
turning once to grease top. Cover and let rise in a
warm place until doubled, about 1 hour. Punch dough
down. On a lightly floured surface, roll into a 16-in.
circle; place on a greased baking sheet (circle will be
larger than the baking sheet). Place a glass in the center. Brush with melted butter. Combine the sugar and
cinnamon; sprinkle over dough. Cut from the glass
to the outside edge, forming 16 wedges (see Fig. 1). Remove glass. Place one slice over the top of the next
slice, cinnamon-sugar sides together; pinch edges to
seal. Continue around circle until there are eight strips
(see Fig. 2). Twist each strip four to five times (see
Fig. 3). Loop to the center to make daisy petals. Cut off
one roll to place in the center (see Fig. 4). Cover and
let rise until doubled, about 1 hour. Beat egg yolk and
water; brush over ring. Bake at 375° for 15-20 minutes.
Remove from pan to a wire rack to cool. Top with preserves. Drizzle with Vanilla Glaze. Sprinkle with almonds. **Yield:** 1 ring loaf.

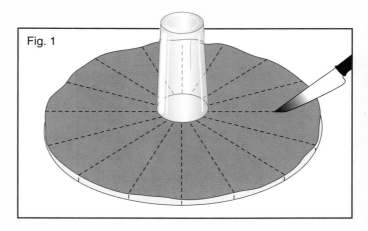

Fig. 1

Fig. 2

Fig. 3

Fig. 4

CRANBERRY CINNAMON CHRISTMAS TREE ROLLS

Margery Richmond, Lacombe, Alberta

(Pictured at left)

These festive rolls are sure to spark lively conversations at your holiday brunch. Colorful cranberries make an appetizing addition to ordinary cinnamon rolls.

    1 tablespoon active dry yeast
1/2 cup warm water (110° to 115°)
1/2 cup sour cream
1/4 cup butter *or* margarine
1/4 cup sugar
    1 teaspoon salt
    2 eggs
-3/4 to 4-1/4 cups all-purpose flour

FILLING:

    2 cups fresh *or* frozen cranberries
1/2 cup water
-1/2 cups packed brown sugar, *divided*
    1 cup chopped pecans
1/3 cup butter *or* margarine, softened
    1 tablespoon ground cinnamon
1/4 cup butter *or* margarine, melted

TOPPING:

1/4 cup corn syrup
3/4 cup confectioners' sugar
    1 tablespoon milk
Cranberries and red and green candied cherries,
    halved

In a mixing bowl, dissolve yeast in warm water. In a small saucepan, heat sour cream and butter to 110°-115°. Add the sour cream mixture, sugar, salt, eggs and 1-1/2 cups flour to yeast mixture. Beat on medium speed for 2 minutes. Stir in enough remaining flour to form a soft dough. Turn onto a floured surface; knead until smooth and elastic, about 6-8 minutes. Place in a greased bowl, turning once to grease top. Cover and let rise in a warm place until doubled, about 1-1/2 hours. Meanwhile, in a saucepan, bring cranberries and water to a boil. Cover and boil gently for 5 minutes. Stir in 1/2 cup brown sugar. Reduce heat; simmer, uncovered, for 5 minutes or until thickened, stirring occasionally. Cool. Combine the pecans, softened butter, cinnamon and remaining brown sugar; set aside. Punch dough down. Turn onto a lightly floured surface; divide in half. Roll each into a 14-in. x 12-in. rectangle. Brush each with 1 tablespoon melted butter. Spread half of the filling to within 1/2 in. of edges. Sprinkle with half of the pecan mixture. Roll up, jelly-roll style, starting with a long side; pinch seam to seal. Brush with remaining

melted butter. To form a tree from each log, cut a 2-in. piece from one end for a tree trunk; set aside. Then cut each log into 15 slices. Cover two baking sheets with foil and grease well. Center one slice near the top of each prepared baking sheet. Arrange slice with sides touching in four more rows, adding one slice for each row, forming a tree. Center the reserved slice lengthwise below the tree for trunk. Cover and let rise until doubled, about 45 minutes. Bake at 350° for 25-30 minutes or until golden brown. In a saucepan, heat corn syrup over low heat. Transfer foil with trees onto wire racks; brush with corn syrup. Cool for 20 minutes. Combine confectioners' sugar and milk. Fill a small pastry or plastic bag; cut a small hole in corner of bag. Pipe on trees for garlands. Garnish with cranberries and candied cherries. **Yield:** 2 trees (16 rolls each).

PEANUT BUTTER ROLLS

Joyce Sprague, Colorado Springs, Colorado

Reach for this recipe when you're looking for a change from typical cinnamon rolls. The unique combination of confectioners' sugar, peanut butter and coffee in the frosting is finger-licking good.

    2 packages (1/4 ounce *each*) active dry yeast
1/2 cup warm water (110° to 115°)
    2 cups warm milk (110° to 115°)
1/4 cup sugar
1/4 cup shortening
    1 teaspoon salt
    2 eggs
    7 to 7-1/2 cups all-purpose flour
2/3 cup peanut butter

FROSTING:

    4 cups confectioners' sugar
1/3 cup peanut butter
1/2 cup hot freshly brewed coffee

In a mixing bowl, dissolve yeast in warm water. Add the milk, sugar, shortening, salt, eggs and 3-1/2 cups flour; beat until smooth. Stir in enough remaining flour to form a soft dough. Turn onto a floured surface; knead until smooth and elastic, about 6-8 minutes. Place in a greased bowl, turning once to grease top. Cover and let rise in a warm place until doubled, about 45 minutes. Punch dough down. Turn onto a lightly floured surface; divide in half. Roll each into a 14-in. x 9-in. rectangle. Spread 1/3 cup peanut butter to within 1/2 in. of edges. Roll up, jelly-roll style, starting with a long side; pinch seam to seal. Cut each into 12 slices. Place, cut side down, in two greased 13-in. x 9-in. x 2-in. baking pans. Cover and let rise until doubled, about 1 hour. Bake at 375° for 20-25 minutes or until light brown. Combine frosting ingredients; frost warm rolls. Cool in pans on wire racks. **Yield:** 2 dozen.

YULETIDE YUMMIES. Pictured at left: Cranberry Cinnamon Christmas Tree Rolls (recipe on this page) and Lemon Candy Canes (recipe on page 82).

LEMON CANDY CANES

Marie Frangpane, Eugene, Oregon

(Pictured above and on page 80)

We enjoy looking at these cute candy cane rolls as much as we love eating them! For even more festive fun, I sometimes decorate them with sliced candied cherries.

>   1 package (1/4 ounce) active dry yeast
>   1/2 cup warm water (110° to 115°)
>   1/3 cup sour cream
>   1 egg
>   3 tablespoons butter *or* margarine, softened
>   3 tablespoons sugar
>   1 teaspoon salt
> 2-3/4 to 3 cups all-purpose flour
> FILLING:
>   1/2 cup finely chopped walnuts *or* pecans
>   1/3 cup sugar
>   3 tablespoons butter *or* margarine, melted
>   1 tablespoon grated lemon peel
> LEMON ICING:
>   1 cup confectioners' sugar
>   1 tablespoon lemon juice
>   1 tablespoon water
>   1/4 teaspoon vanilla extract

In a mixing bowl, dissolve yeast in warm water. Add the sour cream, egg, butter, sugar, salt and 1-1/4 cups flour. Beat until smooth. Stir in enough remaining flour to form a soft dough. Turn onto a floured surface; knead until smooth and elastic, about 6-8 minutes. Place in a greased bowl, turning once to grease top. Cover and let rise in a warm place until doubled, about 1 hour. Punch dough down. Turn onto a lightly floured surface; divide in half. Let rest for 10 minutes. Roll each into a 12-in. x 8-in. rectangle. In a bowl, combine filling ingredients; mix well. Spread half of filling over dough to within 1/2 in. of edges. Fold in half lengthwise; pinch seam to seal. Cut into 12 strips. Holding both ends of strip, twist each strip three or four times. Place 2 in. apart on greased baking sheets. Curve one end to form a cane. Cover and let rise until doubled, about 30 minutes. Bake at 375° for 12-14 minutes or until golden brown. Remove from pans to wire racks to cool. Combine icing ingredients; drizzle over rolls. **Yield:** 2 dozen.

MAPLE OAT BATTER BREAD

Denise Frink, Henderson, Iowa

This moist, hearty bread has a terrific mix of grains and maple flavor. The recipe appeals to me because the dough requires no kneading and only one rising.

> 1-1/4 cups warm milk (120° to 130°)
>   1 cup quick-cooking oats
>   1/4 cup butter *or* margarine, softened
>   1 package (1/4 ounce) active dry yeast
>   1/4 cup warm water (110° to 115°)
>   1/3 cup maple syrup
> 1-1/2 teaspoons salt
>   1 egg
>   3/4 cup whole wheat flour
>   2 cups all-purpose flour
> Additional oats

In a mixing bowl, combine the milk, oats and butter; cool to 110°-115°. In a small bowl, dissolve yeast in warm water; add to oat mixture. Add the syrup, salt, egg, whole wheat flour and 1 cup all-purpose flour. Beat on low speed for 30 seconds. Beat on high for 3 minutes. Stir in remaining all-purpose flour (batter will be thick). Do not knead. Grease a 1-1/2-qt. baking dish and sprinkle with additional oats. Spoon batter into prepared dish. Cover and let rise in a warm place until doubled, about 50 minutes. Bake at 350° for 40-45 minutes or until golden brown. Cool for 10 minutes before removing from pan to a wire rack. **Yield:** 1 loaf.

BLUSHING APPLE BRAID

Cordavee Heupel, Sturgis, South Dakota

Every Christmas for the past 20 years, I've been baking and giving these braids as gifts to shut-ins, special friends and teachers.

>   2 packages (1/4 ounce *each*) active dry yeast
>   1/2 cup warm water (110° to 115°)
> 1-1/4 cups warm buttermilk* (110° to 115°)
>   1/2 cup butter *or* margarine, softened
>   1/2 cup sugar
>   2 teaspoons baking powder
> 1-1/2 teaspoons salt
>   2 eggs
> 5-3/4 to 6-1/4 cups all-purpose flour
>   2 cans (21 ounces *each*) apple pie filling
>   3/4 cup red-hot candies
> GLAZE:
> 1-1/2 cups confectioners' sugar
>   5 to 6 teaspoons water
> Red candied cherries, optional

In a mixing bowl, dissolve yeast in warm water. Add the buttermilk, butter, sugar, baking powder, salt, eggs and 2-1/2 cups flour. Beat on low speed for 30 seconds.

eat on medium for 2 minutes. Stir in enough remaining flour to form a soft dough. Turn onto a floured surface; knead until smooth and elastic, about 6-8 minutes. Place in a greased bowl, turning once to grease top. Cover and let rise in a warm place until doubled, about 1 hour. Punch dough down. Turn onto a lightly floured surface; divide into thirds. Roll each into a 13-in. x 9-in. rectangle. Place on greased baking sheets. Remove apples from pie filling. Discard remaining filling or save for another use. Place a third of the apples down the center third of each rectangle. Sprinkle with a third of the red-hots. On each long side, cut 1-in.-wide strips to the center to within 1/2 in. of the filling. Starting at one end, fold alternating strips at an angle across filling. Pinch ends to seal and tuck under. Cover and let rise until doubled, about 1 hour. Bake at 375° for 25-30 minutes or until golden brown. Cool slightly on baking sheets before removing to wire racks. For glaze, combine sugar and enough water to achieve desired consistency. Drizzle over breads. Decorate with candied cherries if desired. **Yield:** 3 loaves. **Editor's Note:** Warm buttermilk will appear curdled.

CRANBERRY KUCHEN

Linda Bright, Wichita, Kansas

This German coffee cake has been served at family breakfasts for more than five generations. There is no recipe requested more by our large family.

> 2 packages (1/4 ounce *each*) active dry yeast
> 1/4 cup warm water (110° to 115°)
> 1 cup warm milk (110° to 115°)
> 1/4 cup butter *or* margarine, softened
> 1/4 cup sugar
> 1 teaspoon salt
> 1 egg
> 3-1/2 to 4 cups all-purpose flour

CRANBERRY SAUCE:
> 2 cups water
> 1-1/2 cups sugar
> 4 cups fresh *or* frozen cranberries

EGG MIXTURE:
> 8 eggs
> 3/4 cup evaporated milk
> 3/4 cup sugar

TOPPING:
> 2 cups all-purpose flour
> 2 cups sugar
> 1 cup cold butter *or* margarine

In a mixing bowl, dissolve yeast in warm water. Add the milk, butter, sugar, salt, egg and 2 cups flour. Beat until smooth. Stir in enough remaining flour to form a soft dough. Do not knead. Cover and let rise in a warm place until doubled, about 1 hour. Meanwhile, in a saucepan, bring water and sugar to a boil. Add cranberries. Reduce heat; cover and simmer for 10 minutes. Remove from the heat; set aside. In a bowl, combine the eggs, evaporated milk and sugar; beat well. Divide half of the egg mixture between two greased 13-in. x 9-in. x 2-in. baking pans; set remaining egg mixture aside. Punch dough down. Divide in half. Pat each portion over egg mixture in pans. Spoon cranberry sauce over dough. Drizzle with remaining egg mixture. For topping, combine flour and sugar in a bowl. Cut in butter until crumbly; sprinkle over the top. Bake at 350° for 25-30 minutes or until lightly browned. **Yield:** 2 kuchens.

ALMOND CROISSANTS

Patricia Glass, East Wenatchee, Washington

These tender croissants are a little lighter than others I've tried. A close friend of mine serves these every Christmas and Easter.

> 1 package (1/4 ounce) active dry yeast
> 1/4 cup warm water (110° to 115°)
> 4 cups all-purpose flour
> 1/4 cup sugar
> 1 teaspoon salt
> 1 cup cold butter (no substitutes)
> 3/4 cup warm milk (110° to 115°)
> 3 egg yolks

FILLING:
> 1/2 cup almond paste
> 1 egg white
> 1/4 cup confectioners' sugar

EGG WASH:
> 1 egg white
> 1 tablespoon water
> 1/4 cup sliced almonds

In a bowl, dissolve yeast in warm water. In a large bowl, combine the flour, sugar and salt. Cut in butter until crumbly. Add milk and egg yolks to yeast mixture; mix well. Stir into flour mixture; mix well. Do not knead. Cover and refrigerate overnight. In a mixing bowl, beat filling ingredients until smooth. Turn dough onto a lightly floured surface; divide in half. Roll each into a 12-in. circle; cut into eight wedges. Spread filling over wedges. Roll up from wide end and place with pointed end down 3 in. apart on ungreased baking sheets. Curve ends to form a crescent shape. Cover and let rise in a warm place for 1 hour (dough will not double). Beat egg white and water; brush over croissants. Sprinkle with almonds. Bake at 350° for 15-20 minutes. Remove from pans to wire racks to cool. **Yield:** 16 rolls.

CHRISTMAS TREE TWISTS

Sandy Walowski, Delburne, Alberta

Red and green colored sugar peeks out from the twisted "branches" of these lovely loaves. You can have your family enjoy one and give the other as a gift.

2-3/4 to 3-1/4 cups all-purpose flour
  1/4 cup sugar
    1 package (1/4 ounce) active dry yeast
    1 teaspoon salt
  1/4 teaspoon baking soda
    1 cup buttermilk
  1/4 cup shortening
    1 egg
    2 tablespoons butter *or* margarine, softened
    1 tablespoon red colored sugar
    1 tablespoon green colored sugar

In a mixing bowl, combine 1-1/2 cups flour, sugar, yeast, salt and baking soda. In a saucepan, heat buttermilk and shortening to 120°-130°. Add to dry ingredients; beat until moistened. Add egg; beat on medium speed for 30 seconds. Beat on high for 3 minutes. Stir in enough remaining flour to form a firm dough. Turn onto a floured surface; knead until smooth and elastic, about 6-8 minutes. Cover and let rest for 10 minutes. Divide dough in half. Roll each into a 14-in. x 6-in. rectangle; brush with butter. Sprinkle one rectangle with red sugar and one with green sugar. Fold each rectangle in half lengthwise, forming two 14-in. x 3-in. rectangles; pinch seam to seal. Cut each into fourteen 3-in. x 1-in. strips (see Fig. 1). Beginning with the red-sugared strips, twist each strip several times. On a greased baking sheet, arrange strips in a tree shape by placing pinched edge of a strip in the top center of baking sheet and fanning out rounded end, allowing filling to show (see Fig. 2). Use six strips of dough on one side and seven strips on other side. Pinch dough in center to join. Use remaining strip for tree trunk (see Fig. 3). Repeat with green-sugared strips. Cover and let rise in a warm place until doubled, about 1 hour. Bake at 375° for 15-20 minutes or until lightly browned. Remove from pans to wire racks to cool. **Yield:** 2 loaves.

MAPLE NUT COFFEE BREAD

Deanne Roberts, Orem, Utah

This recipe makes one large coffee cake, so it's great to take to potlucks. The maple flavoring is a nice change from the more common fruit fillings.

    1 tablespoon active dry yeast
  1/4 cup warm water (110° to 115°)
    1 cup warm milk (110° to 115°)
  1/4 cup shortening
  1/4 cup sugar
    1 egg
    1 teaspoon salt
    1 teaspoon maple flavoring
  1/8 teaspoon ground cardamom
3-1/2 cups all-purpose flour
FILLING:
    1 cup packed brown sugar
  1/3 cup chopped pecans
    1 teaspoon ground cinnamon
    1 teaspoon maple flavoring
    6 tablespoons butter *or* margarine, softened
GLAZE:
1-1/2 cups confectioners' sugar
  1/4 teaspoon maple flavoring
    2 to 3 tablespoons milk

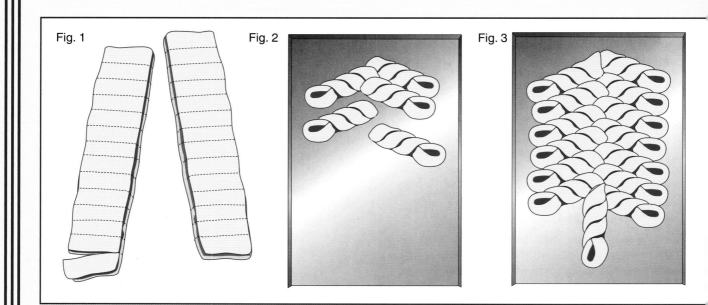

Fig. 1   Fig. 2   Fig. 3

In a mixing bowl, dissolve yeast in warm water. Add milk, shortening, sugar, egg, salt, maple flavoring and cardamom; mix well. Add the flour; beat until smooth. Turn onto a floured surface; knead until smooth and elastic, about 6-8 minutes. Place in a greased bowl, turning once to grease top. Cover and let rise in a warm place until doubled, about 1 hour. Grease a baking sheet or 14-in. pizza pan or line with foil. For filling, combine the brown sugar, pecans, cinnamon and maple flavoring; set aside. Punch dough down. Turn onto a lightly floured surface; divide into thirds. Roll each into a 14-in. circle; place one on prepared pan. Spread with a third of the butter; sprinkle with a third of the filling. Top with a second circle of dough; top with butter and filling. Repeat. Pinch to seal. Carefully place a glass in center of circle. With scissors, cut from outside edge just to the glass, forming 16 wedges. Remove glass; twist each wedge five to six times. Pinch ends to seal and tuck under. Cover and let rise until doubled, about 30 minutes. Bake at 375° for 25-30 minutes or until golden brown. For glaze, combine the sugar, maple flavoring and enough milk to achieve desired consistency; set aside. Carefully remove bread from pan by running a metal spatula under it to loosen. Transfer to a wire rack. Drizzle with glaze. Cool completely or serve while slightly warm. **Yield:** 1 loaf.

HONEY PULL-APART BREAD

Donna Bittinger, Oakland, Maryland

When I came across this recipe in an old family cookbook, I knew it would be an instant hit with my family. We enjoy it fresh from the oven, and it disappears in a flash.

> **2 packages (1/4 ounce *each*) active dry yeast**
> **1/4 cup warm water (110° to 115°)**
> **1 cup warm milk (110° to 115°)**
> **1/2 cup shortening**
> **1/4 cup sugar**
> **2 teaspoons salt**
> **2 eggs**
> **4-1/2 to 5 cups all-purpose flour**
> **FILLING:**
> **2 tablespoons butter *or* margarine, melted**
> **1 cup honey**
> **1 cup chopped pecans**
> **1/2 cup sugar**
> **1/4 cup grated orange peel**
> **2 tablespoons orange juice**
> **2 teaspoons ground cinnamon**
> **GLAZE:**
> **1/3 cup honey**
> **1/3 cup sugar**
> **2 teaspoons grated orange peel**
> **1 tablespoon butter *or* margarine**

In a mixing bowl, dissolve yeast in warm water. Add the milk, shortening, sugar, salt, eggs and 2 cups flour. Beat until smooth. Stir in enough remaining flour to form a stiff dough. Turn onto a floured surface; knead until smooth and elastic, about 6-8 minutes. Place in a greased bowl, turning once to grease top. Cover and let rise in a warm place until doubled, about 1 hour. Punch dough down. Turn onto a lightly floured surface; divide in half. Roll each into a 16-in. x 12-in. rectangle. Brush with butter. Combine remaining filling ingredients; spread over dough to within 1/2 in. of edges. Roll up, jelly-roll style, starting with a long side. Pinch seam to seal. Cut each into 16 slices. Place, cut side down, in a greased one-piece 10-in. tube pan. Cover and let rise until doubled, about 45 minutes. Bake at 350° for 40-45 minutes or until golden brown. Cool in pan for 10 minutes before inverting onto a serving plate. In a small saucepan, combine glaze ingredients; heat until sugar is dissolved. Drizzle over warm bread. **Yield:** 16 servings.

CINNAMON RAISIN BREAD

Joan Ort, Milford, New Jersey

Slices of warm cinnamon bread and a cup of hot tea work wonders for holiday visitors to our home. My mother received this recipe from a friend in West Virginia.

> **2 packages (1/4 ounce *each*) active dry yeast**
> **2 cups warm water (110° to 115°)**
> **1 cup sugar, *divided***
> **1/4 cup vegetable oil**
> **1 tablespoon salt**
> **2 eggs**
> **6 to 6-1/2 cups all-purpose flour**
> **1 cup raisins**
> **Additional vegetable oil**
> **1 tablespoon ground cinnamon**

In a mixing bowl, dissolve yeast in warm water. Add 1/2 cup sugar, oil, salt, eggs and 4 cups flour. Beat until smooth. Stir in enough remaining flour to form a soft dough. Turn onto a floured surface; knead until smooth and elastic, about 6-8 minutes. Place in a greased bowl, turning once to grease top. Cover and let rise in a warm place until doubled, about 1 hour. Punch dough down. Turn onto a lightly floured surface; divide in half. Knead 1/2 cup raisins into each piece; roll into a 15-in. x 9-in. rectangle. Brush with additional oil. Combine cinnamon and remaining sugar; sprinkle to within 1/2 in. of edges. Tightly roll up, jelly-roll style, starting with a short side; pinch seam to seal. Place, seam side down, in two greased 9-in. x 5-in. x 3-in. loaf pans. Cover and let rise until doubled, about 30 minutes. Brush with oil. Bake at 375° for 45-50 minutes or until golden brown. Remove from pans to wire racks to cool. **Yield:** 2 loaves.

SWEET SESAME BREAD

Kristi Parker, Merrimack, New Hampshire

Aniseed gives this festive Greek bread its unusual yet pleasing flavor. Everyone in the family runs to the kitchen for a fresh-from-the-oven slice.

> 1 tablespoon active dry yeast
> 1/2 cup warm water (110° to 115°)
> 1/4 cup butter *or* margarine, softened
> 1/4 cup sugar
> 3 tablespoons instant nonfat dry milk powder
> 1/2 teaspoon salt
> 1/2 teaspoon crushed aniseed
> 2 eggs
> 2-1/2 to 3 cups all-purpose flour
> TOPPING:
> 1 egg
> 1 tablespoon milk
> 2 tablespoons sesame seeds
> 2 tablespoons chopped almonds
> 2 tablespoons sugar

In a mixing bowl, dissolve yeast in warm water. Add the butter, sugar, milk powder, salt, aniseed, eggs and 2 cups flour. Beat on low speed for 3 minutes. Stir in enough remaining flour to form a soft dough. Turn onto a floured surface; knead until smooth and elastic, about 6-8 minutes. Place in a greased bowl, turning once to grease top. Cover and let rise in a warm place until doubled, about 1 hour. Punch dough down. Turn onto a lightly floured surface; divide into thirds. Shape each into a 15-in. rope. Place ropes on a greased baking sheet; braid. Pinch ends to seal and tuck under. Cover and let rise until doubled, about 45 minutes. Beat egg and milk; brush over braid. Sprinkle with sesame seeds, almonds and sugar. Bake at 350° for 25-30 minutes or until golden brown. Remove from pan to a wire rack to cool. Serve warm or at room temperature. **Yield:** 1 loaf.

POPPY SEED LOAVES

Helen Salabak, Sedalia, Colorado

Everyone always looked forward to Grandma Brettin baking these delicious loaves. She didn't use a recipe, so a cousin watched her make them one day and wrote down the ingredients.

> 2 packages (1/4 ounce *each*) active dry yeast
> 1 cup warm water (110° to 115°)
> 1 cup butter *or* margarine, softened
> 1/2 cup sugar
> 3 eggs
> 2 teaspoons grated lemon peel
> 1 teaspoon salt
> 4-1/2 cups all-purpose flour

> 2 cans (12-1/2 ounces *each*) poppy seed filling
> Melted butter *or* margarine
> Confectioners' sugar, optional

In a small bowl, dissolve yeast in warm water. In a mixing bowl, cream butter and sugar. Add eggs, one at a time, beating well after each addition. Add lemon peel and salt; mix well. Beat in yeast mixture. Gradually add flour; beat on medium speed for 5 minutes (dough will be sticky). Do not knead. Place in a greased bowl, turning once to grease top. Cover and refrigerate for at least 2 hours. Punch dough down. Turn onto a lightly floured surface; divide into four pieces. Roll each into a 12-in. x 8-in. rectangle. Spread poppy seed filling over each to within 1/2 in. of edges. Loosely roll up, jelly-roll style, starting with a long side; pinch seam to seal and tuck ends under. Place, seam side down, on two greased baking sheets. With a sharp knife, make five to six deep diagonal slashes across the top of each loaf. Cover and let rise until doubled, about 30 minutes. Brush with melted butter. Bake at 350° for 30-35 minutes or until golden brown. Remove from pans to wire racks. Cool for 20 minutes; dust with confectioners' sugar if desired. **Yield:** 4 loaves.

PINEAPPLE SWEET ROLLS

Bernice Morris, Marshfield, Missouri

These sweet rolls are very similar to the kind found in bakeries…only better! Pineapple adds just the right amount of sweetness. My husband can't eat just one.

> 1 package (1/4 ounce) active dry yeast
> 1/4 cup warm water (110° to 115°)
> 1 tablespoon plus 1/4 cup sugar, *divided*
> 1 cup warm milk (110° to 115°)
> 5 to 5-1/2 cups all-purpose flour
> 2 eggs, beaten
> 1/2 cup butter *or* margarine, melted, *divided*
> 1 teaspoon salt
> TOPPING:
> 1-1/2 teaspoons cornstarch
> 1 can (8 ounces) crushed pineapple, undrained
> GLAZE:
> 1-1/2 cups confectioners' sugar
> 1 teaspoon vanilla extract
> 1 to 2 tablespoons milk

In a mixing bowl, dissolve yeast in warm water. Add 1 tablespoon sugar; let stand for 5 minutes. Add milk and 1-1/2 cups flour. Beat until smooth. Cover and let rise in a warm place until doubled, about 45 minutes. Add the eggs, 1/4 cup butter, salt, remaining sugar and enough remaining flour to form a soft dough. Turn onto a floured surface; knead until smooth and elastic, about 6-8 minutes. Place in a greased bowl, turning once to grease top. Cover and let rise until doubled, about 45 minutes. Punch dough down. Turn onto a floured surface; divide in half. Roll each into a 12-in. x 8-in. rectangle. Brush with some of the remaining butter. Roll up, jelly-roll style, starting with a long side. Pinch seam to seal. Cut each into 12 slices. Place, cut side down, 2 in. apart on greased baking sheets. Brush with remaining butter. Cover and let rise until doubled, about 30 minutes. Meanwhile, in a small saucepan, combine cornstarch and pineapple until blended. Bring to a boil over medium heat; cook and stir for 2 minutes. Remove from the heat. Place a teaspoonful of filling in the center of each roll. Bake at 425° for 12-16 minutes or until golden brown. Remove from pans to wire racks. For glaze, combine sugar, vanilla and enough milk to achieve desired consistency. Drizzle over warm rolls. **Yield:** 2 dozen.

EASY APPLE DANISH

Dorothea Ladd, Ballston Lake, New York

This dough should be refrigerated for at least 2 hours. I often prepare it the night before and bake the rolls fresh in the morning as a special breakfast treat.

>　1 package (1/4 ounce) active dry yeast
> 1/4 cup warm water (110° to 115°)
>　5 cups all-purpose flour
> 1/4 cup sugar
>　1 teaspoon salt
>　1 teaspoon grated lemon peel
>　1 cup cold butter (no substitutes)
>　1 cup warm milk (110° to 115°)
>　2 eggs, beaten

FILLING:
> 1-1/2 cups chopped peeled tart apples
>　3/4 cup chopped walnuts
>　1/3 cup sugar
> 1-1/2 teaspoons ground cinnamon
>　2 tablespoons butter (no substitutes), melted

GLAZE:
>　2 cups confectioners' sugar
>　3 tablespoons milk
> 1/2 teaspoon vanilla extract

In a small bowl, dissolve yeast in warm water. In a large bowl, combine the flour, sugar, salt and lemon peel; cut in butter until crumbly. Stir in the yeast mixture, milk and eggs by hand. Turn onto a floured surface; knead about 20 times (dough will be slightly sticky). Cover and refrigerate for at least 2 hours. For filling, combine the apples, walnuts, sugar and cinnamon; set aside. Punch dough down. Turn onto a lightly floured surface; divide in half. Roll each into an 18-in. x 15-in. rectangle; brush with butter. Sprinkle with filling to within 1/2 in. of edges. Starting with a short side, fold one third of the side over filling; repeat with other side, making a 15-

in. x 6-in. rectangle. Pinch seam to seal. Cut each into 15 slices. Twist each slice a few times; pinch ends together, forming a small circle. Place 2 in. apart on greased baking sheets. Bake at 400° for 12-15 minutes or until golden brown. Remove from pans to wire racks. Combine glaze ingredients; drizzle over warm rolls. **Yield:** 2-1/2 dozen.

CHOCOLATE STICKY BUNS

Jean Seidel, Wadena, Iowa

My husband, Randy, and I are chocoholics, so this recipe has become a favorite. The fudge-like topping pairs well with the chocolate-cinnamon filling.

>　1 package (1/4 ounce) active dry yeast
> 1/3 cup warm water (110° to 115°)
> 3/4 cup warm milk (110° to 115°)
> 1/2 cup butter *or* margarine, softened
> 1/3 cup sugar
>　1 teaspoon salt
>　1 egg
> 4-1/2 to 5 cups all-purpose flour

SYRUP:
>　1 cup packed brown sugar
> 1/2 cup butter *or* margarine
> 1/4 cup corn syrup
>　3 tablespoons baking cocoa
> 1-1/2 cups chopped pecans

FILLING:
>　1 cup sugar
>　2 tablespoons baking cocoa
>　2 teaspoons ground cinnamon
> 1/4 cup butter *or* margarine, melted

In a mixing bowl, dissolve yeast in warm water. Add the milk, butter, sugar, salt, egg and 1-1/2 cups flour. Beat on medium speed for 2-3 minutes or until smooth. Stir in enough remaining flour to form a soft dough. Turn onto a floured surface; knead until smooth and elastic, about 6-8 minutes. Place in a greased bowl, turning once to grease top. Cover and let rise in a warm place until doubled, about 1 hour. Meanwhile, for syrup, combine the brown sugar, butter, corn syrup and cocoa in a saucepan. Bring to a boil; boil and stir for 1 minute. Pour into two greased 9-in. round or square baking pans; sprinkle with pecans. Set aside. For filling, combine the sugar, cocoa and cinnamon; set aside. Punch dough down. Turn onto a lightly floured surface; divide in half. Roll each into a 12-in. x 10-in. rectangle; brush with melted butter. Sprinkle filling to within 1/2 in. of edges. Roll up, jelly-roll style, starting with a short side; pinch seam to seal. Cut each into nine slices; place, cut side down, over syrup and pecans. Cover and let rise until doubled, about 1 hour. Bake at 375° for 20-25 minutes or until well browned. Cool in pans for 1 minute before inverting onto serving plates. **Yield:** 1-1/2 dozen.

Teddy Bear Bread

Edna Hoffman, Hebron, Indiana

(Pictured at left)

I had lots of fun making this adorable bread with one of our granddaughters. I kept one loaf and sent the other home with her. She was so proud of it and kept it in her bedroom! Finally, she reluctantly brought it out to share with her family.

1 package (1/4 ounce) active dry yeast
1-1/2 cups warm water (110° to 115°)
1/2 cup warm milk (110° to 115°)
3 tablespoons butter *or* margarine, softened
3 tablespoons sugar
2 teaspoons salt
5-1/4 to 5-3/4 cups all-purpose flour
12 raisins
1 egg
1 tablespoon cold water
Ribbon, optional

In a mixing bowl, dissolve yeast in warm water. Add the milk, butter, sugar, salt and 3 cups flour. Beat until smooth. Stir in enough remaining flour to form a stiff dough. Turn onto a floured surface; knead until smooth and elastic, about 6-8 minutes. Place in a greased bowl, turning once to grease top. Cover and let rise in a warm place until doubled, about 1 hour. Punch dough down. Turn onto a lightly floured surface; divide into four portions. Cut one portion in half; shape into balls. Cut another portion into 14 pieces; shape into balls. Shape remaining two portions into balls. To form bear body, place each large ball in the center of a greased baking sheet. Place a medium ball above body for head; flatten slightly. Place two small balls on each side of head for ears. Place one small ball in the center of head for nose, and four small balls around body for arms and legs. Cover and let rise until doubled, about 1 hour. With a sharp knife or scissors, cut slits for ears, eyes, nose and belly button. Insert raisins into slits. Beat egg and cold water; brush over dough. Bake at 375° for 25-30 minutes or until golden brown. Remove from pans to wire racks to cool. If desired, tie a bow around bear's neck with ribbon. **Yield:** 2 loaves.

Bird Rolls

Margaret Fowler, Plainfield, Indiana

(Pictured at left)

I make a point of having these tender bird rolls "fly in"

for Easter dinner. With their slightly sweet flavor, the grandchildren can't help but gobble them up.

1 package (1/4 ounce) active dry yeast
1 cup warm milk (110° to 115°)
1/4 cup butter *or* margarine, melted
1/4 cup packed brown sugar
3 eggs
1 teaspoon salt
3-1/2 to 4 cups all-purpose flour
1 tablespoon water
16 whole unblanched almonds

In a mixing bowl, dissolve yeast in warm milk. Add the butter, brown sugar, 2 eggs, salt and 2 cups flour. Beat until smooth. Stir in enough remaining flour to form a soft dough. Turn onto a floured surface; knead until smooth and elastic, about 6-8 minutes. Place in a greased bowl, turning once to grease top. Cover and let rise in a warm place until doubled, about 1 hour. Punch dough down. Turn onto a lightly floured surface; divide into 16 pieces. Roll each into a 12-in. rope; tie each into a knot. To form bird's head, tuck one end back into knot. With a sharp knife or scissors, cut two slits on opposite end to form tail feathers. Place 2 in. apart on greased baking sheets. Cover and let rise until doubled, about 30 minutes. Beat remaining egg with water; brush over dough. Bake at 350° for 15-20 minutes or until golden brown. Insert an almond into each for beak. Remove from pans to wire racks to cool. **Yield:** 16 rolls.

Vanilla Glaze

This classic glaze adds a special sweet finishing touch to a variety of breads, rolls and muffins.

1 cup confectioners' sugar
1/4 teaspoon vanilla extract
1 to 2 tablespoons milk

In a bowl, combine confectioners' sugar, vanilla and enough milk to achieve desired consistency. **Yield:** about 1/2 cup.

GET CREATIVE WITH GLAZES

When making sweet glazes, start with the Vanilla Glaze recipe (above), then make some simple substitutions.

For instance, instead of always moistening the confectioners' sugar with milk, try using orange juice, strong brewed coffee or even plain water. Flavorings like almond and lemon extract are robust replacements for vanilla extract. For a spiced glaze, forgo the vanilla extract and combine confectioners' sugar, 1/4 teaspoon ground ginger and water.

SHAPED SPECIALTIES. Pictured at left: Teddy Bear Bread and Bird Rolls (recipes on this page).

PEANUT BUTTER BRAIDS

Marla Knight, Hillsboro, Indiana

A peanut butter filling sets this sweet bread apart from all the rest. I can picture my grandma making many of these delightful loaves in her cozy kitchen.

2 packages (1/4 ounce *each*) active dry yeast
1/2 cup warm water (110° to 115°)
1/2 cup warm milk (110° to 115°)
1/2 cup sugar
1/4 cup butter *or* margarine, softened
1-1/2 teaspoons salt
2 eggs
4-1/4 to 4-3/4 cups all-purpose flour
FILLING:
1 cup peanut butter
1/2 cup butter *or* margarine, softened
Vanilla Glaze (recipe on page 89), optional

In a mixing bowl, dissolve yeast in warm water. Add the milk, sugar, butter, salt, eggs and 2 cups flour; beat until smooth. Stir in enough remaining flour to form a soft dough. Turn onto a floured surface; knead until smooth and elastic, about 6-8 minutes. Place in a greased bowl, turning once to grease top. Cover and let rise in a warm place until doubled, about 1 hour. Punch dough down. Turn onto a lightly floured surface; divide in half. Divide each half into thirds. Roll each into a 16-in. x 3-1/2-in. rectangle. In a small mixing bowl, beat peanut butter and butter until smooth. Spread down the center third of each rectangle. Fold dough lengthwise over filling; pinch seam and ends to seal. Place three strips, seam side down, on greased baking sheets. Gently braid and pinch ends to seal; tuck ends under. Repeat with remaining strips. Cover and let rise until doubled, about 1 hour. Bake at 350° for 15-20 minutes or until golden brown. Remove from pans to wire racks to cool. Drizzle with Vanilla Glaze if desired. **Yield:** 2 loaves.

CHOCOLATE CARAMEL BREADS

Patty Bourne, Owings, Maryland

Candy bars are the chocolate-caramel surprise in this bread. I invented this braid as a way to make my basic yeast sweet bread recipe a little more decadent.

2 cups (16 ounces) sour cream
1/3 cup sugar
1/4 cup butter *or* margarine
2 packages (1/4 ounce *each*) active dry yeast
1/2 cup warm water (110° to 115°)
1-1/2 teaspoons salt
2 eggs
6 to 6-1/2 cups all-purpose flour

2 packages (13.3 ounces *each*) fun-size Snickers
***or* Milky Way candy bars**
EGG WASH:
1 egg white
1 tablespoon water

In a saucepan, heat the sour cream, sugar and butter to 110°-115°. In a mixing bowl, dissolve yeast in warm water. Add the sour cream mixture, salt, eggs and 2 cups flour. Beat until smooth. Stir in enough remaining flour to form a soft dough. Turn onto a floured surface; knead until smooth and elastic, about 6-8 minutes. Place in a greased bowl, turning once to grease top. Cover and let rise in a warm place until doubled, about 1 hour. Punch dough down. Turn onto a lightly floured surface; divide into thirds. Roll each into a 16-in. x 10-in. rectangle. Place on three greased baking sheets. Place candy bars lengthwise in two rows down the center third of each rectangle. On each long side, cut 1-in.-wide strips into the center to within 1/2 in. of candy bars. Starting at one end, fold alternating strips at an angle across candy bars. Pinch ends to seal and tuck under. Cover and let rise until doubled, about 1 hour. Beat egg white and water; brush over braids. Bake at 375° for 15-20 minutes or until golden brown. Remove from pans to wire racks to cool. **Yield:** 3 loaves.

NO-KNEAD FAN ROLLS

Christine Wahlgren, Sandwich, Illinois

All the men who help on our farm can't wait for me to bake these cinnamon- and raisin-filled rolls. Whether served oven-fresh or at room temperature the next day, they always disappear.

3-1/4 cups all-purpose flour
1/4 cup sugar
1 package (1/4 ounce) active dry yeast
1 teaspoon grated lemon peel
1/2 teaspoon salt
1 cup milk
1/4 cup shortening
1 egg
FILLING:
1/2 cup packed brown sugar
1/2 cup raisins
1 teaspoon ground cinnamon
2 tablespoons butter *or* margarine, softened
Vanilla Glaze (recipe on page 89)

In a mixing bowl, combine 1-1/4 cups flour, sugar, yeast, lemon peel and salt. In a saucepan, heat milk and shortening to 120°-130°. Add to dry ingredients; beat until moistened. Add egg; beat on high speed for 3 minutes. Stir in enough remaining flour to form a soft dough. Do not knead. Cover and refrigerate for 2-24 hours. When ready to bake, let dough stand at room temperature for 10 minutes. Meanwhile, for filling, combine the brown sugar, raisins and cinnamon; set aside. On a lightly floured surface, roll dough into a 16-in. x 12-in. rectangle. Cut in half lengthwise; spread with butter. Sprinkle filling down the center third of each rectangle. Fold one long side of dough over filling, then fold other long side of dough over, forming a 16-in. x 2-in. rectangle. Pat lightly to flatten. Cut each rectangle into four 4-in. rolls. Line a baking sheet with foil and grease the foil. Place rolls, seam side down, 3 in. apart on foil. With a sharp knife, cut five strips two-thirds of the way through each roll. Separate each strip slightly, curving to form a fan shape. Cover and let rise in a warm place until doubled, about 45 minutes. Bake at 350° for 15-20 minutes or until lightly browned. Remove from pan to a wire rack to cool. Drizzle with Vanilla Glaze. **Yield:** 8 rolls.

BLUEBERRY PINWHEELS

Betsy Stoner, Elmira, New York

We grow fresh blueberries at our house, so these fruity rolls are a favorite of my family and our many guests. They also freeze and reheat well.

3-1/2 to 4 **cups all-purpose flour**
   1/4 **cup sugar**
     1 **package (1/4 ounce) active dry yeast**
     1 **teaspoon salt**
     2 **cans (5 ounces *each*) evaporated milk**
     6 **tablespoons butter *or* margarine, softened**
     1 **egg**
FILLING:
     3 **tablespoons butter *or* margarine, melted**
   1/2 **cup sugar**
1-1/2 to 2 **teaspoons ground cinnamon**
     1 **teaspoon grated lemon peel**
     2 **cups fresh *or* frozen blueberries***
GLAZE:
     1 **cup confectioners' sugar**
   1/2 **teaspoon vanilla extract**
    1 to 2 **tablespoons water**

In a mixing bowl, combine 1-1/2 cups flour, sugar, yeast and salt. In a saucepan, heat milk and butter to 120°-130°. Add to dry ingredients; beat until moistened. Add egg; beat on medium speed for 3 minutes. Stir in enough remaining flour to form a soft dough. Turn onto a floured surface; knead until smooth and elastic, about 6-8 minutes. Place in a greased bowl, turning once to grease top. Cover and let rise in a warm place until doubled, about 1-1/4 hours. Punch dough down. Turn onto a floured surface; divide in half. Roll each into a 14-in. x 8-in. rectangle; brush with melted butter. Combine sugar, cinnamon and lemon peel; sprinkle over dough to within 1/2 in. of edges. Top with blueberries; press in-

to dough. Roll up, jelly-roll style, starting with a long side; pinch seam to seal. Cut each into 12 slices. Place, cut side down, in two greased 13-in. x 9-in. x 2-in. baking pans. Cover and let rise until doubled, about 1-1/4 hours. Bake at 375° for 20-25 minutes or until golden brown. For glaze, combine sugar, vanilla and enough water to achieve a desired consistency. Drizzle over warm rolls. Cool in pans on wire racks. **Yield:** 2 dozen. *****Editor's Note:** If using frozen blueberries, do not thaw before adding to the batter.

CHEESE-FILLED COFFEE CAKES

Shirley Hartman, Colorado Springs, Colorado

I began collecting interesting recipes years ago when I had dreams of owning a bed-and-breakfast. I never met that goal but came away with flavorful recipes like this.

     2 **packages (1/4 ounce *each*) active dry yeast**
   1/2 **cup warm water (110° to 115°)**
     1 **cup (8 ounces) sour cream**
   1/2 **cup butter *or* margarine**
   1/2 **cup sugar**
     1 **teaspoon salt**
     2 **eggs**
4-1/2 **cups all-purpose flour**
FILLING:
     2 **packages (8 ounces *each*) cream cheese,**
       softened
   3/4 **cup sugar**
     1 **egg**
     1 **teaspoon almond extract**
   1/8 **teaspoon salt**
GLAZE:
     2 **cups confectioners' sugar**
     3 **tablespoons milk**
   1/2 **teaspoon vanilla extract**

In a mixing bowl, dissolve yeast in warm water. In a saucepan, heat sour cream and butter to 110°-115°. Add the sour cream mixture, sugar, salt and eggs to yeast mixture; mix well. Gradually add flour; mix well. Do not knead. Cover and refrigerate for 2 hours. In a mixing bowl, beat filling ingredients until smooth. Set aside. Turn dough onto a lightly floured surface; divide into four pieces. Roll each into a 12-in. x 8-in. rectangle. Spread filling to within 1/2 in. of edges. Roll up, jelly-roll style, starting with a long side; pinch seam to seal and tuck ends under. Place, seam side down, on two greased baking sheets. With a sharp knife, make deep slashes across the top of each loaf. Cover and let rise in a warm place until doubled, about 1 hour. Bake at 375° for 20-25 minutes or until golden brown. Remove from pans to wire racks. Combine glaze ingredients; drizzle over warm loaves. Cool. Refrigerate leftovers. **Yield:** 4 loaves.

PEACH FLIP

Helen Millhouse, Piqua, Ohio

I've used this recipe for years, especially as Christmas gifts for friends and neighbors. Everyone loves it.

> **2 packages (1/4 ounce *each*) active dry yeast**
> **1/2 cup warm water (110° to 115°)**
> **1/2 cup plus 2/3 cup sugar, *divided***
> **3/4 cup butter *or* margarine, softened, *divided***
> **1/2 cup warm milk (110° to 115°)**
> **2 teaspoons salt**
> **3 eggs**
> **5 to 5-1/2 cups all-purpose flour**
> **1 cup peach preserves**
> **1 cup chopped pecans**
> **2 teaspoons ground cinnamon**

In a mixing bowl, dissolve yeast in warm water. Add 1/2 cup sugar, 1/2 cup butter, milk, salt, eggs and 2-1/2 cups flour. Beat until smooth. Stir in enough remaining flour to form a stiff dough. Turn onto a floured surface; knead until smooth and elastic, about 6-8 minutes. Place in a greased bowl, turning once to grease top. Cover and let rise in a warm place until doubled, about 1-1/4 hours. Punch dough down. Turn onto a floured surface; divide in half. Roll each into a 24-in. x 13-in. rectangle; spread 2 tablespoons butter and 1/4 cup peach preserves to within 1/2 in. of edges. Combine the pecans, cinnamon and remaining sugar. Sprinkle over preserves. Roll up, jelly-roll style, starting with a long side; pinch seam to seal. Place, seam side down, on two greased baking sheets; curve each roll to form a crescent. With a sharp knife, make a lengthwise slash a third of the way through the center of each to within 2 in. of each end. Spoon 1/4 cup preserves into each roll. Bake at 350° for 20-25 minutes or until golden brown. Remove from pans to wire racks to cool. **Yield:** 2 loaves.

CARDAMOM BRAID

Roberta Moellenberg, Idalia, Colorado

I enjoy baking of any kind, but yeast breads are my favorite. This is appropriate since my husband and I raise wheat on the plains of eastern Colorado.

> **1 package (1/4 ounce) active dry yeast**
> **1/2 cup warm water (110° to 115°)**
> **1/2 cup warm evaporated milk (110° to 115°)**
> **1/2 cup sugar**
> **1/4 cup butter *or* margarine, softened**
> **2 eggs**
> **4-1/2 cups all-purpose flour**
> **1-1/2 to 2 teaspoons ground cardamom**
> **1 teaspoon salt**
> **Melted butter *or* margarine**

In a mixing bowl, dissolve yeast in warm water. Add the milk, sugar, butter, eggs and 1-3/4 cups flour. Beat until smooth. Combine cardamom, salt and remaining flour. Gradually add to dough (dough may seem sticky, but do not add more flour); mix well. Turn onto a lightly floured surface; knead until smooth and elastic, about 6-8 minutes. Place in a greased bowl, turning once to grease top. Cover with a damp cloth and let rise in a warm place until doubled, about 1-1/2 hours. Punch dough down. Turn onto a lightly floured surface; divide into thirds. Shape each into a 20-in. rope. Place three ropes on a greased baking sheet; braid. Pinch ends to seal and tuck under. Cover and let rise until doubled, about 1 hour. Bake at 375° for 25-30 minutes or until golden brown. Remove from pan to a wire rack. Brush with melted butter. Cool. **Yield:** 1 loaf.

BANANA NUT YEAST BREAD

Elizabeth Zesiger, Oroville, Washington

A friend gave me this recipe more than 30 years ago. She liked it because it requires no kneading but has the same terrific taste and aroma of traditional banana bread.

> **2 packages (1/4 ounce *each*) active dry yeast**
> **1/3 cup warm water (110° to 115°)**
> **1 cup mashed ripe bananas (2 to 3 medium)**
> **1/2 cup sugar**
> **1/3 cup warm milk (110° to 115°)**
> **1/3 cup butter *or* margarine, softened**
> **1/2 teaspoon salt**
> **2 eggs**
> **5 to 5-1/2 cups all-purpose flour**
> **1/2 cup chopped nuts**

In a mixing bowl, dissolve yeast in warm water. Add the bananas, sugar, milk, butter, salt, eggs and 3 cups flour. Beat on medium speed for 2 minutes. Stir in nuts. Stir in enough remaining flour to form a stiff batter. Do not knead. Spoon into two greased 9-in. x 5-in. x 3-in. loaf pans. Cover and let rise in a warm place until doubled, about 1-1/2 hours. Bake at 375° for 25-30 minutes or until a toothpick comes out clean. Remove from pans to wire racks to cool. **Yield:** 2 loaves.

HAWAIIAN SWEET BREAD

Ruthie Banks, Pryor, Oklahoma

The mother of a high school friend would make 13 of these lightly sweet loaves at a time! I make this bread year-round, but my family insists it's a "must" for the holidays.

7 to 7-1/2 cups all-purpose flour
3/4 cup mashed potato flakes
2/3 cup sugar
2 packages (1/4 ounce *each*) active dry yeast
1 teaspoon salt
1/2 teaspoon ground ginger
1 cup milk
1/2 cup water
1/2 cup butter *or* margarine, softened
1 cup pineapple juice
3 eggs
2 teaspoons vanilla extract

In a mixing bowl, combine 3 cups flour, potato flakes, sugar, yeast, salt and ginger. In a saucepan, heat the milk, water, butter and pineapple juice to 120°-130°. Add to dry ingredients; beat just until moistened. Add eggs, one at a time, beating well after each addition. Beat in vanilla. Stir in enough remaining flour to form a soft dough. Turn onto a floured surface; knead until smooth and elastic, about 6-8 minutes. Place in a greased bowl, turning once to grease top. Cover and let rise in a warm place until doubled, about 1-1/2 hours. Punch dough down. Turn onto a floured surface; divide into thirds. Shape each into a ball. Place in three greased 9-in. round baking pans. Cover and let rise until doubled, about 1 hour. Bake at 375° for 20-25 minutes or until golden brown. Cover loosely with foil if top browns too quickly. Remove from pans to wire racks to cool. **Yield:** 3 loaves.

APRICOT BRAID

Virginia Adams, Prosser, Washington

When I need to feed a crowd, this large lovely loaf comes in handy. Golden raisins and dried apricots give it a nicely sweet flavor while walnuts add a little crunch.

1 package (1/4 ounce) active dry yeast
1/4 cup warm water (110° to 115°)
1 cup warm milk (110° to 115°)
1/2 cup sugar
1/4 cup shortening
2 teaspoons salt
1 egg
1/2 cup chopped golden raisins
1/2 cup chopped dried apricots
1/4 cup chopped walnuts
1 teaspoon grated lemon peel
4-1/4 to 4-3/4 cups all-purpose flour
Vanilla Glaze (recipe on page 89)

In a mixing bowl, dissolve yeast in warm water. Add the milk, sugar, shortening and salt; beat until smooth. Add the egg, raisins, apricots, walnuts, lemon peel and 1 cup flour; mix well. Stir in enough remaining flour to form a soft dough. Turn onto a floured surface; knead until smooth and elastic, about 6-8 minutes.

Place in a greased bowl, turning once to grease top. Cover and let rise in a warm place until doubled, about 1-1/4 hours. Punch dough down. Turn onto a lightly floured surface; divide into five pieces. Shape each into an 18-in. rope. Place three ropes on a greased baking sheet; braid. Pinch ends to seal and tuck under. Twist the two remaining ropes together. Pinch ends to seal. Place on top of braid; tuck ends under. Cover and let rise until doubled, about 1 hour. Bake at 350° for 40-45 minutes or until golden brown. Remove from pan to a wire rack to cool. Drizzle with Vanilla Glaze. **Yield:** 1 loaf.

HOT CROSS BUNS

Rose Marie Dehner, Knox, Pennsylvania

These traditional buns with a delicate orange flavor are always on our Easter menu. But my family enjoys them so much that I also prepare them throughout the year.

2 packages (1/4 ounce *each*) active dry yeast
1/2 cup warm water (110° to 115°)
3/4 cup warm milk (110° to 115°)
1/2 cup sugar
1/3 cup butter *or* margarine, melted
1 teaspoon salt
1 teaspoon ground cinnamon
1/2 teaspoon ground allspice
3 eggs
3/4 cup raisins
1 tablespoon grated lemon peel
1 tablespoon grated orange peel
4-1/2 cups all-purpose flour
1 tablespoon cold water
ICING:
1 cup confectioners' sugar
1-1/2 teaspoons butter *or* margarine, softened
1/4 teaspoon vanilla extract
3 to 4 teaspoons milk

In a mixing bowl, dissolve yeast in warm water. Add the milk, sugar, butter, salt, cinnamon and allspice; mix well. Beat in 2 eggs. Stir in raisins, lemon and orange peel and enough flour to form a soft dough. Turn onto a floured surface; knead until smooth and elastic, about 10 minutes. Place in a greased bowl, turning once to grease top. Cover and let rise in a warm place until doubled, about 1 hour. Punch dough down. Turn onto a lightly floured surface; divide into 24 pieces. Shape each into a ball. Place 2 in. apart on greased baking sheets. Cover and let rise until doubled, about 30 minutes. Beat remaining egg with water; brush over rolls. Bake at 375° for 20-25 minutes or until browned. Remove from pans to wire racks to cool. For icing, combine sugar, butter, vanilla and enough milk to achieve a piping consistency. Pipe an "X" on top of each bun. **Yield:** 2 dozen.

Biscuits and Beyond

Hand-held goodies like biscuits, doughnuts, scones, breadsticks and pretzels may be small in size, but they're big on flavor!

DOUBLE ORANGE SCONES

Margaret Frayser, Linton, Indiana

(Pictured at left)

I first used this recipe several years ago for a church break-fast and received rave reviews. Orange butter adds the perfect finishing touch on each hearty bite.

- 1 cup all-purpose flour
- 1 cup whole wheat flour
- 3 tablespoons sugar
- 2-1/2 teaspoons baking powder
- 2 teaspoons grated orange peel
- 1/4 teaspoon salt
- 1/3 cup cold butter *or* margarine
- 1/3 cup milk
- 1 egg
- 1/2 cup chopped mandarin oranges, well drained
- Additional sugar

ORANGE BUTTER:
- 1/2 cup butter (no substitutes), softened
- 2 tablespoons orange marmalade

In a bowl, combine the first six ingredients. Cut in butter until mixture resembles coarse crumbs. In a bowl, whisk milk and egg; add to dry ingredients. Stir in oranges just until moistened. Turn onto a floured surface; knead 10 times. Pat into a 6-in. circle. Sprinkle with additional sugar. Cut into eight wedges. Separate wedges and place on a greased baking sheet. Bake at 400° for 15-20 minutes or until golden brown. Meanwhile, in a small mixing bowl, beat butter and marmalade until fluffy. Serve with warm scones. **Yield:** 8 scones.

MASHED POTATO DOUGHNUTS

Tammy Evans, Nepean, Ontario

(Pictured at left)

As a special treat in winter, my parents would make a double batch of these doughnuts to welcome us six kids home from school. This recipe from my great-aunt has been handed down through the generations.

- 1 package (1/4 ounce) active dry yeast
- 1 cup warm buttermilk (110° to 115°)*
- 3 cups sugar, *divided*
- 3 eggs
- 1-1/2 cups warm mashed potatoes (without added milk or butter)
- 1/3 cup butter *or* margarine, melted
- 6 cups all-purpose flour
- 4 teaspoons baking powder
- 1-1/2 teaspoons baking soda
- 1 teaspoon salt
- 1 teaspoon ground nutmeg
- Oil for deep-fat frying
- 1/2 teaspoon ground cinnamon

In a mixing bowl, dissolve yeast in warm buttermilk. Add 2 cups sugar and eggs; beat well. Add potatoes and butter; mix well. Add flour, baking powder, baking soda, salt and nutmeg; mix well. Do not knead. Cover and refrigerate for 2 hours. Turn onto a floured surface; divide into fourths. Roll each portion to 1/2-in. thickness. Cut with a floured 3-in. doughnut cutter. In an electric skillet or deep-fat fryer, heat oil to 375°. Fry doughnuts, a few at a time, until golden brown on both sides. Drain on paper towels. Combine remaining sugar and cinnamon; roll doughnuts in cinnamon-sugar while warm. **Yield:** about 2 dozen. *Editor's Note:** Warmed buttermilk will appear curdled.

SWEET AND SAVORY. Pictured at left, top to bottom: Mashed Potato Doughnuts (recipe on this page), Soft Italian Bread Twists (recipe on page 96) and Double Orange Scones (recipe on this page).

BETTER BISCUITS

- *For the flakiest biscuits, use a pastry blender or fork to thoroughly cut shortening into the dry ingredients. Don't over-mix or overknead the dough.*
- *Roll or pat the dough to an even thickness so that the biscuits will be more attractive and bake evenly.*
- *Dip the biscuit cutter into flour after each cut to prevent sticking. Press the floured cutter into the dough and lift straight up; don't twist it.*
- *To keep the dough from turning tough and dry, handle it as little as possible when reworking the trimmings and use as little additional flour as needed on the working surface.*
- *Bake biscuits until golden brown on the top and bottom. The sides will be a little lighter.*

Soft Italian Bread Twists

Marcia Rand, Adams, Nebraska

(Pictured above and on page 94)

Although my heritage is strictly Dutch, my family loves Italian food. These seasoned breadsticks are a great accompaniment to lasagna or pizza.

    1 teaspoon sugar
    1 teaspoon salt, *divided*
    1 package (1/4 ounce) quick-rise yeast
  2 to 2-1/2 cups all-purpose flour
  2/3 cup warm water (120° to 130°)
    1 tablespoon vegetable oil
    3 tablespoons butter *or* margarine, melted
  1/2 teaspoon garlic powder
  1/4 teaspoon paprika
Italian seasoning *or* grated Parmesan cheese,
  optional

In a food processor, combine the sugar, 3/4 teaspoon salt, yeast and 2 cups flour. Cover and process for 5-10 seconds. While processing, gradually add warm water and oil in a steady stream. Process for 1 minute or until smooth and elastic. Check dough; add 1 to 2 tablespoons of water or flour if needed. Turn onto a floured surface. Roll into a 15-in. x 12-in. rectangle. Cut into 12 strips. Fold each strip in half lengthwise; twist each strip several times. Pinch ends to seal. Place 2 in. apart on a greased baking sheet. In a bowl, combine butter, garlic powder, paprika and remaining salt. Brush some over dough. Sprinkle with Italian seasoning or Parmesan cheese if desired. Cover and let rise in a warm place until doubled, about 25 minutes. Bake at 425° for 6-8 minutes or until golden brown. Brush with remaining butter mixture. **Yield:** 1 dozen.

Frosted Cinnamon-Raisin Biscuits

Deb Lusby, Sunbury, Pennsylvania

I created this recipe several years ago after sampling something similar at a popular chain restaurant. These easy drop biscuits are a great accompaniment to a country-style breakfast.

  2 cups all-purpose flour
  1/4 cup sugar
    2 teaspoons baking powder
    1 teaspoon salt
  1/4 teaspoon baking soda
  1/3 cup shortening
  2/3 cup buttermilk
  1/3 cup raisins
1-1/2 teaspoons ground cinnamon
FROSTING:
1-1/2 cups confectioners' sugar
    2 tablespoons butter *or* margarine, softened
1-1/2 teaspoons vanilla extract
    3 to 5 teaspoons warm water

In a bowl, combine the first five ingredients; cut in shortening until mixture resembles coarse crumbs. Stir in buttermilk just until moistened. Turn onto a floured surface; sprinkle with raisins and cinnamon. Knead 8-10 times (cinnamon will have a marbled appearance). Drop batter into 12 mounds 2 in. apart on a greased baking sheet. Bake at 425° for 12-16 minutes or until golden brown. For frosting, combine the sugar, butter, vanilla and enough water to achieve desired consistency. Frost warm biscuits. Serve immediately. **Yield:** 1 dozen.

Long Johns

Twilla Eisele, Wellsville, Kansas

The tattered recipe in my files is a good indication of how popular these doughnuts have been in our family over the years. They disappear in a hurry, so I typically double the recipe.

    1 package (1/4 ounce) active dry yeast
  1/4 cup warm water (110° to 115°)
    1 cup warm milk (120° to 130°)
  1/4 cup butter *or* margarine, softened
  1/4 cup sugar
  1/2 teaspoon salt
    1 egg
3-1/4 to 3-3/4 cups all-purpose flour
Oil for deep-fat frying
GLAZE:
1-1/4 cups confectioners' sugar
    1 tablespoon brown sugar
    1 tablespoon water
  1/2 teaspoon vanilla extract
  1/8 teaspoon salt

In a mixing bowl, dissolve yeast in warm water. Add the milk, butter, sugar, salt and egg; mix well. Stir in enough flour to form a soft dough. Do not knead. Place in a greased bowl, turning once to grease top. Cover and let rise in a warm place until doubled, about 1 hour. Punch dough down. Turn onto a lightly floured surface; roll into a 12-in. x 8-in. rectangle. Cut into 3 in. x 1-in. rectangles. Place on greased baking sheets. Cover and let rise in a warm place until doubled, about 30 minutes. In an electric skillet or deep-fat fryer, heat oil to 400°. Fry doughnuts, a few at a time, until golden brown on both sides. Drain on paper towels. Combine glaze ingredients; brush over warm long johns. **Yield:** 2-1/2 dozen.

CHEDDAR PUFF BISCUITS

Mary Burrows, Rome, New York

This is one of my favorite biscuit recipes because it's fast, simple and doesn't require any special ingredients. I sometimes freeze some baked puffs, then reheat in foil.

    1/2 cup milk
      2 tablespoons butter *or* margarine
    1/2 cup all-purpose flour
      2 eggs
    1/2 cup shredded cheddar cheese
    1/4 cup chopped onion
    1/4 teaspoon garlic powder
    1/4 teaspoon pepper

In a saucepan, bring milk and butter to a boil. Add flour all at once and stir until a smooth ball forms. Remove from the heat; let stand for 5 minutes. Add eggs, one at a time, beating well after each addition. Add the cheese, onion, garlic powder and pepper; beat until mixture is smooth and shiny. Drop by rounded teaspoonfuls 2 in. apart onto greased baking sheets. Bake at 350° for 25-30 minutes or until golden brown. Serve warm. Refrigerate leftovers. **Yield:** about 2 dozen.

CRUMPETS

Carol Craig, Summerville, Oregon

I save clean water chestnut and pineapple cans so I can make crumpets whenever my family requests them. (You can also use a circle cookie cutter or mason jar ring.) I first made these for a 4-H project.

      1 package (1/4 ounce) active dry yeast
    1/4 cup warm water (110° to 115°)
      1 teaspoon sugar
    1/3 cup warm milk (110° to 115°)
      4 tablespoons butter *or* margarine, melted, *divided*
      1 egg
      1 cup all-purpose flour
    1/2 teaspoon salt

In a mixing bowl, dissolve yeast in warm water. Add sugar; let stand for 5 minutes. Add the milk, 1 table-

spoon butter and egg; mix well. Add flour and salt; beat until smooth. Cover and let rise in a warm place until doubled, about 45 minutes. Brush griddle and 3-in. metal rings or open-topped metal cookie cutters with remaining butter. Place rings on griddle; heat over low heat. Pour 3 tablespoons of batter into each ring. Cook for 7 minutes or until bubbles begin to pop and the top appears dry. Remove rings. Turn crumpets; cook 1-2 minutes longer or until the second side is golden brown. Serve warm or let cool on a wire rack and toast before serving. **Yield:** 8 crumpets.

STICKY APPLE BISCUITS

Edna Hoffman, Hebron, Indiana

Instead of the typical drop or cut biscuits, this hearty version is rolled up like a cinnamon roll. Tender apples, crunchy pecans and sweet honey make these a wonderful breakfast treat.

    1/4 cup honey
    1/4 cup packed brown sugar
      2 tablespoons butter *or* margarine, melted
      2 tablespoons water
    1/3 cup pecan halves
  BISCUITS:
      2 cups all-purpose flour
      2 teaspoons baking powder
    1/2 teaspoon salt
    1/2 teaspoon ground cinnamon
      3 tablespoons shortening
      3 tablespoons cold butter *or* margarine
    2/3 cup milk
    1/2 cup diced peeled tart apple
  FILLING:
      3 tablespoons butter *or* margarine, softened
      2 tablespoons applesauce
      1 tablespoon honey
    1/4 cup packed brown sugar
      3 tablespoons raisins

In a small bowl, combine the honey, brown sugar, butter and water. Divide between 12 greased muffin cups. Sprinkle with pecans; set aside. In a large bowl, combine the flour, baking powder, salt and cinnamon. Cut in shortening and butter until mixture resembles coarse crumbs. Stir in milk and apple just until moistened. Turn onto a floured surface. Pat into a 10-in. x 8-in. rectangle, about 1/2 in. thick. Spread with butter, then applesauce; drizzle with honey. Sprinkle with brown sugar and raisins. Roll up, jelly-roll style, starting with a long side. Cut into 12 biscuits. Place, cut side down, over pecan mixture in muffin cups. Bake at 425° for 20-25 minutes or until golden brown. Cool for 1 minute before inverting onto a serving platter. Serve warm. **Yield:** 1 dozen.

SAGE CORNMEAL BISCUITS

Mary Kincaid, Bostic, North Carolina

My family loves these outstanding savory biscuits with eggs and sausage at breakfast or with meats at dinner. They bake up light and tender and have just the right amount of sage.

1-1/2 cups all-purpose flour
  1/2 cup cornmeal
    3 teaspoons baking powder
  1/2 to 3/4 teaspoon rubbed sage
  1/2 teaspoon salt
  1/3 cup shortening
  3/4 cup milk

In a bowl, combine the first five ingredients. Cut in shortening until mixture resembles coarse crumbs. Stir in milk just until moistened. Turn onto a lightly floured surface. Roll to 3/4-in. thickness; cut with a floured 2-in. biscuit cutter. Place 2 in. apart on an ungreased baking sheet. Bake at 450° for 10-12 minutes or until browned. Serve warm. **Yield:** 10 biscuits.

MOM'S BUTTERMILK BISCUITS

Judith Rush, Katy, Texas

Rich buttermilk biscuits baking in the oven will bring back warm memories of your own mom's kitchen. These have a classic old-fashioned flavor that's stood the test of time. You can make them with little effort.

    2 cups all-purpose flour
2-1/4 teaspoons baking powder
  3/4 teaspoon salt
  1/4 teaspoon baking soda
  1/3 cup shortening
  3/4 cup buttermilk

In a large bowl, combine the dry ingredients. Cut in shortening until mixture resembles coarse crumbs. Stir in buttermilk just until moistened. Turn onto a lightly floured surface. Roll to 1/2-in. thickness; cut with a floured 2-1/2-in. biscuit cutter. Place 1 in. apart on an ungreased baking sheet. Bake at 450° for 8-10 minutes or until golden brown. Serve warm. **Yield:** 1 dozen.

WHOLE WHEAT PITA BREAD

Ruby Witmer, Goshen, Indiana

After a trip to Israel, I fell in love with the rustic pita breads enjoyed with just about every meal. These nutritious whole wheat pitas are a favorite with young and old alike.

  2 packages (1/4 ounce *each*) active dry yeast
  2 cups warm water (110° to 115°), *divided*
  1/2 teaspoon honey
  1/4 cup olive *or* vegetable oil
    1 tablespoon salt
    5 to 6 cups whole wheat flour
All-purpose flour
Cornmeal

In a mixing bowl, dissolve yeast in 1/2 cup warm water. Add honey; let stand for 5 minutes. Add the oil, salt and remaining water; mix well. Stir in enough whole wheat flour to form a soft dough. Turn onto a surface dusted with all-purpose flour; knead until smooth and elastic, about 6-8 minutes. Place in a greased bowl, turning once to grease top. Cover and let rise in a warm place until doubled, about 1-1/2 hours. Punch dough down; let rest for 10 minutes. Turn onto a lightly floured surface; divide dough into 12 pieces. Shape each into a ball. Knead each ball for 1 minute. Cover and let rest for 20 minutes. Grease baking sheets and sprinkle with cornmeal. Roll each ball into an 8-in. circle. Place on prepared baking sheets. Cover and let rise in a warm place until doubled, about 30 minutes. Bake at 475° for 8-10 minutes or until browned. Remove from pans to wire racks to cool. To serve, cut in half and split open. Stuff with fillings of your choice. **Yield:** 1 dozen.

PEPPERY HUSH PUPPIES

Carolyn Griffin, Macon, Georgia

For our family, a good fish dinner just isn't complete without these zesty hush puppies. You can also serve them alone as a satisfying snack.

    2 cups cornmeal
    1 cup plus 3 tablespoons all-purpose flour
    2 teaspoons baking powder
1-1/2 teaspoons sugar
    1 teaspoon salt
  1/2 teaspoon baking soda
    1 egg
  2/3 cup water
  1/2 cup buttermilk
  1/2 cup butter *or* margarine, melted
    1 cup grated onion
    2 jalapeno peppers, seeded and chopped*
    1 small green pepper, chopped
Oil for deep-fat frying

In a bowl, combine the cornmeal, flour, baking powder, sugar, salt and baking soda. In another bowl, beat the egg, water, buttermilk and butter. Stir in onion, jalapenos and green pepper. Stir into dry ingredients just until moistened. In an electric skillet or deep-fat fryer, heat oil to 375°. Drop batter by teaspoonfuls, a few at a time, into hot oil. Fry until golden brown on both sides. Drain on paper towels. Serve warm. **Yield:** 5 dozen. *****Editor's Note:** When cutting or seeding hot peppers, use rubber or plastic gloves to protect your hands. Avoid touching your face.

BACON ONION BREADSTICKS

Michelle Buerge, Ithaca, Michigan

With a delicious blend of bacon, butter and onion, these soft breadsticks are hard to resist. Our family enjoys them with soup and salad.

    2 tablespoons active dry yeast
    2 cups warm milk (110° to 115°), *divided*
    1 teaspoon sugar
1/2 cup butter *or* margarine, melted
1-1/4 teaspoons salt, *divided*
5-1/2 to 6 cups all-purpose flour
    1 pound sliced bacon, diced
    1 medium onion, chopped
1/4 teaspoon pepper
    1 egg, beaten
Coarse salt

In a mixing bowl, dissolve yeast in 1 cup warm milk. Add sugar; let stand for 5 minutes. Add butter, 1 teaspoon salt and remaining milk; mix well. Stir in enough flour to form a soft dough. Turn onto a floured surface; knead until smooth and elastic, about 6-8 minutes. Place in a greased bowl, turning once to grease top. Cover and let rise in a warm place until doubled, about 1-1/2 hours. Meanwhile, in a skillet, saute bacon and onion until bacon is crisp; drain. Add pepper and remaining salt. Cool completely. Punch dough down. Turn onto a floured surface; knead bacon mixture into dough. Roll dough into a 14-in. square. Brush with egg; sprinkle with coarse salt. Cut dough in half lengthwise and in thirds crosswise. Cut each section into six strips. Place 2 in. apart on greased baking sheets. Cover and let rise in a warm place until doubled, about 30 minutes. Bake at 375° for 15-20 minutes or until golden brown. Remove from pans to wire racks to cool. **Yield:** 3 dozen.

LEMON BLUEBERRY DROP SCONES

Jacqueline Hendershot, Orange, California

I enjoy serving these fruity scones for baby and bridal showers. They're a bit lower in fat than other scone recipes, so you can indulge with little guilt.

    2 cups all-purpose flour
1/3 cup sugar
    2 teaspoons baking powder
    1 teaspoon grated lemon peel
1/2 teaspoon baking soda
1/4 teaspoon salt
    1 cup (8 ounces) lemon yogurt
    1 egg
1/4 cup butter *or* margarine, melted
    1 cup fresh *or* frozen blueberries*
GLAZE:
1/2 cup confectioners' sugar
    1 tablespoon lemon juice
1/2 teaspoon grated lemon peel

In a large bowl, combine the first six ingredients. In another bowl, combine the yogurt, egg and butter. Stir into dry ingredients just until moistened. Fold in blueberries. Drop by heaping tablespoonfuls 2 in. apart onto a greased baking sheet. Bake at 400° for 15-18 minutes or until lightly browned. Combine glaze ingredients; drizzle over warm scones. **Yield:** 14 scones. *****Editor's Note:** If using frozen blueberries, do not thaw before adding to the batter.

NEW YEAR'S RAISIN FRITTERS

Jaycille Zart, Kamloops, British Columbia

Folks who like raisins will love these fritters, which have been a traditional New Year's treat in our family for at least five generations. Dipping warm fritters in sugar makes them extra special.

    1 tablespoon active dry yeast
1/2 cup warm water (110° to 115°)
    2 teaspoons plus 1/4 cup sugar, *divided*
    2 cups warm milk (110° to 115°)
1/4 cup butter *or* margarine, melted
1-1/2 teaspoons salt
    2 eggs
    4 to 4-1/2 cups all-purpose flour
    1 package (15 ounces) raisins
Oil for deep-fat frying
Additional sugar

In a mixing bowl, dissolve yeast in warm water. Add 2 teaspoons sugar; let stand for 5 minutes. Add milk, butter, salt, eggs and remaining sugar; mix well. Stir in enough flour to form a thick batter. Stir in raisins. Cover and let rise in a warm place until doubled, about 1 hour. Stir down batter; cover and let rise again until doubled. In an electric skillet or deep-fat fryer, heat oil to 375°. Drop batter by tablespoonfuls, a few at a time, into hot oil. Fry until golden brown on both sides. Drain on paper towels. Roll in additional sugar while warm. **Yield:** 6 dozen.

SOFT PRETZELS

Lucinda Walker, Somerset, Pennsylvania

(Pictured at left)

Big soft pretzels are all the rage in shopping malls across the country. I think it's worth the time to make them from scratch to get the incomparable homemade taste.

   2 packages (1/4 ounce *each*) active dry yeast
   2 cups warm water (110° to 115°)
   1/2 cup sugar
   1/4 cup butter *or* margarine, softened
   2 teaspoons salt
   1 egg
6-1/2 to 7-1/2 cups all-purpose flour
   1 egg yolk
   2 tablespoons cold water
Coarse salt

In a mixing bowl, dissolve yeast in warm water. Add the sugar, butter, salt, egg and 2 cups flour. Beat until smooth. Stir in enough remaining flour to form a stiff dough. Place in a greased bowl, turning once to grease top. Cover and refrigerate for 2-24 hours. Punch dough down. Turn onto a lightly floured surface; divide in half. Cut each into 16 pieces. Roll each piece into a 20-in. rope. Shape into a pretzel. Place on greased baking sheets. Beat egg yolk and cold water; brush over pretzels. Sprinkle with coarse salt. Cover and let rise in a warm place until doubled, about 25 minutes. Bake at 400° for 15-20 minutes or until golden brown. Remove from pans to wire racks to cool. **Yield:** 32 pretzels.

CHEESY DROP BISCUITS

Milly Heaton, Richmond, Indiana

(Pictured at left)

I wanted to capture the flavor of cheese biscuits from a popular restaurant. So I took my favorite buttermilk biscuit recipe and added to it.

   2 cups all-purpose flour
   2 teaspoons baking powder
   1 teaspoon salt
1/4 teaspoon baking soda
1/4 teaspoon garlic powder
   1 cup (4 ounces) shredded cheddar cheese
1/4 cup grated Parmesan cheese
2/3 cup buttermilk
1/3 cup vegetable oil
Additional Parmesan cheese, optional

In a large bowl, combine the first five ingredients. Add cheeses. In a small bowl, combine buttermilk and oil. Stir into dry ingredients just until moistened. Drop by 1/4 cupfuls 2 in. apart onto a greased baking sheet. Sprinkle with additional Parmesan cheese if desired. Bake at 450° for 10-12 minutes or until golden brown. Serve warm. Refrigerate leftovers. **Yield:** about 1 dozen.

COUNTRY SCONES

Martha Plassmeyer, St. Elizabeth, Missouri

(Pictured at left)

These tempting triangles perfectly balance a light and airy texture with a rich and moist flavor. I serve them frequently for breakfast with fresh fruit, coffee and juice.

   3/4 cup dried currants *or* raisins
   2 cups all-purpose flour
   3 tablespoons sugar
   2 teaspoons baking powder
3/4 teaspoon salt
1/2 teaspoon baking soda
   5 tablespoons cold butter *or* margarine
   1 cup (8 ounces) sour cream
   2 egg yolks
TOPPING:
   1 egg white
   1 teaspoon sugar
1/8 teaspoon ground cinnamon

Place currants in a bowl. Cover with hot water and let stand for 5 minutes. Drain well and set aside. In a bowl, combine the flour, sugar, baking powder, salt and baking soda. Cut in butter until mixture resembles coarse crumbs. Combine sour cream and egg yolks; add to crumb mixture. Stir in currants just until blended. Turn onto a floured surface; knead gently 8-10 times. Pat into a 9-in. circle. Cut dough into 4-in. circles; place on ungreased baking sheets. Cut each into four wedges but do not separate. Beat egg white; brush over dough. Combine sugar and cinnamon; sprinkle over tops. Bake at 425° for 15-18 minutes or until golden brown. Serve warm. **Yield:** about 1-1/2 dozen.

PRETZEL PARTNERS

- *Instead of simply sprinkling homemade pretzels with coarse salt before baking, try topping with sesame or poppy seeds.*
- *Brush plain, just-baked pretzels with melted butter, then sprinkle with grated Parmesan cheese, Cajun seasoning or cinnamon-sugar.*
- *Serve savory pretzels alongside cheese sauce or vegetable dips like ranch, spinach and French onion.*

LUSCIOUS LITTLE BREADS. Pictured at left, top to bottom: Soft Pretzels, Cheesy Drop Biscuits and Country Scones (recipes on this page).

Buttery Oatmeal Breadsticks

Joan Hansen, Forest City, Iowa

I grew up on a South Dakota farm and watched my mother bake all the bread for our family of 10. The aroma of freshly baked bread often welcomed us home and is a memory I'll always treasure.

>   3 cups all-purpose flour
>   1 tablespoon sugar
>   1 package (1/4 ounce) active dry yeast
>   1/2 teaspoon salt
> 1-1/4 cups water
>   2 tablespoons butter *or* margarine
>   1 cup quick-cooking oats
> **Melted butter *or* margarine**

In a mixing bowl, combine 1-1/2 cups flour, sugar, yeast and salt. In a saucepan, heat water and butter to 120°-130°. Add to dry ingredients; beat on low speed for 30 seconds. Beat on high for 3 minutes. Stir in oats and enough remaining flour to form a soft dough. Turn onto a floured surface; knead until smooth and elastic, about 6-8 minutes. Place in a greased bowl, turning once to grease top. Cover and let rise in a warm place until doubled, about 1 hour. Punch dough down. Let rest for 10 minutes. Turn onto a lightly floured surface; divide into 24 pieces. Shape each into a 10-in. rope that is 1/2 in. thick. Place 2 in. apart on greased baking sheets. Cover and let rise in a warm place until doubled, about 30 minutes. Bake at 375° for 20-25 minutes or until golden brown. Brush with melted butter. **Yield:** 2 dozen.

Homemade Bagels

Rebecca Phillips, Burlington, Connecticut

I always wanted to make my own bagels, so I searched to find a recipe I could try. For variation and flavor, I sometimes add cinnamon and raisins or honey and sesame seeds to the dough.

>   1 teaspoon active dry yeast
> 1-1/4 cups warm milk (110° to 115°)
>   1/4 cup butter *or* margarine, softened
>   2 tablespoons sugar
>   1 teaspoon salt
>   1 egg yolk
> 3-3/4 to 4-1/4 cups all-purpose flour

In a mixing bowl, dissolve yeast in warm milk. Add the butter, sugar, salt and egg yolk; mix well. Stir in enough flour to form a soft dough. Turn onto a floured surface; knead until smooth and elastic, about 6-8 minutes. Place in a greased bowl, turning once to grease top. Cover and let rise in a warm place until doubled, about 1 hour. Punch dough down. Shape into 12 balls. Push thumb through centers to form a 1-in. hole. Place on

a floured surface. Cover and let rest for 10 minutes; flatten. In a large saucepan, bring water to a boil. Drop bagels, one at a time, into boiling water. When bagels float to the surface, remove with a slotted spoon and place 2 in. apart on greased baking sheets. Bake at 400° for 20-25 minutes or until golden brown. Remove from pans to wire racks to cool. **Yield:** 1 dozen.

Baking Powder Drop Biscuits

Sharon Evans, Rockwell, Iowa

One day I had company coming and realized I had run out of biscuit mix. I'd never made biscuits from scratch before, but I decided to give this recipe a try. Now this is the only way I make them!

>   2 cups all-purpose flour
>   2 tablespoons sugar
>   4 teaspoons baking powder
> 1/2 teaspoon cream of tartar
> 1/2 teaspoon salt
> 1/2 cup shortening
> 2/3 cup milk
>   1 egg

In a bowl, combine the first five ingredients. Cut in shortening until the mixture resembles coarse crumbs. In a bowl, whisk milk and egg. Stir into crumb mixture just until moistened. Drop by heaping spoonfuls 2 in. apart onto an ungreased baking sheet. Bake at 450° for 10-12 minutes or until golden brown. Serve warm. **Yield:** 1 dozen.

New Orleans Beignets

Beth Dawson, Jackson, Louisiana

These sweet French doughnuts are square instead of round and have no hole in the middle. They're a traditional part of breakfasts in New Orleans.

>   1 package (1/4 ounce) active dry yeast
> 1/4 cup warm water (110° to 115°)
>   1 cup evaporated milk
> 1/2 cup vegetable oil
> 1/4 cup sugar
>   1 egg
> 4-1/2 cups self-rising flour*
> **Oil for deep-fat frying**
> **Confectioners' sugar**

In a mixing bowl, dissolve yeast in warm water. Add the milk, oil, sugar and egg; mix well. Add flour; mix to form a soft dough (dough will be sticky). Do not knead. Cover and refrigerate overnight. Punch dough down. Turn onto a floured surface; roll into a 16-in. x 12-in. rectangle. Cut into 2-in. squares. In an electric skillet or deep-fat fryer, heat oil to 375°. Fry squares, a few at a time, until golden brown on both sides. Drain on paper towels. Roll warm beignets in confectioners' sugar. **Yield:** 4 dozen. *****Editor's Note:** As a substitute for *each* cup of self-rising flour, place 1-1/2 teaspoons baking powder and 1/2 teaspoon salt in a measuring cup. Add all-purpose flour to measure 1 cup. For 1/2 cup self-rising flour, use 3/4 teaspoon baking powder, 1/4 teaspoon salt and a 1/2-cup measuring cup. Add all-purpose flour to measure 1/2 cup.

GARLIC POTATO BISCUITS

Diane Hixon, Niceville, Florida

We grow our own potatoes and garlic, so these delectable biscuits are on our table often. I make biscuits a lot because they're quicker and easier than rolls.

> 1/2 pound diced peeled potatoes (about 1 large)
> 3 to 4 garlic cloves, peeled
> 1/3 cup butter *or* margarine, softened
> 1 teaspoon salt
> 1/4 teaspoon pepper
> 2 cups all-purpose flour
> 1 tablespoon baking powder
> 1/3 cup milk

Place potatoes and garlic cloves in a saucepan. Add enough water to cover. Bring to a boil. Reduce heat; cover and simmer until tender. Drain well. Mash potatoes and garlic with butter, salt and pepper. In a bowl, combine flour and baking powder; stir in potato mixture until mixture resembles coarse crumbs. Add milk and stir well. Turn onto a lightly floured surface. Roll to 1/2-in. thickness; cut with a floured 2-in. biscuit cutter. Place 1 in. apart on an ungreased baking sheet. Bake at 450° for 10-12 minutes or until golden brown. Serve warm. **Yield:** 15 biscuits.

PINEAPPLE DROP DOUGHNUTS

Deanna Richter, Elmore, Minnesota

These light, cake-like treats warm you up on a cold winter morning. They satisfy your hunger for doughnuts with less effort and time.

> 3 cups all-purpose flour
> 3/4 cup sugar
> 2 tablespoons baking powder
> 3/4 teaspoon salt

> 3 eggs
> 1 cup milk
> 1 can (20 ounces) crushed pineapple, drained
> **Oil for deep-fat frying**
> **Confectioners' sugar**

In a large bowl, combine the flour, sugar, baking powder and salt. In another bowl, beat eggs and milk. Stir in pineapple. Stir into dry ingredients just until blended. In an electric skillet or deep-fat fryer, heat oil to 375°. Drop batter by heaping teaspoonfuls, a few at a time, into hot oil. Fry until golden brown, about 1-1/2 minutes on each side. Drain on paper towels. Dust with confectioners' sugar. **Yield:** about 10 dozen. **Editor's Note:** Doughnuts may be frozen in an airtight container for up to 1 month. To reheat, place on a microwave-safe plate and microwave on high for 5-10 seconds or until warm. Dust with confectioners' sugar.

CINNAMON CHIP RAISIN SCONES

Mary Ann Morgan, Cedartown, Georgia

This creative recipe features raisins and homemade cinnamon "chips" to produce rich, mouth-watering scones. I think they're best served warm with lemon curd or butter and jelly.

CINNAMON CHIPS:
> 3 tablespoons sugar
> 2 teaspoons shortening
> 2 teaspoons corn syrup
> 1 tablespoon ground cinnamon

SCONES:
> 1-2/3 cups bread *or* all-purpose flour
> 2 tablespoons sugar
> 2 teaspoons baking powder
> 1/2 teaspoon salt
> 1/3 cup cold butter *or* margarine
> 1/2 cup evaporated milk
> 1/2 cup raisins

Additional evaporated milk

In a bowl, combine the sugar, shortening, corn syrup and cinnamon with a fork until crumbly and evenly blended. Spread onto a foil-lined baking sheet. Bake at 250° for 30-40 minutes or until melted and bubbly. Cool completely; break into small pieces. In a bowl, combine the flour, sugar, baking powder and salt. Cut in butter until the mixture resembles coarse crumbs. Stir in milk just until moistened. Gently stir in raisins and cinnamon chips. Turn onto a lightly floured surface. Roll to 1/2-in. thickness; cut with a floured 2-in. biscuit cutter. Line a baking sheet with foil and grease the foil. Place scones 1 in. apart on foil. Brush tops lightly with additional milk. Bake at 400° for 14-16 minutes or until golden brown. Serve warm. **Yield:** 15 scones.

PUFFY SOPAIPILLAS

Deanna Naivar, Temple, Texas

Our teenage son requests these sweet doughnut puffs for dessert whenever we have enchiladas. They're similar to sopaipillas we used to enjoy at a favorite Mexican restaurant.

    1 teaspoon active dry yeast
3/4 cup warm water (110° to 115°)
1/2 cup warm evaporated milk (110° to 115°)
1/4 cup sugar
    2 tablespoons shortening
1/2 teaspoon salt
    1 egg
3-3/4 cups all-purpose flour
Oil for deep-fat frying
Honey, optional

In a mixing bowl, dissolve yeast in warm water. Add the milk, sugar, shortening, salt, egg and 2 cups flour. Beat until smooth. Stir in enough remaining flour to form a soft dough. Do not knead. Cover and refrigerate for 2-24 hours. Turn onto a floured surface; roll into a 16-in. x 14-in. rectangle. Cut into 2-in. squares. In an electric skillet or deep-fat fryer, heat oil to 375°. Fry squares, a few at a time, until golden brown on both sides. Drain on paper towels. Serve warm with honey if desired. **Yield:** 4-1/2 dozen.

MINI FRENCH PUFFS

Eleanor Dunbar, Peoria, Illinois

These delicious bite-size treats are the perfect ending to a breakfast or brunch. My family also enjoys nibbling on them throughout the day.

1/3 cup shortening
1/2 cup sugar
    1 egg
1-1/2 cups all-purpose flour
1-1/2 teaspoons baking powder
1/2 teaspoon salt
1/4 teaspoon ground nutmeg
1/2 cup milk
TOPPING:
1/2 cup sugar
    1 teaspoon ground cinnamon
    6 tablespoons butter *or* margarine, melted

In a mixing bowl, cream shortening and sugar. Beat in egg. Combine flour, baking powder, salt and nutmeg. Add to creamed mixture alternately with milk (batter will be stiff). Fill greased miniature muffin cups two-thirds full. Bake at 350° for 20-25 minutes or until a toothpick comes out clean. Combine sugar and cinnamon in a bowl. Remove puffs from pans; immediately roll in butter, then in cinnamon-sugar. Serve

warm. **Yield:** 2-1/2 dozen. **Editor's Note:** Twelve regular-size muffin cups may be used; bake for 15-20 minutes.

OATMEAL BISCUITS

Barbara Chornoboy, Thunder Bay, Ontario

This recipe has been in the family for generations, and my sister and I make these biscuits often for our families. When I bake them first thing in the morning, the house soon smells delicious.

    2 cups all-purpose flour
1/2 cup packed brown sugar
    2 teaspoons baking powder
    1 teaspoon baking soda
    1 teaspoon salt
1/2 cup shortening
1-1/4 cups quick-cooking oats
3/4 cup milk

In a bowl, combine the first five ingredients. Cut in shortening until mixture resembles coarse crumbs. Stir in oats and milk just until moistened. Turn onto a lightly floured surface. Roll to 3/4-in. thickness; cut with a floured 2-in. biscuit cutter. Place 1 in. apart on an ungreased baking sheet. Bake at 375° for 15-20 minutes or until lightly browned. Serve warm. **Yield:** 15 biscuits.

MANDARIN ORANGE BREAKFAST BITES

Delores Thompson, Clear Lake, Iowa

These taste like doughnuts without the hassle of rolling out and frying. Our daughter likes me to have them waiting for her and her friends after school.

1-1/2 cups all-purpose flour
1/2 cup sugar
1-3/4 teaspoons baking powder
1/2 teaspoon salt
1/2 teaspoon ground nutmeg
1/2 cup cold butter *or* margarine
    1 egg
1/2 cup milk
    1 teaspoon almond extract
    1 can (11 ounces) mandarin oranges, drained and diced
TOPPING:
1/3 cup sugar
    1 teaspoon ground cinnamon
1/2 cup butter *or* margarine, melted

In a large bowl, combine the first five ingredients. Cut in butter until mixture resembles coarse crumbs. In another bowl, whisk the egg, milk and extract. Stir into crumb mixture just until moistened. Fold in oranges. Fill greased or paper-lined miniature muffin cups two-thirds full. Bake at 350° for 15-20 minutes. Cool for 5 minutes before removing from pans to wire racks. Combine sugar and cinnamon. Dip tops of warm muffins in melted butter, then in cinnamon-sugar. **Yield:** 2-1/2 dozen.

DILLY BISCUIT SQUARES

Lorene Corbett, Ringgold, Nebraska

My husband grew up in the South, where biscuits are practically daily fare. So early in our marriage, I began adding variety to this ordinary quick bread. These are good with seafood, beef and pasta dishes.

    2 cups all-purpose flour
    4 teaspoons baking powder
    1 tablespoon sugar
    1/2 teaspoon salt
    1 cup (4 ounces) shredded cheddar cheese
    1/4 cup shortening
    3/4 cup plus 1 tablespoon milk
DILL BUTTER:
    1/4 cup butter (no substitutes), melted
    1/2 teaspoon dill weed
    1/8 teaspoon garlic salt

In a large bowl, combine the first four ingredients. Add cheese. Cut in shortening until mixture resembles coarse crumbs. Stir in milk just until moistened. Turn onto a lightly floured surface. Roll into a 3/4-in.-thick square. Cut into 12 squares. Place 1/8 in. apart on an ungreased baking sheet. Bake at 450° for 10-12 minutes or until golden brown. Combine butter, dill and salt; brush over hot biscuits. Serve warm. Refrigerate leftovers. **Yield:** 1 dozen.

TRADITIONAL PITA BREAD

Lynne Hartke, Chandler, Arizona

My husband taught me how to make this pita bread when we were first dating. He always has his eye out for good recipes.

    1 package (1/4 ounce) active dry yeast
1-1/4 cups warm water (110° to 115°)
    2 teaspoons salt
    3 to 3-1/2 cups all-purpose flour

In a mixing bowl, dissolve yeast in warm water. Stir in salt and enough flour to form a soft dough. Turn onto a floured surface; knead until smooth and elastic, about 6-8 minutes. Do not let rise. Divide dough into six pieces; knead each for 1 minute. Roll each into a 5-in. circle. Cover and let rise in a warm place until

doubled, about 45 minutes. Place upside down on greased baking sheets. Bake at 500° for 5-10 minutes. Remove from pans to wire racks to cool. **Yield:** 6 pita breads.

PARMESAN BUTTER DIPS

Ruby Seaman, Bonners Ferry, Idaho

I always get compliments when I serve these breadsticks with homemade soup. They're quick and easy to make, even for folks who've never tried their hand at baking homemade bread.

2-1/4 cups all-purpose flour
    2 tablespoons sugar
    3 teaspoons baking powder
    1 teaspoon salt
    1 cup milk
    1/2 cup butter *or* margarine, melted
    1/4 cup grated Parmesan cheese

In a bowl, combine the first four ingredients. Stir in milk just until moistened. Turn onto a floured surface; divide into 18 pieces. Roll each into a 5-in. rope. Pour butter into a shallow pan. Dip ropes in butter. Place 2 in. apart on greased baking sheets. Sprinkle with Parmesan cheese. Bake at 400° for 12-15 minutes or until golden brown. Serve warm. **Yield:** 1-1/2 dozen.

RYE BREADSTICKS

Mary Johnston, Fredericktown, Pennsylvania

I love to experiment with bread recipes. This one is a favorite of my children and grandchildren. The soft, chewy breadsticks are delicious with a casserole or hearty bowl of soup.

    1 tablespoon active dry yeast
1-1/2 cups warm water (110° to 115°), *divided*
    2 tablespoons honey
    2 cups whole wheat flour
    1 cup rye flour
    1 to 1-1/2 cups all-purpose flour

In a mixing bowl, dissolve yeast in 1/2 cup warm water. Add honey; let stand for 5 minutes. Stir in the remaining water, whole wheat flour, rye flour and enough all-purpose flour to form a soft dough. Turn onto a floured surface; knead until smooth and elastic, about 6-8 minutes. Do not let rise. Divide dough into 16 pieces. Roll each into a 10-in. rope. Place 2 in. apart on a greased baking sheet. Cover and let rise in a warm place until doubled, about 30 minutes. Bake at 350° for 20-25 minutes or until golden brown. **Yield:** 16 breadsticks.

Breads in Brief

By relying on such convenience foods as frozen bread dough, refrigerated biscuits and baking mixes, busy cooks can make "homemade" breads in a hurry.

SPEEDY CINNAMON ROLLS

Nicole Weir, Hager City, Wisconsin

(Pictured at left)

On special occasions when we were growing up, my mother would make as many as four batches of these delicious cinnamon rolls to satisfy the appetites of her eight ravenous children. Today this recipe is still a hit.

  1 loaf (1 pound) frozen bread dough, thawed
  2 tablespoons butter *or* margarine, melted
2/3 cup packed brown sugar
1/2 cup chopped walnuts
  1 teaspoon ground cinnamon
1/2 cup whipping cream

On a floured surface, roll dough into an 18-in. x 6-in. rectangle; brush with butter. In a bowl, combine the brown sugar, walnuts and cinnamon; sprinkle over dough. Roll up, jelly-roll style, starting with a long side; pinch seam to seal. Cut into 16 slices. Place, cut side down, in two greased 8-in. round baking pans. Cover and let rise until doubled, about 50 minutes. Pour 1/4 cup cream over each pan. Bake at 350° for 25-30 minutes or until golden brown. Immediately invert onto serving plates. **Yield:** 1-1/2 dozen.

BROCCOLI CORN BREAD

Colleen Goodwin, Livingston, Texas

This moist bread with a sweet corn flavor can be served as a side dish with any meaty entree. The broccoli and cottage cheese combination is delicious.

  2 packages (8-1/2 ounces *each*) corn bread/muffin mix
  4 eggs
  1 carton (12 ounces) small-curd cottage cheese
3/4 cup butter *or* margarine, melted
  1 package (10 ounces) frozen chopped broccoli, thawed

  1 large onion, chopped

In a large bowl, combine corn bread mixes. In another bowl, beat eggs, cottage cheese and butter. Stir into corn bread mixes just until moistened. Fold in broccoli and onion. Transfer to a greased 13-in. x 9-in. x 2-in. baking pan. Bake at 350° for 40-45 minutes or until a toothpick comes out clean. Let stand for 10 minutes before cutting. Serve warm. Refrigerate leftovers. **Yield:** 12-15 servings.

CHEDDAR CHILI BRAID

Katie Dreibelbis, State College, Pennsylvania

(Pictured at left)

Hot roll mix gives me a head start when making this savory bread. I usually make it with a big pot of chili and serve thick warm slices for "dunking".

  1 package (16 ounces) hot roll mix
  1 cup warm water (120° to 130°)
  2 eggs
  2 cups (8 ounces) shredded cheddar cheese
  2 tablespoons canned chopped green chilies, drained
  2 tablespoons grated Parmesan cheese

In a bowl, combine contents of roll mix and yeast packet; stir in water, one egg, cheddar cheese and chilies. Turn onto a floured surface; knead until smooth and elastic, about 5 minutes. Cover and let rest for 5 minutes. Divide into thirds. Shape each into a 14-in. rope. Place ropes on a greased baking sheet and braid; pinch ends to seal and tuck under. Cover and let rise in a warm place until doubled, about 30 minutes. Beat remaining egg; brush over dough. Sprinkle with Parmesan cheese. Bake at 375° for 30 minutes or until golden brown. Remove from pan to a wire rack. **Yield:** 1 loaf.

BRAIDING BREADS

To braid breads with ease, place the ropes of bread side by side on a baking sheet so they're almost touching. Braid from the center to the ends. Turn the pan; repeat braiding. Pinch ends to seal; tuck under.

FAST FLAVORFUL FARE. Pictured at left, top to bottom: Cheddar Chili Braid and Speedy Cinnamon Rolls (recipes on this page).

BRAIDED PIZZA LOAF

Debbie Meduna, Plaza, North Dakota

Working women can take the frozen bread dough out in the morning and then prepare this hearty loaf when they get home. It's important to let the filling cool completely before spreading on the dough.

>   1 loaf (1 pound) frozen bread dough, thawed
>   1 pound ground beef
>   1 medium onion, finely chopped
>   1 teaspoon salt
>   1 teaspoon pepper
>   1 can (8 ounces) tomato sauce
>   1 teaspoon dried oregano
>   1 teaspoon paprika
> 1/2 teaspoon garlic salt
>   1 cup (4 ounces) shredded cheddar cheese
>   1 cup (4 ounces) shredded mozzarella cheese

Melted butter *or* margarine

Place dough in a greased bowl, turning once to grease top. Cover and let rise in a warm place until doubled, about 1 hour. Meanwhile, in a skillet, cook the beef, onion, salt and pepper over medium heat until meat is no longer pink; drain. Stir in tomato sauce, oregano, paprika and garlic salt. Bring to a boil. Reduce heat; cover and simmer for 30 minutes, stirring occasionally. Cool completely. Punch dough down. Turn onto a lightly floured surface; roll into a 15-in. x 12-in. rectangle. Place on a greased baking sheet. Spread filling lengthwise down center third of rectangle. Sprinkle with cheeses. On each long side, cut 1-1/2-in.-wide strips about 2-1/2 in. into center. Starting at one end, fold alternating strips at an angle across filling. Brush with butter. Bake at 350° for 30-35 minutes or until golden brown. Serve warm. Refrigerate leftovers. **Yield:** 1 loaf.

MONKEY BREAD

Charlene Wilson, Williamsburg, Ohio

The dear friend who shared this recipe has since passed away, but I think of her every time I prepare this sweet bread. Maple syrup provides a saucy caramel flavor. I enjoy developing original recipes or altering others to suit my tastes.

>   2 tubes (7-1/2 ounces *each*) refrigerated
>   buttermilk biscuits
>   1 cup packed brown sugar
>   1 teaspoon ground cinnamon
>   1 teaspoon ground nutmeg
> 1/2 cup butter *or* margarine, melted
> 1/2 cup chopped nuts
> 1/2 cup maple syrup

Cut each biscuit into quarters. In a small bowl, combine brown sugar, cinnamon and nutmeg. Dip biscuits in butter, then roll in sugar mixture. Layer half the biscuits in a 10-in. fluted pan; sprinkle with half the nuts. Repeat layers. Pour syrup over top. Bake at 350° for 25-30 minutes or until golden brown. Immediately invert onto a serving platter. Serve warm. **Yield:** 1 loaf.

DISAPPEARING MARSHMALLOW PUFFS

Linda Livers, Chaska, Minnesota

Kids love making these tasty treats for Sunday breakfast. While baking, the marshmallows melt and blend with the cinnamon-sugar.

>   2 tubes (8 ounces *each*) refrigerated crescent
>   rolls
> 1/4 cup sugar
>   1 teaspoon ground cinnamon
>   16 large marshmallows
> 1/4 cup butter *or* margarine, melted

GLAZE:
> 1/2 cup confectioners' sugar
> 1/2 teaspoon vanilla extract
>   2 to 3 teaspoons milk
> 1/4 cup chopped nuts

Separate crescent dough into 16 triangles. In a bowl, combine sugar and cinnamon. Roll marshmallows in butter, then in cinnamon-sugar. Place marshmallows at wide end of crescents. Fold corners over marshmallow. Roll up each triangle, beginning at the wide end. Pinch seams to seal. Dip bottom of dough in butter. Place, butter side down, in ungreased muffin cups. Place muffin pans on baking sheets. Bake at 375° for 10-15 minutes or until golden brown. Immediately remove from pans to wire racks. For glaze, combine confectioners' sugar and vanilla. Stir in enough milk to achieve desired consistency. Drizzle over puffs. Sprinkle with nuts. Serve warm. **Yield:** 16 rolls.

TOMATO-CHEESE SNACK BREAD

Karen Farruggia, West Winfield, New York

My family is fond of cheese, so I have many recipes calling for that delectable ingredient. This rich bread is a great way to showcase garden-fresh tomatoes. Serve it as a snack or with your favorite grilled meats.

>   2 cups biscuit/baking mix
> 2/3 cup milk
>   3 medium tomatoes, peeled and cut into
>   1/4-inch slices

1 medium onion, finely chopped
2 tablespoons butter *or* margarine
1 cup (4 ounces) shredded cheddar cheese
3/4 cup sour cream
1/3 cup mayonnaise
3/4 teaspoon salt
1/4 teaspoon pepper
1/4 teaspoon dried oregano
Paprika

In a bowl, combine biscuit mix and milk just until moistened. Turn onto a floured surface; knead 10-12 times. Press onto the bottom and 1 in. up the sides of a greased 13-in. x 9-in. x 2-in. baking dish. Arrange tomato slices over top. In a skillet, saute onion in butter until tender; remove from the heat. Stir in the cheese, sour cream, mayonnaise, salt, pepper and oregano. Spoon over tomatoes. Sprinkle with paprika. Bake at 400° for 20-25 minutes or until browned. Let stand for 10 minutes before cutting. Serve warm. Refrigerate leftovers. **Yield:** 12-15 servings.

QUICK CALZONES

Clarice Brender, North Liberty, Iowa

These individual stuffed pizzas taste delectable with or without the sauce on the side. If you can't make up your mind, prepare half of the calzones with ham and the other half with pepperoni.

2 cups (8 ounces) shredded mozzarella cheese
1 carton (15 ounces) ricotta cheese
6 ounces diced fully cooked ham *or* sliced pepperoni
1 teaspoon garlic powder
2 loaves (1 pound *each*) frozen bread dough, thawed
Warmed spaghetti *or* pizza sauce, optional

In a large bowl, combine the cheeses, ham and garlic powder; mix well. Divide each loaf into eight pieces. On a floured surface, roll each portion into a 5-in. circle. Place filling in the center of each circle. Bring dough over filling; pinch seams to seal. Place, seam side down, on greased baking sheets. Bake at 375° for 30-35 minutes or until golden brown. Serve warm with sauce if desired. Refrigerate leftovers. **Yield:** 16 servings.

LEMON-GLAZED POPPY SEED RING

Betty Hass, Fort Myers, Florida

I like to modify existing recipes to be more interesting.

This bread is a combination of three old standbys: the poppy seed kolaches my Ukranian grandmother used to make, the cinnamon rolls I learned to make in Girl Scouts and the lemon glaze from my favorite bundt cake.

1 tube (17.3 ounces) large refrigerated biscuits
1/2 cup poppy seed filling
GLAZE:
1 cup confectioners' sugar
2 tablespoons lemon juice

Open biscuit tube; do not separate biscuits. Place on a greased baking sheet and pat into a 14-in. x 8-in. rectangle. Spread poppy seed filling to within 1/2 in. of edges. Roll up, jelly-roll style, starting with a long side; pinch seam to seal. Bring ends together to form a ring; pinch ends to seal. With scissors, cut from outside edge to two-thirds of the way toward center of ring at 1-in. intervals. Gently stretch ring to form a 4-1/2-in. center. Separate strips slightly; twist to allow filling to show. Bake at 375° for 15-17 minutes or until golden brown. Remove from pan to a wire rack. Combine glaze ingredients; drizzle over warm coffee cake. Cool. **Yield:** 1 loaf.

PECAN BREAKFAST LOAF

Darlene Richardson, Independence, Missouri

This quick bread has the terrific taste of caramel yeast rolls but with the convenience of refrigerated crescent rolls. Each Thanksgiving, I make several breads for my husband to share with his fellow teachers.

2 tubes (8 ounces *each*) refrigerated crescent rolls
2 tablespoons butter *or* margarine, softened
1/2 cup sugar
1/4 cup chopped pecans
2 teaspoons ground cinnamon
1/4 cup pecan halves
GLAZE:
1/4 cup confectioners' sugar
2 tablespoons butter *or* margarine
2 tablespoons honey
1 teaspoon vanilla extract

Separate crescent dough into 16 triangles. Spread each with butter. Combine sugar, chopped pecans and cinnamon; sprinkle over triangles. Beginning at the wide end, roll up each triangle. In a greased 9-in. x 5-in. x 3-in. loaf pan, place rolls, point side down, widthwise in two layers. Bake at 375° for 35-40 minutes or until golden brown. Cool for 10 minutes before removing from pan to a wire rack. Top with pecan halves. In a saucepan, combine glaze ingredients; bring to a boil, stirring constantly. Cool for 5 minutes. Drizzle over warm bread. **Yield:** 1 loaf.

POTATO DROP BISCUITS

Roberta Strohmaier, Lebanon, New Jersey

When you don't have time to make biscuit dough from scratch and cut out the biscuits, you can rely on this four-ingredient recipe.

2-1/4 cups biscuit/baking mix
1/3 cup mashed potato flakes
2/3 cup milk
2 tablespoons sour cream

In a bowl, combine biscuit mix and potato flakes. In another bowl, whisk the milk and sour cream. Stir into dry ingredients just until moistened. Drop by heaping tablespoonfuls onto a greased baking sheet. Bake at 400° for 10-12 minutes or until tops begin to brown. Serve warm. **Yield:** 1 dozen.

SHOOFLY COFFEE CAKE

Kezia Sullivan, Sackets Harbor, New York

A sugar crumb topping lends to this moist coffee cake's appeal. The rich molasses flavor really shines through. Slices are good served warm or at room temperature.

2 cups buttermilk pancake mix
1/2 teaspoon ground cinnamon
1/4 teaspoon ground ginger
2/3 cup milk
1/3 cup molasses
1/4 cup sugar
2 tablespoons cold butter *or* margarine

In a bowl, combine the pancake mix, cinnamon and ginger. Set aside 1/3 cup for topping. In another bowl, combine milk and molasses. Stir into dry ingredients just until moistened. Transfer to a greased 9-in. pie plate. In a small bowl, combine sugar and reserved pancake mix mixture. Cut in butter until mixture resembles coarse crumbs. Sprinkle over batter. Bake at 350° for 25-30 minutes or until a toothpick comes out clean. Serve warm. **Yield:** 8 servings.

CHEERY CHERRY CHRISTMAS BREAD

Robyn Wegelin, Bridgeport, Nebraska

This recipe was given to me by my mother-in-law, who was a wonderful country cook. She always went the extra mile to make every meal special. Her breads were simply the best…this is one of my favorites.

1 package (16 ounces) hot roll mix
1 can (21 ounces) cherry pie filling
FILLING:
1/2 cup sour cream
1 egg

2 tablespoons sugar
1/2 teaspoon almond extract
TOPPING:
1 cup all-purpose flour
1/4 cup sugar
1/2 cup cold butter *or* margarine

Prepare roll mix and knead dough according to package directions. Cover and let rest for 5 minutes. Turn onto a lightly floured surface; roll into a 15-in. x 10-in. rectangle. Press dough onto the bottom and up the sides of a greased 15-in. x 10-in. x 1-in. baking pan. Cover and let rise in a warm place until doubled, about 30 minutes. Spread with pie filling. Combine filling ingredients; drizzle over pie filling. For topping, combine flour and sugar. Cut in butter until mixture resembles coarse crumbs; sprinkle over filling. Bake at 375° for 30-35 minutes or until golden brown. **Yield:** 16-20 servings.

CHEESY ROUND BREAD

Ruthe Krohne, Fort Wayne, Indiana

This bread, which looks similar to focaccia, has a light olive and garlic flavor. We enjoy generous slices with soup.

1 package (16 ounces) hot roll mix
3/4 cup warm water (120° to 130°)
1 egg
1 tablespoon butter *or* margarine, softened
1-1/2 teaspoons garlic salt
1/2 teaspoon dried oregano
1/2 teaspoon paprika
3/4 cup shredded cheddar cheese
1/2 cup chopped ripe olives, well drained
1 egg white, beaten

In a mixing bowl, combine contents of roll mix and yeast packet. Add warm water; mix well. Add the egg, butter and seasonings. Turn onto a floured surface. Knead in cheese and olives. Place in a greased bowl, turning once to grease top. Cover and let rise in a warm place until doubled, about 1 hour. Punch dough down. Press into a 12-in. pizza pan. Cover and let rise in a warm place until doubled, about 30 minutes. With a sharp knife, make three or four slashes across top of loaf. Brush with egg white. Bake at 325° for 40-45 minutes or until golden brown. Cool for 5 minutes before removing from pan to a wire rack. **Yield:** 1 loaf.

PIMIENTO-STUFFED OLIVE BREAD

Val Wilson, Wabasha, Minnesota

Salty olives pair well with this bread's cream cheese and chives. Even folks who normally avoid olives can't resist slices of this colorful bread.

3 cups biscuit/baking mix
2 tablespoons sugar
1 egg
1-1/2 cups buttermilk
1 cup (4 ounces) shredded Swiss cheese
1 cup stuffed olives
3/4 cup chopped walnuts
1 package (8 ounces) cream cheese, softened
1 teaspoon minced chives

In a large bowl, combine biscuit mix and sugar. In another bowl, beat egg and buttermilk. Stir into dry ingredients just until moistened. Fold in the Swiss cheese, olives and walnuts. Transfer to a greased 9-in. x 5-in. x 3-in. loaf pan. Bake at 350° for 50-55 minutes or until a toothpick comes out clean. Cool for 10 minutes before removing from pan to a wire rack. In a mixing bowl, combine cream cheese and chives; mix well. Serve with bread. Refrigerate leftovers. **Yield:** 1 loaf.

Sugar-Topped Applesauce Muffins

Shelley Goodfellow, Fruitland, Idaho

My five brothers, two sisters and I grew up on a farm and built up hearty appetites doing various chores. It seemed no matter what I helped Mom cook was gobbled up. That encouraged me to spend more time in the kitchen!

2 cups biscuit/baking mix
1/4 cup sugar
1 teaspoon ground cinnamon
1 egg
1/2 cup applesauce
1/4 cup milk
2 tablespoons vegetable oil
TOPPING:
1/4 cup sugar
1/4 teaspoon ground cinnamon
2 tablespoons butter *or* margarine, melted

In a bowl, combine the biscuit mix, sugar and cinnamon. In another bowl, beat the egg, applesauce, milk and oil. Stir into dry ingredients just until moistened. Fill greased or paper-lined muffin cups two-thirds full. Bake at 400° for 10-12 minutes or until a toothpick comes out clean. Cool for 5 minutes before removing from pan to a wire rack. In a small bowl, combine sugar and cinnamon. Dip muffin tops in melted butter, then in cinnamon-sugar. **Yield:** 1 dozen.

Italian Sausage Bread

Debbie Connett, Painted Post, New York

This Italian-style stuffed bread is packed with eggs, sausage, pepperoni and cheese. When I know I'll really be pressed for time, I bake this a day in advance and reheat slices for breakfast, lunch or dinner.

1 package (16 ounces) hot roll mix
6 eggs
1 pound bulk Italian sausage, cooked and drained
8 ounces pepperoni, thinly sliced
2 cups (8 ounces) shredded mozzarella cheese
8 ounces provolone cheese, shredded
Garlic powder to taste
1 egg yolk
1 tablespoon water

Prepare roll mix and knead dough according to package directions. Cover and let rise for 30 minutes. Meanwhile, scramble eggs in a skillet over medium heat until completely set. In a large bowl, combine the eggs, sausage, pepperoni and cheeses; mix well. Punch dough down. Turn onto a floured surface; roll into a 14-in. x 12-in. rectangle. Sprinkle with garlic powder. Spread filling to within 1/2 in. of edges. Roll up, jelly-roll style, starting with a short side; pinch seams to seal. Place, seam side down, on a greased baking sheet. Beat egg yolk and water; brush over bread. Bake at 350° for 25-30 minutes or until golden brown. Serve warm. Refrigerate leftovers. **Yield:** 1 loaf.

Onion Shortcake

Helen Greenleaf, Chehalis, Washington

My dear friend, Barbara Gruis, is asked to bring this bread for just about every type of gathering. She was kind enough to share the recipe with me.

1 package (8-1/2 ounces) corn bread/muffin mix
1/3 cup milk
1/4 cup vegetable oil
1 egg
1 large onion, chopped
1 can (8-1/2 ounces) cream-style corn
1-1/2 cups (6 ounces) shredded cheddar cheese, *divided*
1 cup (8 ounces) sour cream
1/2 cup mayonnaise*
1 teaspoon salt
2 drops hot pepper sauce

In a bowl, combine the corn bread mix, milk, oil and egg. Spread in a greased 9-in. square baking pan. In another bowl, combine the onion, corn, 1 cup cheddar cheese, sour cream, mayonnaise, salt and hot pepper sauce; mix well. Spoon over batter. Top with remaining cheese. Bake at 425° for 25-30 minutes or until golden brown. Cool for 15 minutes before cutting. Refrigerate leftovers. **Yield:** 12 servings. *****Editor's Note:** Light or fat-free mayonnaise may not be substituted for regular mayonnaise.

INDEX